JEAN
HARLOW

JEAN HARLOW

Tarnished Angel

DAVID BRET

BOOKS

First published in Great Britain in 2009 by
JR Books, 10 Greenland Street, London NW1 0ND
www.jrbooks.com

A catalogue record for this book is available from the British Library.

ISBN 978-1-906779-34-4

1 3 5 7 9 10 8 6 4 2

Printed by MPG Books, Bodmin, Cornwall

CONTENTS

This book is dedicated to Eartha Kitt and Yma Sumac and
Les Enfants de Novembre.

N'oublie pas la vie sans c'est comme

Un jardin sans fleurs.

Acknowledgements

Writing this book would not have been possible had it not been for the inspiration, criticisms and love of that select group of individuals who, whether they be in this world or the next, I will always regard as my true family and *autre coeur*: Barbara, Irene Bevan, Marlene Dietrich, René Chevalier, Axel Dotti, Dorothy Squires and Roger Normand, *que vous dormez en paix*. Lucette Chevalier, Maria da Fé, Jacqueline Danno, Doris Day, Héléne Delavault, Tony Griffin, Betty and Gérard Garmain, Annick Roux, John and Anne Taylor, Terry Sanderson, Charley Marouani, David and Sally Bolt. Also a very special mention for Amália Rodrigues, Joey Stefano, those *hiboux*, *fadistas* and *amis de foutre* who happened along the way, and *mes enfants perdus*. Thanks too to Mikey Blatin and Theo Morgan. And where would I be without Jeremy Robson and the munificent team at JR Books? Likewise my agent Guy Rose and his lovely wife, Alex? Also to my wife, Jeanne, for putting up with my bad moods and for still being the keeper of my soul.

And finally a *grand chapeau bas* to Jean Harlow, for having lived.

David Bret

Introduction

Her lodestar was extinguished no sooner than it had ascended, yet her legacy has endured for more than 70 years. On the screen she epitomised the fun-loving, wisecracking trollop. She was the original tart with the heart who drove men wild, and made wives jealous of their husbands' thoughts – but unlike contemporaries such as Mae West, she conducted herself on and off the screen with such coarse innocence that rarely caused offence save to the stuffy National League of Decency and the Hays Office, in whose 'Black Book' virtually every Hollywood star eventually ended up, therefore minimalising the power of these moral fools. And yet away from the spotlight she was nothing like the public perceived her to be.

Throughout her short life she was cruelly manipulated by just about everyone who came into contact with her. Her megalomaniac mother – obsessed by money and the religious cult she latched on to – failed to achieve anything in life, so she set out to make life hell for those around her, most especially the daughter she always referred to, even in adulthood, as 'The Baby'. Her father was a weak man who could not have cared less – his one desire had been to get his troublesome wife out of his hair once and for all. Jean Harlow's stepfather mixed with gangsters and low-life, and both mentally and sexually abused her while spending half of her salary on needless luxuries and a string of mistresses. Hypocritical movie moguls pretended to like her but only used her, paying her a pittance of what their other stars were earning while they were earning 10 times the amount she was for the same studio.

Considering her natural beauty and sparkling personality she could have had only the very best, yet her choice of men bordered on the amorously blind. She never showed the remotest interest in any of her handsome, matinee idol co-stars, not until William Powell came along, towards the end of her life – and only then because he slotted into the sophisticated older-man category she had become obsessed with, while searching for a father figure to offer her the spiritual comfort she had missed out on as a child.

When her first husband announced that he wanted her to settle down and have a family, her stepfather menaced him into granting her a divorce she did not want, and forced her to have the first of several abortions. His successor, a man who beat her mercilessly and almost certainly contributed to her death, was more than twice her age and subjected her to one of the messiest scandals in Hollywood history, a mystery which has never been properly solved to this day. Her third husband, also many years her senior, failed to keep up with the pace of being mere 'Mr Harlow'. Between these spouses were mobster, bootlegger and drug-dealer lovers, a gay journalist who took her most closely guarded secrets to the grave, and the actor William Powell, who almost married her, unceremoniously dumped her, then came back to fork out $25,000 – an enormous sum at the time – for her tomb.

Jean Harlow was an enigma, the original Blonde Bombshell, completely uninhibited. She made no secret of the fact that she never wore underwear, bleached her pubic hair to match that on her head – and was never afraid of showing this to journalists, if they asked. She answered the door to her dressing room in the nude, with such a lack of exhibitionism that most visitors did not blink. Most people thought her fearless, yet deep inside she was little more than a timid, confused child. Her first few films were nothing short of appalling because she was typecast as the heartless

Introduction

slut who uses men, and pays the price. Then all of a sudden her career spiralled when, having been given roles to suit her innate screwball talents, MGM realised that they had struck gold – not that this made the studio treat her with even a fraction of the respect she deserved.

Jean Harlow was the original *monstre sacré*. This is her story....

CHAPTER ONE

The Girl From Missouri

'She filled the eye and imagination with the impact of her looks and personality. I never saw a star with more personal magnetism. Her stardom was of the immediate moment of her presence, of stunning good looks, of unbounded vitality which needed no grafted additions or embellishment.'

Jesse Lasky Jr

She was born a little before 8pm on 3 March 1911, at 3344 Olive Street, in one of Kansas City's more opulent districts. Her mother was a handsome, 22-year-old society climber born Jean Harlow, who always insisted on being called Mama Jean – and who in most contemporary reports was noted as having wildly eccentric behaviour. Her father was Montclair Carpenter, who practised at the local dental college.

Later in life, the Jean Harlow everyone knew and loved would apply the dictum, 'Fuck 'em and forget 'em', to most of the men in her life. It was a trait she inherited from a hard-edged mother whose morals left much to be desired. And just as the future Jean Harlow would spend much of her life under her mother's thumb, so Mama Jean lived in fear of her staunch Presbyterian father, Samuel, a wealthy property developer, largely because he was the one financing her schemes and foibles.

The Harlows lived in a huge, 24-room mansion overlooking the Skaw River, and it was Samuel (always known as Skip) who railroaded his daughter down the aisle at the end of 1908 – having defined Montclair Carpenter of being of good breeding stock. Mama Jean entered the bridal suite with one thought in mind – having a child but not with him – and between then and what she later called 'the immaculate conception', she tolerated her new husband forcing himself upon her. Then, once the family doctor had confirmed the good news, Montclair was not just ousted from her bed, but from her life, though for the time being – so as not to displease Skip who was paying most of their bills – they still lived under the same roof.

As with some of the other great, yet controversial stars of this and the next generation – instinctively one thinks of Judy Garland and Elizabeth Taylor – Mama Jean Carpenter opted to live out her own failed aspirations through her daughter, almost always indiscriminately and with little thought of anyone but herself. There seems no denying that this martinet loved her daughter, but throughout her tragically short life Harlean, as she was baptised – an amalgamation of Mama Jean's first and maiden names – would be treated like a chattel, not just by her immediate family but by just about everyone who came in close contact with her.

Yet in spite of this, Harlean's was a privileged upbringing, to say the least. Soon after her birth, the Carpenters moved to a much bigger house at 4409 Robert Gillam Road – Montclair's way of trying to hang on to his domineering wife, who demanded that she be provided with a personal maid, housekeeper, major-domo, and liveried chauffeur. Baby, as everyone called her – Harlean claimed that, until starting school, she had actually believed this to have been her real name – had her own nanny and private nurse. 'Until I was five I spoke French almost exclusively, as I had a Parisian governess', she later told her celebrity journalist friend, Ben

Maddox – though this may have been another Harlow 'tall tale'. She was confined beyond belief by her mother, who kept her away from other children but afforded her plenty of winged and four-legged playmates: the several acres of grounds were populated with pigs, ducks, chickens and lambs, while within the house Harlean had several dogs, cats and birds. Skip Harlow also bought his granddaughter a pony, but so as not to frighten the other animals, she was only permitted to ride it at his place.

Mama Jean was ultra-possessive, and prone to exaggeration. Theirs was the best house in town, hers was the lustiest husband – though by now she and Montclair were sleeping in separate rooms. Harlean was a sickly infant who seems to have contracted every childhood ailment. If any child in the neighbourhood fell ill, then whatever ailment laid Harlean low had to be more severe than the others, if not life threatening. In 1916, Kansas City was hit by the influenza epidemic which would result in a bigger worldwide death-toll than all the casualties of World War 1. Harlean did not contract mere influenza, Mama Jean later declared – she almost died of spinal meningitis. This was refuted by relatives, speaking to biographer David Stenn (*Bombshell*, 1993) – though by this time, with all of the major characters in her story dead, there is no knowing whether this and other anecdotes recounted to Stenn were accurate. He simply repeated them as they had been told, perhaps at a time when memories may have been fading.

Harlean was not allowed to play with other local children. Occasionally she was escorted to a birthday party, but that is as far as it went. She was perpetually on display, clinging to her mother's hand, wearing only the most expensive clothes, clutching the costliest dolls money could buy – a possession more than a child. Setting a precedent for the future, and to set her aside from every other youngster, Mama Jean dyed Harlean's mousey hair not just blonde, but almost white. This, she declared, went well with her blue eyes. The situation between Mama Jean and Harlean brings to mind the later one between another less privileged Kansas City girl, Joan Crawford, and her adopted daughter, Christina – save that Jean Harlow would not repay her mother with an odious, mostly invented kiss-and-tell of their years together.

For the first 12 years of her life, as throughout much of her later career, Harlean Carpenter was hardly ever addressed by her first name – only as Baby. When she was six, her grandfather enrolled her at Barstow's, a prestigious private academy for children from privileged backgrounds whose families hoped the experience would turn them into genteel young ladies. This coincided with Skip Harlow buying an 18-room mansion on the city's opulent East 79th Street – not for himself, but for Mama Jean and Montclair, in the hope of getting them reunited not just for Harlean's sake, but to stop the local gossips who saw Mama Jean as a harlot.

Mama Jean promised she would make a go of things, moved into the property – and promptly filed for divorce. Montclair could have contested the suit and triumphed in any courthouse by branding his wife a scarlet woman. What lies Mama Jean told the judge are not known – suffice to say, along with the $200 a month alimony, *she* was awarded sole custody of their daughter, and Harlean would hardly ever see her father again. The divorce was made final on 22 September 1922, whence Mama Jean announced that she was heading for Hollywood to seek her fortune – as if she was not rich enough! And naturally, Harlean would be going with her.

In 1923, when Mama Jean and Harlean arrived in Tinseltown, Hollywood's marquee names were Rudolph Valentino, Pola Negri, Mary Pickford and Douglas Fairbanks, Clara Bow and Richard Barthelmess. Within a few years, the advent of sound would see some of these stars falling by the wayside, while Valentino would succumb to peritonitis, aged just 31. Mama Jean still had aspirations for her daughter, but she saw only herself working opposite the likes of Valentino and Richard Arlen, and even as a stooge for funnymen Harold Lloyd and Laurel & Hardy.

It mattered little to her that, now in her mid-thirties, most producers considered her far too old – the average age of a Hollywood leading lady then was just 20. If these vamps could make themselves look older, she declared, then with the right application of make-up she could reverse the process. She was told that maybe she could find work as an extra, in caricature or matronly parts – the undisputed queen of which was Marie Dressler – but for Mama Jean Carpenter, this was not good enough. She wanted to play Ibsen heroines, like the great Russian actress Alla Nazimova!

Mama Jean rented a small apartment, within a Sunset Boulevard mansion. Skip picked up the tab, but only because Mama Jean fulfilled his instruction to enrol his granddaughter at the Hollywood School For Girls. Despite its title, the pupils here included Mary Pickford's son, Douglas Fairbanks Jr. Harlean later said that her first unrequited love was cowboy star Buck Jones (1889–1942), whose movies she would see every Saturday afternoon, unchaperoned, while her mother went off socialising in search of some well-heeled benefactor to help launch her movie career.

It was during one of these social jaunts – cynics have suggested for the want of something better to do – that Mama Jean discovered Christian Science, regarded by some sections of the Hollywood community as the latest fad. Mary Pickford, Conrad Nagel, Leatrice Joy – big stars of the day – and director King Vidor were all practitioners. The movement had been founded by Mary Baker Eddy (1821–1910), who although raised a Catholic had rejected the formal teachings of her faith because of 'divine intervention' during a series of illnesses and a spinal injury, from which she claimed she had 'miraculously' recovered without medical help.

Thrice married, and not the role model she made herself out to be, Eddy's theory – which if introduced today would see her lampooned as a crank, but which in 1866 with medical knowledge limited was taken very seriously by gullible believers – was that 'illness is but an illusion which can be healed through a clearer conception of God.' As such, she had founded the Christian Science movement, whose edicts as detailed in her *Science With A Key To*

The Scriptures, published in 1875, profess that since God is good and is a spirit, matter and evil are ultimately unreal. Suffice to say, no reputable publisher had wished to risk the scandal of taking on such a project, so Eddy had financed the first print run herself. It sold just 800 copies, but most of the 'students' who had bought it had moved around the country spreading the word, so by the time of Eddy's death the movement had attracted many thousands of followers and had spawned several publications including *The Christian Science Monitor*, still going strong today. As a consequence, true followers of the religion still shy away from orthodox medical treatment, preferring to rely on healing which they believe is brought about by 'operation of truth within the human conscience'.

Mama Jean Carpenter joined the movement chiefly for social advancement – she would only apply its edicts when this suited her, most disastrously some years later when her 'beliefs' would cost her daughter her life. What makes the movement hypocritical is that one of its laws 'shuns the cult of celebrity' – not that this, like the cult of Scientology, has seen some stars accused of augmenting its ranks as a publicity exercise *just* to get themselves noticed. Three future recruits into Christian Science were Joan Crawford, Doris Day and Elizabeth Taylor.

Aside from a few Christian Science meetings and parties where Mama Jean flaunted herself in front of movie executives and talent scouts who showed no interest in her whatsoever, this particular sojourn in Hollywood did not prove fruitful. Aware that his daughter was up to no good, Skip Harlow cut Mama Jean's weekly allowance, forcing her to 'slum it' in a cheaper apartment on North La Brea Avenue. She stuck this out until March 1925, then returned with Harlean to Kansas City. Here, there was a furious row with Skip, who accused Mama Jean of leading Harlean astray by having introduced her to all the wrong people in Hollywood. In an attempt to instil a little discipline into her life, not to mention a few morals, he enrolled Harlean at Notre Dame de Sion (despite his distrust of any other religion but his own), a strict convent boarding school. She lasted a single term before running home to her mother, who found her a place at Bigelow's, a school within easy travelling distance of her home.

During that summer of 1925, in yet another attempt to separate Harlean from a mother who was preoccupied with socialising, Skip sent her to summer camp at Camp Cha-ton-ka, in Michigamme, Michigan. She would subsequently remember this as the worst experience of her life because, knowing nothing of country life, she had grabbed the first thing at hand to wipe her bottom during a field trip – poison oak leaves – and caught an infection. During the same trip she claimed she had also contracted scarlet fever, though she cannot have been too ill because she also found time to lose her virginity to a fellow camper called David Thornton Arnold. Years later, Thor, as he was popularly known, would dine out on his Jean Harlow stories and recall the event – which he nevertheless described as unexciting – in clinical detail.

The real reason for Harlean Carpenter being asked to leave Cha-ton-ka is unclear, though almost certainly it was on account of her wayward behaviour. Mama Jean collected her, and the two travelled back to Kansas via Chicago, where they stayed at the ultra plush Sherman Hotel. It was here that Marino Bello entered their lives. 'He's a phoney son of a bitch,' Jean Harlow would later say, 'I hate him as much as my mother loves him. His idea of heaven is his side of the bed.'

Sicilian by birth, schizophrenic by nature and an all-round unsavoury character, Marino Bello (1883–1953) had links with the Mafia and was a close friend of mobster Johnny Rosselli. Described by Joan Crawford as 'an ersatz, smarmy middle-aged Valentino with no charisma whatsoever', Bello was balding, wore cheap spectacles, dressed spivvishly, and carried a cane within which was concealed a rapier – he claimed for fighting duels. Like the younger, much better looking Valentino he kissed women on the *palm* of the hand, and kissed the sugar lump before dropping it into their coffee; also like Valentino in his formative years, he charged his wealthy conquests for sex. Curiously, he was considered something of a catch. In 1914 he had married Mildred Maas, a wealthy American widow who had paid for his services while visiting Italy. This marriage had enabled him to emigrate to Chicago, where he had been employed by Mildred's cousin, who ran the Sherman Hotel. Bello had stayed with her just long enough to acquire American citizenship, though he and Mildred were still married when he met Mama Jean Carpenter.

Skip Harlow loathed Marino Bello on sight, and opted to keep his granddaughter away from him at all costs. Like many of his generation he distrusted foreigners, but this one he immediately recognised from the outset as an opportunist. Because he disapproved, Mama Jean decided against returning to Kansas, and in September 1926 rented a room at the Sherman which she shared with her lover.

Skip dispatched Harlean to Ferry Hall School in Lake Forest, Illinois, in those days *the* establishment which taught young girls the basics of deportment and social graces – the latter a quality which Jean Harlow could never be accused of having in excess. And it was during one of her weekend trips back to Chicago that Harlean met the first important man in her life.

Born in Chicago in 1906, Charles Freemont McGrew – Chuck to his intimates – had led a privileged but tragic existence which would not improve during his involvement with Harlean Carpenter. His immensely wealthy parents died in 1922 when their boat capsized during a trip to their private island in Wisconsin. Chuck's grandparents had agreed to look after him until he came of age, obviously with one eye on his inheritance. They had enrolled him in the boy's half of Ferry Hall, where he is supposed to have met Harlean on a blind date.

Despite learning that the boy stood to come into a sizeable fortune, Mama Jean and Marino Bello disapproved. Chuck was nowhere near as well off as the man they had in mind for their daughter – Bello's 'confirmed bachelor' brother, Eugene Byfield, a millionaire by today's standards. Harlean was compelled to date this man whom she later remembered as being repulsive, and wrote to her grandfather, begging him to intervene. Skip Harlow offered Mama Jean an ultimatum: to return home where he could keep an eye on her, or to marry Bello so that he could have the responsibility of looking after her. Upon reading Skip's letter, Bello gave Mama Jean a beating 'to show her who was boss' – then promptly proposed. When his wife Mildred refused to grant him a divorce, he visited her house daily and beat her black and blue until she conceded defeat. The wedding took place in Waukegan, Illinois, on 18 January 1927, and Harlean was conspicuous by her absence.

Though she hated her stepfather, Harlean put up with his loutish behaviour just to be close to Chuck, who lived nearby, when he too came home on a weekend. She was well developed for her age, forward, and made no secret of the fact that she never wore a brassiere. She should therefore not have been surprised when Bello began making advances towards her. Initially, this began as mild flirtation, but the more Harlean snubbed him, the more persistent he became, to such an extent that he began leaving 'love notes' in her bed – into which he had masturbated. Indeed, Bello may even have raped her, according to what some friends have said, declaring that she alone was to blame for being so attractive. Her biographer, Irving Shulman, who penned his novel-style biography, *Harlow*, after being given access to her agent Arthur Landau's so-called 'secret' diaries, observed of her at this stage of her life: 'She had her full height of five feet two inches and weighed about a hundred and 18 pounds. A creamy type of blonde with expressive blue eyes and a kewpie mouth that made boys wet their lips.'

In fact, Harlean saw nothing of Chuck during these weekend breaks because Mama Jean and Bello were still trying to pair her up with Eugene Byfield. Perhaps this is what pushed Chuck into asking her to marry him at once, instead of waiting until he came of age. On 21 September, they skipped school and jumped into Chuck's car, and dove to Waukegan, where they were married by the same justice of the peace who had conducted the ceremony for Harlean's mother and stepfather. Chuck lied that he was 21, Harlean that she was 20, and no questions were asked. Two months later, Chuck turned 21 and inherited over $200,000; upon hearing that this was but the first portion of his inheritance – that there would be much more to come – Mama Jean began warming to him. Too late, of course, for from now on, Chuck's sole aim in life would be to place as much distance as possible between mother and daughter.

In January 1928, the two embarked on a belated honeymoon to Los Angeles – travelling the sea-route via Cuba and the Panama Canal. Chuck had purchased a house at 618 North Linden Drive, in Beverly Hills – not far from Aunt Jetta Chadsey, her favourite relative who was actually Mama Jean's aunt. Compared with Jetta, one might almost describe Mama Jean as a saint. Married and divorced by the age of 18, she had next born twins to an Osage Indian common-law husband and, within weeks of his death fallen pregnant to another man who she had married. In January 1928, when Harlean and Chuck moved in with her while their own house was being refurbished, Aunt Jetta had just divorced her third husband for the second time, and was planning on tying the knot again!

It was by way of a friend of Aunt Jetta's, an aspiring actress named Rosalie Roy, that Harlean gained access to the Hollywood society which would open the door to her movie career. Rosalie had an appointment with someone at one of the studios and, as she was in a hurry and had no car, Harlean offered to drive her there – though it is not on record when or even if she possessed a car. And at the studio, of course, all eyes were on the blonde beauty. This was an age when studio scouts engaged extras after a cursory glance – usually after walking among the long line of hopefuls who gathered outside the studio gates each morning. If an actor was very tall, like Clark Gable or Rock Hudson, then getting discovered was not that hard. Similarly if someone stood out in some other way – as

Harlean did with her hair and ample cleavage which was always on display – then offers of work were often forthcoming. Much to Rosalie Roy's consternation, the representatives of several studio executives approached Harlean, handing her business cards or taking her address to send her letters of introduction. So far, the only interest Harlean showed in these was to thank everyone politely, shove the letters and cards into her handbag, and say she would think about it. The last thing she wanted at the time, she said, was to become an actress because her grandfather considered the acting profession 'common'.

Harlean changed her mind, but only as a wager, a few weeks later when Rosalie and some of her friends taunted her, accusing her of being too timid to follow up on the business cards. She approached one of the casting directors at Fox, who must have thought all his birthdays had come at once when he saw a potential extra decked out in satin gown, jewels and furs which many of the major stars would not have been able to afford. She made it quite clear, however, that she was a happily married woman – not that this would stop her in the future – who had no intention of hopping onto the casting couch. She was therefore directed to the Central Casting Bureau, a body which hired extras and distributed them around the studios. Interestingly, she announced that she was in town for just a few months visiting relatives, and registered under her mother's maiden name – for no other reason, it appears, than she was still legally a minor and doing this without her parents' written approval. If anyone checked up on her they would find an authentic Jean Harlow living at the 'home' address she had given them.

Harlean later claimed never to have expected a reply from the Central Casting Bureau, and was surprised when, a few days later, they contacted her with an offer of work – so much so that she declined. It is likely that Jean Harlow Snr was also contacted: a few days later, Mama Jean and Marino Bello showed up at Aunt Jetta's with a mountain of luggage. By now, Mama Jean had abandoned all hope of a movie career for herself. From now on she would invest every minute of every day launching and 'maintaining' that of her daughter, whether Harlean wanted this or not. Indeed, it seems very likely that Mama Jean, still a very attractive woman, ended up on the casting couch on her daughter's behalf. For just as Marino Bello continued sleeping around after their marriage – he would still be offering his services as a gigolo 10 years later when well into his forties – so Mama Jean played the field. At whatever cost, it was she who landed Harlean her first movie contract.

Between February 1928 and October 1930, Harlean Carpenter appeared in around 20 films as an extra or bit-part – some have been lost, and there is no way of knowing in which order they were made. As they were released out of sequence, audiences watching her would see her pronouncing (vocally or with titles in this silents-to-Talkies transitional period) a few lines in one, then catch a fleeting glimpse of her in the next. Unlike many of her near contemporaries – Greta Garbo, Marlene Dietrich, Joan Crawford – she is instantly recognisable on account of her hair and slouchy pose. Her first release was *Honor Bound*, a prison drama with musclebound George O'Brien. Working in this led to Harlean being approached by Paramount's Joseph Egli, who for the princely sum of $10 and a night on the town put her into *Moran Of The Marines* with Richard Dix and Ruth Elder. On the same daily salary, she worked for one week at the Hal Roach Studios in a dire Charley Chase two-reeler, *Chasing Husbands* – a title which would later prove most appropriate.

Next, First National put Harlean into *Why Be Good?*, and this was followed by Fox's *Fugitives*, with Colleen Moore. By the end of 1928 she was back with Hal Roach in three bizarrely-titled two-reelers: *Thundering Toupees*, *The Unkissed Man* (with Laurel & Hardy) and *Why Is A Plumber?* All of these saw her unbilled, and the turning point, as such, came with Roach's *Liberty*. Its stars once again were Laurel & Hardy, and it was after completing this one – on Boxing Day – that Roach signed her to a five-year contract, starting out at $100 a week, a tidy sum for a bit-part in those days. The name on the contract read 'Harlean McGrew aka Jean Harlow' – the latter insisted upon by Mama Jean, who over the next nine years would live out her movie star fantasies through her daughter.

Celebrating her newfound success – though aside from Laurel & Hardy and the other actors who had chatted to her in the studio canteens, no one knew who she was – Harlean and Chuck travelled to San Francisco, where she achieved slight notoriety by getting blind drunk and having a row with him in their hotel suite. When Chuck slapped her, she screamed that she wanted a divorce, and stormed off into the night. Chuck retaliated by trashing the suite, causing hundreds of dollars worth of damage. Paramount had promised Harlean a bigger part in her next picture, but for stepping out of line she was demoted to extra for *Close Harmony*, a hammy musical comedy with Charles 'Buddy' Rogers and Nancy Carroll. Within weeks, however, Hal Roach welcomed her back into the fold and she was put into one of the last Laurel & Hardy silents, *Double Whoopee*. In this she sowed the seeds for the inimitable Jean Harlow image which millions would later love – and not inadvertently caused mayhem on the backlot with her antics, setting a valuable precedent for the future.

The scene called for Harlean, a society guest at a plush hotel, to climb out of a cab driven by hapless bellboy Stan Laurel, who traps her dress in the door so that she saunters off and leaves this behind, entering the foyer in just her slip. Some years later it would be in part emulated by Katharine Hepburn and Cary Grant in *Bringing Up Baby*. Neither the actors nor the film crew, naturally, were aware of Harlean's fondness for *not* wearing underwear. Therefore, when the dress came off, the powerful klieg lights shone straight though her see-through underskirt, giving everyone on the set a perfect view of what she called her 'silver clitty bush' – she had dyed her pubic hair to match that on her head!

Hal Roach and most of those involved with *Double Whoopee*

may have initially been shocked, but such was Harlean's reaction
to the episode – according to contemporary reports, throwing the
cameraman a look of 'innocent surprise', as if this sort of thing
happened every day in Hollywood – that she was not even disci-
plined. Hal Roach simply escorted her to the costumes department,
where she was kitted out with a pair of silk knickers and a more
serviceable underskirt. In fact, the incident worked in her favour,
for it led to a meeting with underground photographer Edwin
Bower Hesser, who hired her for what was ostensibly a 'French
postcards' photo-shoot in Griffith Park.

Born in New Jersey, Hesser (1893–1962) had risen to
prominence during World War I, commissioned by Sam
Goldwyn's New York office to oversee land and battlefield
photography of US soldiers. He had relocated to New York in 1923,
combining his expertise of photographing landscapes with his
passion for naked women by launching his own *Arts Monthly*
magazine – his way of beating the moralists who denounced his
very classy portraits as pornographic. His subjects, shot against
parkland and backdrops, included Norma Talmadge, Marion
Davies and the usually staid Mary Pickford. No stranger to
controversy, only weeks before working with Harlean Carpenter,
Hesser had been arrested on suspicion of narcotics peddling, and
for impersonating a police officer during the Helen St Clair Evans
investigation – the starlet murdered by her husband – and all his
operations were closed down. As such, the Jean Harlow session
would re-launch his career.

The previous year, Chuck McGrew had taken a series of
'publicity' shots of Harlean in Griffith Park during one of their
regular Sunday afternoon picnics – or at least ones he assumed the
studios would be interested in, wearing a cardigan and below-the-
knee floral print cotton skirt. Hesser had a different idea. He got her
– without much tempting – to remove everything she was wearing
except her long chiffon scarf, which she wrapped around the most
voluptuous body he claimed he had ever seen. As a bonus, she

pinched her nipples into stiff peaks, setting another precedent, though in the future she would frequently rub them with ice-cubes. The result was sensational, and ended up on sale under counters all over America, initially without her name because she was still an unknown. Many years later, one of Hesser's postcards of Jean Harlow ended up in Marlene Dietrich's possession, and she emulated the pose for her sell-out concerts in South America. One, of her wearing a diaphanous red chiffon gown and showing considerably more flesh than would have been allowed anywhere in late-Fifties Britain or America, appears on the sleeve of her *Dietrich In Rio* album. 'I wore knickers, of course,' she told me, 'and the audience who had by then probably forgotten who Jean Harlow was went wild!'

The Hesser photographs appalled Chuck and he further hit the roof upon seeing the rushes for *Double Whoopee*. His wife's body, he angrily declared, was for his eyes only, and not to be used as masturbation fodder for half of the country's male population. He issued her with an ultimatum – that she should get out of the movies at once, or give him a divorce. Harlean gave every impression of siding with him, breaking her contract with Hal Roach in March 1929, one week before her 18th birthday, with the excuse that she wanted to settle down and have Chuck's children. Not wishing to be criticised for opposing Hollywood's family values clause, dictated verbally but as yet not written into contracts, Roach had no option but to grant her leave of absence. It was however a ploy organised by Mama Jean who, in these last few days that Harlean was legally acknowledged as a child star, 'acted in her best interests' to get her away from Roach, whom she considered stingy and fixed her up with a studio which would pay her more money. Marino Bello had recently become unemployed, and Mama Jean now felt that, after all they had done for her – ostensibly not much – it was Harlean's turn to support *them*. She therefore completed the movie she had just begun working on – Laurel & Hardy's *Bacon Grabbers* – and moved to Fox, where, until they could find her a more suitable vehicle, she was hired as an unbilled bit-part in *Masquerade*.

Halfway through shooting the film, Harlean discovered to her delight that she was pregnant, and made up her mind once and for all to quit the movies, work on her already shaky marriage, and settle down to motherhood. The tyrannical Mama Jean would not hear of this, however. Her daughter would have all the children she wanted, and with a more suitable husband – but only once her career was well and truly underway and she was getting better parts. When Harlean protested, Bello intervened. He offered her a choice – she would consent to having an abortion, or he would beat the baby out of her. Bello personally arranged for her to enter a clinic, which *she* paid for, and the pregnancy was terminated in May 1929.

On 11 June, Chuck McGrew moved out of his own house, terrorised into doing so by Bello's mob associates, and Bello and Mama Jean moved in.

CHAPTER TWO
Hell's Angel

'One day he was eating a cookie and offered me a bite. Don't under-estimate that. The poor guy's so frightened of germs, it could darn near have been a proposal!'

Jean Harlow on Howard Hughes

For Harlean Carpenter, there followed walk-ons and bit-parts in numerous films which ranged from the crass to the sublime. Blink and one missed her in *This Thing Called Love* – while Charlie Chaplin, the connoisseur of underaged girls, steered well clear of this one, chaperoned by an eagle-eyed mother, when he hired her for *City Lights*. She appeared in *New York Nights*, a dire Prohibition drama of which there was currently a glut, and shared a table with Gallic charmer Maurice Chevalier during a break while shooting Paramount's *The Love Parade*. Chevalier was more interested in ogling her cleavage than he was in eating his sandwiches, and it was only after they had been chatting for 15 minutes that he realised she had been in his film. Again, Mama Jean had to step into the breach to prevent him from whisking her off to his trailer.

What Mama Jean did not know was that her daughter was having an affair with bandleader Roy Fox (1901–82), for which he could have been arrested and charged with statutory rape – so far as she had been told, Harlean was sneaking off into the night to meet up with Chuck McGrew, in the hope of a reconciliation. In fact, there was little chance of this ever happening. Chuck was still sticking to his ultimatum – if she wanted him back, she would have to give up her movie career. Additionally, he refused to pay one cent towards her keep, knowing only too well that she would have handed the money straight over to her mother and Marino Bello. When things grew desperate and she had but a few dollars to her name, Harlean cabled Skip Harlow in Kansas, and the response was more or less the same. So long as she remained in Hollywood there would be no more support from her grandfather, because she had brought shame on the clan by stripping down to her shimmy in *Double Whoopee*. One shudders to think what his reaction would have been, had he been witness to the entire incident on the backlot!

Salvation came in the form of Joseph Egli, who had cast Harlean in *Moran Of The Marines* and *The Love Parade*. It was he who introduced her to Edward Sutherland, currently shooting *The Saturday Night Kid* for Paramount with Clara Bow and James Hall. Just two years earlier, Bow (1905–65) had attained megastardom as 'The It Girl', the phrase coined by British novelist Eleanor Glyn for sex-appeal: women across America had emulated her bright red painted bee-stung lips and frizzy hairdo which in time would be adopted by the cartoon character, Betty Boop. Tastes had rapidly changed, however. Bow's horrendously nasal Brooklyn twang had not transcribed well to sound: the critics had been relentless. She had hit the bottle, begun taking drugs and piled on the pounds, and there were rumours that at just 25 she was already suffering from the mental illness that had afflicted her father and other members of her family.

When Clara Bow was introduced to Harlean Carpenter, she flew into a tantrum and yelled at Edward Sutherland, 'Either that broad goes, or I do!' Harlean had not helped matters by wearing a near-transparent dress, flopping onto a stool in the rehearsal room, hoisting this up and spreading her legs wide enough to reveal that she was wearing nothing underneath. Sutherland's reaction was to point to the door – whence Bow and Harlean became reasonably good friends, even when Harlean stole Bow's lover and co-star, James Hall, right from under her nose.

The film is remembered today only because it was the first to feature the name Jean Harlow in the end credits – though this does not feature in the opening ones. Otherwise it is a lame affair, a precursor to the Joan Crawford 'shopgirl' movies of the next decade. She, Clara Bow and Jean Arthur play salesgirls in a department store who are all interested in the James Hall character. Its only lively moment is when Harlow dances the Charleston.

Harlean had already been hired as an extra in *Weak But Willing*, a tepid comedy featuring Billy Bevan, and it was while this was shooting that she met Arthur Landau, the agent who would represent her for the rest of her life. A curious little man – he was just 4 feet 10 inches tall – Landau tried, but failed to seduce her within hours of their meeting, and henceforth would carry an unrequited torch for her. According to Landau, she shrugged off his advances with a wisecracking, 'Mr Landau, I'm hungry, but if you buy me a steak I'll let you pretend I'm a whore!' Of their dinner date, Irving Shulman later recalled, 'As they drove off the Roach lot Arthur stared at Jean's high, firm breasts. Never before had he seen a connection between hunger and passion, but as she licked her lips in anticipation of the food her nipples hardened until they were the size of marbles.'

It was Landau, and not James Hall, who introduced her to Howard Hughes, then producing and directing what would be widely regarded as a landmark World War I aerial epic, *Hell's Angels*, starring James Hall, Ben Lyon and Norwegian actress Greta Nissen – the latter two also clients of Landau.

Born in Houston, Texas, Hughes (1905–76) was the only son of a millionaire who had invented and marketed revolutionary oil-drilling equipment. Indolent as a child, he had made his mark at 18 following the death of his father (his mother had died two years earlier), taking his legal guardians to court, and winning his case to have him legally declared an adult. He had subsequently bought out his relatives' share of the business and become a millionaire at 19, whence he had moved to Hollywood to indulge in his twin fancies – women and making movies. Later, he would found the Hughes Aircraft Company, take over Trans-World Airlines, and become one of the wealthiest men in the world conducting very public affairs with such luminaries as Hedy Lamarr, Lana Turner and Carole Lombard – though it is not thought with Jean Harlow – besides discreet ones with Cary Grant and Errol Flynn.

Towards the end of 1927, Howard Hughes had begun shooting *Hell's Angels* as a silent production, with Hall and Lyon as the aviators who fall for the same woman, only to be duped by her. There had been so many problems and personality clashes that, by the spring of 1929, and with Hughes already having spent over $2 million on the budget, the movie was nowhere near completion. Hughes had fired two directors before settling for the current one – himself – and shelled out a small fortune to the families of the mechanic and two stunt pilots who had died in on-set accidents. Unable to cope with his obsession for the project, his wife had left him, and now he faced having to deal with the advent of sound. This prevented few problems for the aerial sequences – sound effects were added to the finished footage. For the leads, however, who are all supposed to be English, Hughes was faced with a palpable dilemma. Neither Ben Lyon nor James Hall were competent with accents other than their own, and Hughes was compelled to drop Greta Nissen on account of her thick Norwegian drawl.

Hughes' lothario reputation preceded him, therefore few actresses were willing to work with him. Alternatively, most of the Hollywood agents regarded him as a joke – a rich kid who had so much money, he did not know what to do with it. Then, during the break in production brought about by Greta Nissen's dismissal, Hughes won an Oscar for his most recent film, *Two Arabian Nights*, and suddenly he was flavour of the month as agents bombarded him with requests to screen-test their clients. Not surprisingly, Hughes would have nothing to do with them, and announced that the female lead in *Hell's Angels* would go to *his* discovery, and that she would be a complete unknown. It took him within five minutes of meeting her to decide that this would be Harlean Carpenter who, prompted by her mother (though the press were never told this) should henceforth be known as Jean Harlow. The legend had begun.

Harlow signed her contract with Hughes' Caddo Company (so-named after the site in Louisiana where his father had first struck oil) on an auspicious date – 24 October 1929, the day of the Wall Street Crash. Though he knew from the outset that she would only appear in a single film, Hughes insisted on keeping her on a retainer for five years – *Hell's Angels* had already been shooting for two years, and he was unsure when it would be finished. He had paid Greta Nissen – a big star then but forgotten today – a staggering $2,500 a week, and United Artists advised him to leave her in the film, but dub her voice. Hughes demanded authenticity, and so as not to bankrupt the studio shrewdly signed Harlean on the same take it or leave it $100 a week salary she had been getting from Hal Roach. Later, he would raise this to $250 a week when she was working, $200 when she was not, still a fraction of what he had paid Nissen and never ceasing to remind her of the fact.

The following morning, when America was still reeling after the biggest stock exchange disaster in its history, Hughes' press office issued a statement announcing details of his new leading lady: 'Jean Harlow: 19-year-old Chicago Society Girl' – she was actually 18. With it were released the contents of a letter of gratitude to Hughes, part of which read, 'Your faith in me has been a great influence in my life...It is something also that I shall never let you regret.' The letter had been signed 'Jean Bello' – by Mama Jean who, though she had been the first to condemn the Hesser photographs, was so confident of her daughter's future success that she now had several thousand of them printed so that they could be sent out to future fans, with an 'authentic' Jean Harlow autograph, which she and her helpers forged. When reminded of the *type* of role she had been offered, Harlow told a hastily assembled press conference, 'If it gives me a break, I don't care how bad the character is. There's plenty of time to live it down afterwards!' Over the course of the next few years, she would be made to eat those words.

There seems little doubt that Howard Hughes acquired Jean Harlow solely as an investment, and not to add another notch to his bedpost. Indeed, there is more than enough evidence that he disliked her, and she him, so much so that rather than work with her personally, he hired British director James Whale to oversee the dialogue sequences she appeared in. For Harlow, this was but the lesser of two evils. Whale (1889–1957) loathed Hollywood and women in that order, most especially beautiful women, and made no secret of the fact. 'Hollywood is just *too* marvellous,' he told a press conference before starting work on *Hell's Angels*. 'One feels the footprints of all the immortals here, but has a terrible feeling that they are in sand and won't last when civilisation comes this way!' When Whale announced that Harlow was perfect to portray the sluttish Helen, because in his opinion Helen was 'nothing less than a pig' and 'a cock magnet', few expected shooting to run smoothly. Many years later the film's scriptwriter, Joseph Moncure March, would recall Whale's nasty treatment of Harlow in an interview with *Look* magazine (March 1954). She had politely asked Whale how, in his opinion, the part of Helen should be played, bringing the tarty response, 'My dear girl, I can tell you how to be an actress, but I cannot tell you how to be a woman!'

No other producer would have made such a comment, particularly one renowned for his astute professionalism, but Whale had already attracted adverse criticism for his own lifestyle. Later, his final tragic years would be turned into a biopic, *Gods And*

Monsters, starring Ian McKellen and Brendan Fraser. Openly gay in a society which malevolently condemned such things, Whale was dating producer David Lewis (David Levy, 1903–87), who visited the set most days. Their union would endure until Whale's suicide by drowning in May 1957, and after *Hell's Angels* both would move on to better things – Levy producing *Dark Victory* for Bette Davis, Whale directing a clutch of classic horror movies, including *Frankenstein* and *Bride Of Frankenstein*, before falling into obscurity because of peer prejudice against his sexuality. For now, the pair made Jean Harlow's working life hell, never ceasing to remind her that Howard Hughes had contracted the worst actress in America to ruin what could have been his finest achievement.

It was probably Howard Hughes' intention that the characters in *Hell's Angels* and much of the plot be secondary to the aerial sequences. Yet despite the panning it received, it is not that bad. To best appreciate it, one has to view it as a transitional exercise between silence and sound – the sections with the old full-screen titles, and those where the movement suddenly speeds up were filmed pre-1929. Also, in some of the dialogue sequences, the actors hesitate before pronouncing their lines, which again is in keeping with the time. The accents *do* leave much to be desired, particularly as the three main protagonists are supposed to be English. In typical Hollywood fashion, we are reminded of this by the 'expletives' delivered by the Tommy officers who accentuate their dialogue with phrases such as 'bloody hell', 'for Christ's sake' and 'what the blazes' (cut from some early prints), while Hall and Lyon just play extensions of themselves, and Harlow at least attempts to sound like a Londoner. The scenario opens in Munich on the eve of World War I, with English and German students mingling contentedly at a *bierkeller*. Monte and Roy Rutledge (Lyon, Hall) are vacationing here with fellow Oxford student Karl (John Darrow), but are forced to make a hasty return to England when Monte is caught making love to the wife of a German general, and wounds him during a duel. No sooner do they arrive

back at Oxford than war is declared and the friends separate –
Monte and Roy joining the Flying Corps, while pacifist Karl is
inveigled into the German Air Force.

Before leaving for their base, Roy introduces his brother to his
sweetheart, Helen (Harlow), at a charity ball – the film's first all-
colour sequence as opposed to the blue or purple two-tone used for
the action scenes. She makes her appearance, wearing a low-cut
gown and quite obviously no bra, emerging from the bushes with
another soldier, though Roy is so besotted with her, he does not
realise what she has been up to. She never takes her eyes off Monte
all evening, and even when she admits to Roy that she is thinking
only about Monte, and when Monte drives her home, Roy still does
not see her for the loose woman she is. They return to her place
(and monochrome), where Helen pronounces her classic line,
'Would you be shocked if I put on something more comfortable' –
bringing the response, 'I'll try to survive!' There is nothing
seductive in the way she says this, though when she emerges from
her bedroom wearing a bathrobe, it is only too obvious what she has
in mind. At first, Monte tries to resist – until she says of the stuffy
but honourable Roy, in such a way that Harlow could have been
describing Chuck McGrew:

> He wouldn't approve of me if he knew what I was really
> like…When I'm with Roy, I'm the way Roy wants me to be.
> That's caddish, isn't it? But I can't help it…Roy's love means
> marriage and children, never anyone but Roy! I couldn't bear
> that! I want to be free! I want to be gay and have fun! Life's
> short and I want to *live* while I'm alive!

Monte wants to leave, but stays. They spend the night together, and
next morning he regrets what has happened. 'God, I'm rotten. And
you're rotten, too,' he growls. They argue, she kicks him out.

It then cuts to the section of the film that Howard Hughes excels
with: the first aerial sequence which retains its original captions,

and to which he added sound effects. A Zeppelin air balloon is en route to bomb Trafalgar Square, and the Rutledge brothers are two of the quartet of pilots dispatched to bring it down. What they do not know is that their friend Karl is on board, and that it is he who has been winched down in a chariot to guide the bombing crew. Still opposed to the war, Karl misleads them and the bombs drop into the Channel. As the British aircraft move in on their target, however, the German pilot is compelled to lighten his load so that the airship can rise above the clouds and out of firing range. He cuts Karl's winch and he plummets into the sea, then orders most of the crew to bale out to their deaths – moments before a British kamikaze pilot brings the airship down. Roy and Monte are shot down too and end up in France where, shell-shocked, Roy has a fit of hysterics after one of the men calls him 'yellow' for refusing to take up a plane in which a pilot was killed – the film's only unintentionally hilarious moment. Then the brothers discover that Helen has joined up and been posted here to run the NAAFI canteen, where of course she spends much of her time chatting up the soldiers.

When the British commander in France elects to blow up a German munitions dump, risking a few of his men's lives to save hundreds, Monte and Roy volunteer – their only snag being that they will complete the mission in a captured German plane so as not to be detected. Aware of the danger and the fact that this might be their last night on earth, the pair seek out Helen, but instead of finding her at the NAAFI store, she is at a local dive, no more than a brothel, getting it on with a soldier. Roy knocks the man out, and now it is Helen's turn to get hysterical, looking like an over made-up villainess from a bad silent movie. She would not belong to him if he were the last man on earth, she screams, then levels, 'You're too good to live – you're just a stupid prig!'

The brothers get drunk and end up with a couple of doxies and, half-drunk, get into their plane for the film's longest – some thought too long – sequence. They and their comrades complete their mission, only to be pursued by the mighty Baron Von Richtofen (1892–1918), who naturally has to have the slice of the action, and his cronies in rickety-looking biplanes – Hughes had overlooked the fact that the Red Baron had more often than not flown a Fokker Triplane to distinguish himself during such manoeuvres. And so that American audiences could work out who was who, bearing in mind the good guys are also flying a German plane, the German pilots have their names written on the fuselages! Von Richtofen wins the day, of course – even Hughes would never have got away with 'Hollywoodising' this part of aviation history – and the brothers are shot down and captured by the enemy, who Hughes typecasts into shouting all the time just to remind us that they are the baddies.

Ben Lyon, who had trained as a pilot for the US Air Force, insisted on applying realism to this scene by piloting the plane himself – only to refuse, when the crunch came, to get into the machine because of the dream he had had the night before. A few years later he explained to *Screen Book*'s Jerry Lane that he had witnessed himself baling out of a plane with a group of airmen, and that his parachute had failed to open. Howard Hughes had tried to convince him that it had been *just* a dream, but Lyon had gone home to wife Bebe Daniels – where later that day, Hughes had called to say that one of the planes had plummeted out of the sky, killing the pilot. Even so, once his nerves had settled, and despite Hughes' willingness to use a stuntman, Lyons had taken the plane up.

The brothers are given an ultimatum. If they reveal details of the British invasion, their lives will be spared and they will spend the rest of the war in an internment camp before being released. If not, they will be shot. Monte wants to spill the beans and save his skin, but the success of the British attack will now save thousands of lives. Roy therefore cons the German general – the same man whose wife he slept with at the beginning of the picture – into giving him a gun. He shoots Monte to silence him, and allows him to die eloquently in his arms before bravely walking off to face the firing squad. The film ends when the British arrive and decimate the place. What has happened to Helen, know one knows, and by this stage of the proceedings, no one probably cares!

Halfway through shooting, Howard Hughes and James Whale had an almighty row over the rushes, with Hughes blaming Whale for Harlow's 'lacklustre' performance so far. Whale's reaction to this was, 'Direct her yourself if you can do any better!' Hughes therefore commissioned crude Technicolor for the charity ball sequence, at tremendous expense for a production which had already set him back $3 million. This, he declared, would draw more attention to her hourglass figure, hair and blue eyes. In these primitive days of colour photography, the effects on the actors was near catastrophic, particularly during facial close-ups, on account of them having to stand only inches away from the powerful klieg lights. These colour segments took just two days to complete, but Whale summoned all the actors to the set for the 16-hours duration of each shoot, whether they were required for the segment or not. In full evening attire, several fainted, but Harlow soldiered on despite a headache which she complained was getting progressively worse by the hour. Once the colour footage was in the can, Whale permitted her to see the studio doctor – paid to make sure everyone worked, whether they were ill or not – who informed her that she was suffering from mere eye strain, and that the headache would diminish once she got out into the fresh air. Little did she know that she had suffered permanent damage to her eyes.

Shooting wound up a few days before the Christmas of 1929, with Howard Hughes ending up with over two million feet of film, which United Artists asked to be trimmed to 15,000 feet, still much longer than the average film of the day. Because she disliked Hughes so much, Harlow tried to break her contract – or rather Mama Jean did, as had happened with Hal Roach. Hughes, the megalomaniac, refused to budge – she would be offered for loan-out, he said, but only after cutting was finished, just in case any of her scenes had to be redone.

This she found frustrating. The critics, having viewed the rushes, were tearing apart her so-called non-acting abilities – and on the other hand announcing to the world that Hollywood had another major star on its hands. Yet while established stars were living lives of unbridled luxury, most of the $200 Hughes was now paying her was being handed over to greedy relatives who, legally, still had the last say in her welfare. In February 1930, unable to keep the place going – and in any case, it belonged to Chuck McGrew – Harlow, Mama Jean and Marino Bello moved out of the North Linden Drive house, and into a rented bungalow at 300 North Maple Drive.

In January 1930, with no sign of her headaches diminishing, Harlow consulted her own doctor. He sent her to an eye specialist, and the initial prognosis was not good. She had suffered possible irreparable damage to her eyes, and this required immediate surgery. She was secreted into a clinic in the middle of the night, and the press informed that she was 'resting' – the last thing Howard Hughes wanted as he was preparing his greatest achievement for release were salacious rumours about his star, for with Harlow they almost certainly would have jumped to the conclusion that she had had an abortion, or emergency treatment for some sexual malady. It would only be four years later, when she was a major star, that the truth would emerge. Then, in an interview with *Screen Book*'s Jack Grant, her vocabulary would demonstrate that she was by no means the 'dumb blonde' everyone had assumed. 'What is known as the conjunctiva – I believe that is the correct name for the mucous membrane covering the eyeball with a transparent epithelium or film – had been burned by the excessive lights just as the exposed skin of your body becomes sunburned,' she told an astonished Grant.

The surgeon performed what was then a rare and dangerous procedure – to remove the peeling membrane from her damaged eyes. Howard Hughes picked up the tab – it was either that, or Mama Jean would have sued him for neglect. Harlow was told to wear dark glasses day and night, and a sleeping mask, and forbidden to read or go to the cinema. Her indisposition had its good side, however, for one of the visitors sent to cheer her up – as was his wont – would both offer her solace, and become the most controversial man in her life: Paul Bern.

Known as 'Little Father Confessor' on account of his puny build and his fondness for listening to other people's problems – though not always helping them to resolve them, or indeed facing up to his own tribulations – German-born Bern (Paul Levy, 1889–1932) was Irving Thalberg's right-hand man at MGM. With him he would soon produce *Grand Hotel*, with Garbo, Crawford and John Barrymore, all close friends, and later he would take newcomer Clark Gable under his wing. A talented scriptwriter, he had worked with Ernst Lubitsch and Josef von Sternberg.

Sophisticated, intellectual but unattractive, Bern's all-powerful position with MGM enabled him to date some of the biggest names in Hollywood, of both sexes. After his death, however, various inquests revealed that on account of grossly under-developed genitals, he had been incapable of consummating any relationship – that his always younger conquests had merely looked upon him as a kindly father figure. A recent failure had been 29-year-old Barbara Lamarr, six times married, who early in 1926 had died of a drugs overdose – 'Hollywoodised' for the press by studio chiefs as 'death by over-rigorous dieting'. Bern moulded and promoted Joan Crawford to take over where the luckless Lamarr – described in one obituary as 'The Girl Who Was *Too* Beautiful' – had left off. In 1927, he had put Crawford in *The Taxi Dancer*, since which time she had not looked back. And now his intention, he said, was to transform Jean Harlow into the biggest star the movie world had ever seen.

In the spring of 1932, before leaving on a trip to Europe, Joan Crawford gave an interview to *Photoplay*'s Hale Horton, hardly aware that Bern would be dead by the time it reached the printed page. Bern had given her a copy of the book he handed out to all of his intimates: *In Tune With The Infinite*. It was, he said, his own private Bible which he studied daily in the hope of becoming a better person. Written in 1897 by philosopher Ralph Waldo Trine (1866–1958) and several times revised, the editorial prescribes it, 'For all who would like to strengthen their connection to the Infinite Mind in order to enjoy a free-flow of abundance, personal blessings, intuitive knowledge and the strong sense of well-being that results from a solid connection.'

Cynics might have argued that, as a fellow practitioner of Christian Science (enforced by her mother), Harlow like Crawford latched on to Trine's frequently warbled theories for the want of something better to do and to draw attention to herself, as happens with many of today's stars. Even so, Joan's interview offered a candid insight into what he had been like, and when it appeared in the magazine's July issue, Horton had kept it in the present tense, himself refusing to believe that Bern was dead:

> He possesses a great mind and an ability to listen. He lets me rave on about my troubles, troubles which to such a man must seem pitifully small. He never makes me feel that I'm acting in anything but a normal manner. It's not that I'm necessarily getting religion [from the book]. It's only that I'm gradually learning to *believe* in things, in life, in people, most especially in myself. He is making me realise than unless you believe in a thing you can never understand it, and as a result it frightens you. Furthermore he's teaching me to laugh at myself by explaining why it's foolish to take life so hard. Perhaps if I learn to believe in myself utterly and chuckle at myself when I'm doing something perfectly absurd, I shall lose my fear of the future. Perhaps I'm finding permanent relief. If so, I shall face life bravely.

This, then, was Paul Bern. At 40, he was more than twice Harlow's age, but the two got on like a house on fire and would continue to do so, despite the persistent efforts of friends like Joan Crawford – who could not stand Harlow – trying to put him off by informing him that he would only end up making a fool of himself.

It was Bern who escorted her to the premiere of *Hell's Angels* on 27 May 1930, an event that quickly turned into the biggest panic attack Hollywood had seen since Rudolph Valentino's funeral, four years earlier. Tickets for the event, average price $10, had been sold for 10 times that amount by touts. In keeping with the film's scenario, Hughes had organised a fighter squadron to encircle Grauman's Chinese Theater while the guests were arriving, and dancing spotlights – total cost $20,000. All the way along Hollywood Boulevard and its connecting streets there were traffic jams, and the night air was filled with the cursing of frustrated drivers and the blaring of horns. Most of the invited guests managed to get inside the building, but when Harlow's car pulled up in front of the theatre, 50,000 baying fans surged forwards, and cops waved it on while the Los Angeles Chief of Police summoned the National Guard to restore order. Gloria Swanson's car was pounced upon by fans, who began dancing on the roof until mounted police wielding sticks swatted them like flies. By the time Harlow's car returned – at 10pm, two hours after the screening was supposed to start – more than a hundred arrests had been made, but the crowd was now under control. As per her doctor's instructions, she had worn dark glasses until the very last moment, and the spotlights shining in her face caused her to stagger. The ones standing closest to her assumed that she had been drinking, but when Bern advised her to put her glasses back on, she opted to suffer. Clad in white and with a huge corsage of cream orchidae, she presented a vision of loveliness, but was visibly shaking. Bern, seen clinging to her arm, wears an expression of bemusement in the filmed footage. Behind them were Mama Jean, looking almost as glamorous as her daughter – and Marino Bello, looking more like Mama Jean's father than her husband.

The critics were almost unanimously merciless. The *New York*

Times labelled the film 'a most mediocre piece of work', which was
going too far, while the *New York Herald* singled out Harlow as
'plain awful', again an exaggeration. The *New York Post*'s Thornton
Delehanty liked the action scenes, but that was all: 'In contrast with
its pictorial realism, the acting of *Hell's Angels* is not so convincing.
Even in pantomime it would be hard to accept Jean Harlow as an
English girl, or Ben Lyon and James Hall as Oxford students.'
Variety on the other hand was spot-on with its prediction:

> Jean Harlow wafts plenty of 'that' across the screen, and
> dresses to accentuate it. It doesn't make much difference
> what degree of talent she possesses here, for the boys are apt
> to go in an uproar over this girl who is the most sensuous
> figure in front of a camera for some time…She'll probably
> always have to play these kind of roles, but nobody ever
> starved possessing what she's got.

The film was a huge success despite this panning, though Hughes
knew before its release that he would not recover all of the $3.8
million he had lavished on it. James Hall would fall by the wayside,
a victim of sound, and Ben Lyon would go on to better things with
his actress wife, Bebe Daniels. As for Jean Harlow, she became an
overnight sensation. The film also opened a debate which
continues to this day. Were the man-eating trollops she was
typecast into portraying, and Harlow the woman, one and the
same? Detractors have said that she was, while the more zealous
fans have declared her overpowering, on-screen sexuality just a
front for a quiet, home-loving girl who, though interested in men,
was not that keen on sex itself. She certainly was no different
regarding her appetite for lovers than the other great sirens of her
generation: Crawford, Dietrich, Bette Davis, Hepburn and Garbo.

Also, like Carole Lombard, who became a close friend, Harlow's
colourful vocabulary ruined her chance of ever being thought of as
a lady. Yet her vulgarity, like Lombard's, was readily accepted as an

essential component of her complex persona, and was never held against her by those who knew and loved her. Marlene Dietrich coined the phrase, 'tart with a heart', and this is exactly what she was, save that it was usually *she* who was picking up the tab with some of the men in her life.

Becoming a hit with the public, and having her picture on the covers of all the top movie magazines lured Chuck McGrew out of the woodwork. He'd been the first to bemoan her 'femme fatale eccentricities', but now suddenly decided that maybe she *did* belong in the movies, even if she was playing a loose woman. Harlow had not heard from him in months, and he now began calling her every day. It was not a question of money, he said – indeed, he had just received the final instalment of his inheritance, and was extremely wealthy – he just wanted to get her away from her greedy mother and stepfather, and take care of her. As soon as Mama Jean heard of this, she had the calls intercepted, then had the number changed. This resulted in Chuck following her from the Caddo offices on 28 June – the incident made the papers – and slipping into her bedroom, where she was offered an ultimatum – he had rented out the house on Linden Drive, and was returning to Chicago the next day. The choice was hers: to stay with her family, or return with him to the life of luxury he believed she warranted. Rather than decide for herself, Harlow left the matter with Mama Jean. Within the hour, her attorney had served Chuck with divorce papers. The next morning, en route to the airport, Chuck stopped off at Maple Drive just long enough to slap his wife across the face and call her a 'fucking whore'. They would never meet again, not even for their divorce hearing six months later.

For reasons known only to himself, Howard Hughes denied *Hell's Angels* a nationwide release until the November, six months after the premiere. When Mama Jean complained that he was not paying her daughter enough, he upped her retainer to $300 a week, far less than she deserved considering that she had put his name on the map, and the amount of revenue she was earning United Artists.

There was also one condition to the raise. Though Hughes had made it clear that she would never work for him again – in his opinion, she was but 'a nice pair of tits that sold tickets' – she was compelled to embark on a promotional tour with the rest of the cast. Mama Jean, naturally, would be permitted to chaperone her, but Hughes did not want Marino Bello in on the act. Mama Jean took the totally unexpected step of starting divorce proceedings against him, but these got no further than the preliminary stage. Bello was still out of work and being supported by his wife – who in turn was being supported by her daughter. Mama Jean was told that if she went ahead with the divorce, then he would make public 'certain photographic poses' of his stepdaughter. Bello may have been referring to the Edwin Bower Hesser pictures, as yet not captioned with Harlow's name. Equally there could have been others. While making *Honor Bound*, Harlow had learned that its star, George O'Brien, had augmented his income during his formative years by visiting Helen MacGregor's studio in Los Angeles' Post Street, where he had posed for a series of 'health and strength' shots. In these, the actor is totally nude and emulates a number of famous Greek and Roman statues: Cupid, the Discus Thrower and Michelangelo's David all circulated among the Hollywood underground in the 1920s. There is every possibility that Harlow did the same. Though tastefully done, such photographs were considered pornographic at the time, and to have these presented as 'evidence' at a divorce hearing by this spiteful man – even though they had absolutely nothing to do with the case – would have brought Harlow's career to an abrupt halt.

Needless to say, Mama Jean dropped the proceedings, and Bello accompanied her and Harlow on the tour – always with the threat of handing over the mysterious photographs, should either 'step out of line'. First step on the road was Kansas City where Harlean was promoted as the local girl made good. The *Saturday Evening Post* ran a feature headed 'Kansas City Platinum' where, ahead of the 'official' biography penned by the studio publicity department (these were often wildly fabricated), journalist Frank Condon told his version of the Jean Harlow story. Condon remembered her (or so he said) as a simple student, 'A light-hearted schoolgirl hurrying down the Boulevard with her books in a strap, peeking into shop windows and considering the general wisdom of having a chocolate ice-cream soda with vanilla cream.' Nothing was mentioned of her absconding from school to get married, the failure of that marriage, and her induction into the Hollywood circus. According to Condon, a director had seen this girl with 'the Kansas City hair, the likes of which can be found on neither land nor sea', standing outside Kehoe's Drug Store, thinking of nothing but that ice-cream soda. He had turned to his assistant and exclaimed, 'Sweet spirits of Pomona, look at that hair! Go on over, Joe, and ask that girl if she would like to bust into the movies!'

It was all hogwash, of course, and few believed it. There were too many people in Kansas City who remembered the *real* Harlean Carpenter.

Despite Mama Jean's protests, Howard Hughes was urged to invite Montclair Carpenter to the premiere. This, the studio declared as part of its new 'family values' campaign, would prevent the press from asking awkward questions. For the first time, Harlow met her new stepmother, Maude, and to end the rumour that he hated her working in the movies, Montclair fixed his daughter's slightly crooked teeth so that she would look better on the screen – with Hughes paying the bill. During the subsequent press conference, he, Mama Jean and their daughter posed for 'happy family reunion' photographs and someone in the crowd asked Harlow if she really *was* the same as Helen off the screen – bringing the not so ladylike response, 'Why don't you go shove your head up your ass?' Another asked her how she was coping with the tag, 'the worst actress in pictures', and she replied more calmly, 'I hope that in the future that I will learn from all the mistakes I made while shooting *Hell's Angels*.'

The tour continued. In Philadelphia, Harlow wept while

explaining to reporters that, despite her sudden fame, Howard Hughes was not paying her nearly as much as she should have been getting – true – and that she was in debt. In Cleveland, she executed a little routine at the premiere with boxer Jack Dempsey, who had just lost his championship crown. Dempsey strode up to her on the stage, flexing his biceps and punching the air – Harlow kissed him, he hit the deck. Like Tallulah Bankhead, she had become an expert at delivering one-liners. When a plane encircled the theatre in Brooklyn and began scattering publicity leaflets, a female reporter innocently asked if this was a mail plane. 'No, my dear,' Harlow shot back, 'those are its landing wheels!' When asked if, in her opinion, a woman should take a lover as well as a husband, Harlow quipped, 'I'd advise her to take all she can get, and keep on shopping. But I would never steal another woman's husband. It'd be like shopping in a second-hand store!' When another female reporter asked her if it was true that she did not like underwear, she replied: 'Underwear makes me uncomfortable. And besides, my parts have to breathe!' Her most outrageous comment came when she was informed of Joan Crawford's own one-liner, 'Harlow should do well for herself – she's on the studio's lay-roll!' Imitating Crawford's then Kansas drawl, she hit back, 'She should know. When snakes get drunk they fuck her. I know she doesn't like me, but I've promised to go see her on visiting days!'

By the time the tour reached New York for the second time, however, Harlow was starting to show the strain. By now she was compelled to wear her dark glasses most of the time – her eyes were almost healed, but the slightest bright light caused them to stream, and resulted in questions appertaining to her 'unhappiness' and what might have been causing this. Always the same questions, the routine answers – more often than not peppered with anticipated expletives. She wanted to work again, she said, and had been offered parts, but Hughes would neither release her from her contract with him nor put her into another movie. When her agent Arthur Landau tried to intervene, Hughes threatened to have him shanghaied out of Hollywood. Blaming Landau for the fiasco, Mama Jean tried to fire him so that she could take over as her daughter's agent, but the United Artists executives advised her against this. No studio, they declared in this sexist era, would even consider entering into negotiations with a woman. Landau was kept on, but henceforth it would be Mama Jean making all the decisions.

CHAPTER THREE
Gangster's Moll

'The men like me because I don't wear a brassiere. The women like me because I don't look like a girl who would steal a husband – least not for long.'

Jean Harlow

It was Paul Bern who persuaded Howard Hughes to loan Harlow to MGM for *The Secret Six*, featuring Johnny Mack Brown, Wallace Beery, fluffing his lines all the way through the film – and newcomer Clark Gable who had recently grabbed good notices opposite Joan Crawford in *Dance, Fools, Dance*. The slant of *The Secret Six* owed much to director George Hill's passion for the German cinema, and in particular the sinister-looking but amiable Conrad Veidt, who Gable could almost be mistaken for now with his narrow eyes and feline stealth as he moves across the screen.

The story, by Frances Marion, was based on a *Saturday Evening Post* exclusive about a real-life group of Chicago businessmen (including newspaper magnate William Randolph Hearst) who had joined forces with the authorities to stamp out crime in the city. Louis 'Slaughterhouse' Scorpio – (Wallace Beery) never

ceases to remind us that he is 'a gentle, honest soul'. We see him
sledgehammering cattle at the abattoir, then striding off to a local
cafe where he drinks only milk and sets up his bootlegging
operation, sponsored by mobster Richard Newton (Lewis Stone)
with pals Franks and Mizoski (Ralph Bellamy, Paul Hurst), who are
only marginally less obnoxious than he is. Currently, the Scorpio
gang are only small town, but they plan on branching out in the big
city, once they have dispensed with its kingpin mobster, Joe
Colimo (John Miljan). When Franks and his boys turn up at
Colimo's club, the mobster sends his heavies to fix them, including
his weakling brother, Ivan (Oscar Rudolph), who is desperate to
prove himself a man. When Ivan dies in a hail of bullets,
masterfully executed while the pianola plays, we instinctively know
what the outcome of the film will be – particularly when Franks
tells Colimo that it was Scorpio who killed his brother. Colimo
goes after Scorpio and wounds him: he retaliates by shooting
Franks dead.

Enter investigative reporters Hank Rogers (Brown) and Carl
Luckner (Gable), working for rival newspapers but drawn together
by their interest in Anne Courtland (Harlow, 30 minutes into the
picture), Scorpio's cashier-moll who he keeps in a $20,000 a year
apartment, and who he now pays to seduce them and throw them
off his scent. 'Baby,' Gable drawls, 'you got a pair of the most
beautiful blues eyes I've ever seen. I'd sure like to take you around
to and introduce you to my Aunt Emma!' Irving Thalberg was so
bowled over, watching Gable in the rushes for this scene, that he
recommissioned Frances Marion to make his part bigger – from
this point in the film, Gable runs rings around everyone he comes
into contact with. Even so, Marion refused to let Gable get the girl
– it is Hank who Anne falls for.

Scorpio takes unofficial control of the city by putting up Mizoski
for Mayor and pressurising the people into voting for him. Colimo
is disposed of and, as the police are in Scorpio's pocket, it is up to
the local big-wigs to bring him to justice by way of 'The Secret Six'.

In a rather silly scene where these all don masks, Hank is hired to help them gather evidence – silly because their names have already been plastered all over the newspapers. While Carl takes pay-offs from Scorpio and lets the mobster think he is on his side so that he can pass evidence on to the Secret Six, Hank learns that the bullets which killed Colimo and Franks came from the same gun. Finding this, he sets off for the precinct to hand it in as evidence, but Scorpio is on to him, and has him followed on the subway. Anne gets there first and tries to warn him, but Hank is murdered. Scorpio is arrested at Hank's funeral – he has even had the audacity to send a wreath – but at his subsequent trial is acquitted after fixing the jury. Even the judge denounces it an outrageous miscarriage of justice. Exacting his revenge, Scorpio kidnaps Anne and Carl, but the police seek out his lair, just as he and Newton are fighting over their illicit takings. Scorpio shoots Newton dead before getting arrested, and the film ends with him being sent to the electric chair. As with several of Harlow's early films, the scriptwriter appears to have forgotten about her by this stage, so we never find out what really happens to her.

Gable aside, the acting in *The Secret Six* is intensely wooden. The film was shot quickly, and it shows: even the usually reliable Johnny Mack Brown seems at a loss for words much of the time, and Harlow, minus her trademark wisecracks, appears woefully miscast when one watches this production in retrospectives with her other work. Few of the reviews mentioned Harlow, but the critics, surprisingly, liked the film, with the *New York Daily Mirror* applauding it as 'another neat gangland melodrama, genuinely thrilling', while the *New York Post* considered the direction and acting as 'only on the highest level'.

The Secret Six very quickly fell foul of the Hays Office, though one wonders today what all the fuss was about with most of the productions they bellyached about. Former Postmaster General Will Hays (1879–1954) had set up his code in conjunction with the Bank of America and the Catholic Church in 1922. To 'rid

Hollywood of its filth and corruption', Hays, on a $100,000 a year salary, prescribed a powerful censorship law (which had not gone into full force until 1930) prohibiting 'immoral' on-screen activities such as open-mouth kissing, sexual innuendo, drinking, gambling, the mockery of religion, childbirth, swearing, sexual perversion (homosexuality, venereal disease), violence and substance abuse. Also forbidden was the displaying of navels, and chest and underarm hair. Additionally, the Hays Code dictated how stars and studio employees should conduct themselves away from the set, including how they treated their families – in Harlow's and Joan Crawford's case, no matter how badly these families treated them. Will Hays – described by Kenneth Anger in his *Hollywood Babylon* as 'a prim-faced, bat-eared, mealy-mouthed political chiseler' – compiled a 'Black Book' containing the names of movie stars whom he deemed guilty of 'moral turpitude'. By the end of 1931 Harlow, along with Joan Crawford and Clark Gable, would find their names added to this most illustrious roster, bringing the total to 117.

The Hays Office censors deemed *The Secret Six* so gratuitously violent that many of its key scenes were trimmed before it reached the screen. Indeed, in some US states it was banned following a spate of copycat shootings involving children – a twist of the usual 'Cowboys and Injuns' playground games when, in New Jersey, one boy used a real gun belonging to his father to shoot another boy in the head.

Harlow loathed Wallace Beery, who had just completed the phenomenally successful *Min And Bill* with Marie Dressler – a tremendous pastiche of tragi-comedy which had audiences rolling in the aisle one minute, weeping the next. Yet while the public adored this seemingly kindly old grouch (though Beery was only 45 when he made the film), away from the screen, Beery was generally regarded as one of the most unpleasant actors in Hollywood. Once married to Gloria Swanson, she had divorced him because of his drinking and abusive ways. Child star Jackie Gleason, who appeared with him in the tearjerker, *The Champ*, called him the most sadistic person he had ever known, and only wished that the actor could have died as well as the character he played. Beery (1885–1949) also hailed from Kansas City, and never ceased to remind her that, though her family had more money than his, she was still trash who belonged in the gutter. When this little snippet reached Marino Bello's ears, he threatened to have Beery 'taken out' by one of his boys. In fact, Harlow handled herself rather well during shooting because she discovered a valuable ally in co-star Johnny Mack Brown, who had suffered Beery's insults for just one day on the set of *Billy The Kid* before giving as good as he got. From Brown's point of view, if Beery could call him a 'dirty faggot', then he could call Beery 'child molester' on account of his reputation for liking under-aged girls. Between them, Harlow and Brown would make the next few weeks hell for the older actor.

Many of those involved with the production expected Gable to make a play for Harlow. At 30, he already had a fearsome reputation as a womaniser: twice married, and currently having a not so very discreet affair with Joan Crawford. In fact, his first wife Josephine Dillon had been a lesbian used by him in her capacity as theatrical agent to gain his footing on the Hollywood ladder. His wealthy second wife, Ria Langham, had always been there to pay the bills and support him, and rumour had it that their marriage was well and truly on the rocks. What almost no one knew at the time was that, since arriving in Hollywood, Gable had been 'gay for pay', having relationships with former silents stars William Haines and Rod La Rocque solely for the advancement of his career. Later, when rumours of these affairs began circulating, Gable would out Haines and La Rocque to the press and virtually destroy their careers to keep the heat off himself. Harlow certainly flaunted herself in front of Gable, and no doubt would have given her eye-teeth for a roll in the hay with this otherwise (then) unattractive man with big ears, bad teeth, and halitosis which was legendary.

What Harlow had not reckoned with was that Gable was far

more attracted to Johnny Mack Brown (1904–75), William Haines' former fuck-buddy, whose screen debut four years earlier had been in Haines' baseball movie, *Slide, Kelly, Slide*. A big hunk of a man, Alabama-born Brown was the former all-American halfback who scored the winning touchdown for the University of Alabama's Crimson Tide team in the 1926 NCAA Division Rose Bowl final. This led to his picture appearing on cereal boxes, and a Hollywood contract which had seen him partnering Norma Shearer, committing suicide opposite Garbo, and appearing in two major films with Joan Crawford. Brown was also a close friend of Humphrey Bogart, then starting to make his name. Unlikely as it may seem, Bogart and Brown may have been lovers.

Bogart (1899–1957) is known to have been very gay-friendly, and according to one biographer (Darwin Porter: *The Secret Life Of Humphrey Bogart*) enjoyed oral sex with men *and* acted as a benevolent pimp for the gay acting fraternity. In his book, Porter claims that Brown and George O'Brien were procured by Bogart, again solely for career advancement, to have sex with Howard Hughes. This may explain why Hughes fought so hard to prevent Harlow from working with Brown in *The Secret Six*, though he did well out of the deal – MGM paid him $2,000 a week for Harlow's services, out of which she received just $200. At 19 she was already 'one of the guys' and, like Carole Lombard after her, was never more content than when hanging out with Hollywood's gay crowd – and one outburst from her concerning his personal life would have been curtains for Hughes' movie career. She must therefore have been at least slightly amused – one cannot possibly imagine her taking offence – to learn that, while rejecting her advances, Brown and Gable ended up with each other while making the film. The fact that she was among men who were more interested in each other also brought out her irascible side.

Just as Lombard would walk around the house stark naked when entertaining one or more of her many gay friends, knowing that this would neither offend nor turn them on, so Harlow took to 'icing' her breasts in front of her co-stars – popping them out before each scene which called for her to don a revealing dress, rubbing her nipples with an ice-cube so that these would show through the flimsy fabric. There were even reports of Mama Jean doing this for her, if she was tired towards the close of a long day on the set. On the last day of shooting, Wallace Beery stomped up to her and growled, in font of the whole set, 'Working with you, you little minx, has almost been the death of me!' – bringing the quickfire response, 'I wish it had, then I'd be able to piss on your grave, you old toad!' What is remarkable is that, despite these insults which never stopped, both would insist on working with each other time and time again over the next few years.

Within days of Harlow finishing the film, Howard Hughes loaned her out again – this time to Universal for *The Iron Man*, a boxing movie directed by Tod Browning, who the previous year had triumphed with *Dracula* and made Bela Lugosi a household name. Young Mason (Lew Ayres) lives only for the ring and dotes on his pretty wife, Rose (Harlow), while for her part she is interested only in money. When Young loses a fight, therefore, she leaves him and heads for Hollywood in search of fame and fortune. He puts more effort into his training, and wins his next fight. When Rose learns of his success and newfound wealth she is back like a shot, much to the chagrin of his manager (Robert Armstrong), whose recompense for telling Young that his wife is a gold-digger is a sock in the jaw before he tears up his contract. Young hires a new manager (John Miljan, the mobster from *The Secret Six*), who just happens to be Rose's lover. All ends badly when his wife learns of the affair and cites Rose as correspondent in their divorce. Young ousts his manager and wife from his life, loses the fight of his life – though as the credits prepare to roll we are assured that he is now a better man by way of his unfortunate experiences.

Yet again, the critics were harsh. Richard Watts of the *New York Herald* found it 'an earnest and interesting motion picture', but said of Harlow by way of a back-handed compliment, 'Even an unfriendly witness must confess that her artificial qualities fit her present role perfectly and result in a genuinely effective portrayal.' The *New York Times'* André Sennwald begrudgingly observed, 'It is unfortunate that Jean Harlow, whose virtues as an actress are limited to her blonde beauty, has to carry a good share of the picture.' And *Variety* likened the actress to the character she was portraying: 'Miss Harlow typifies the Broadway moll who by no means can be classified as a good actress here…but she will likely aid the male reaction to the film with her proverbial low cut and flimsy raiment.' Twenty years later, the film would be remade, with Jeff Chandler and, in a supporting role, a young Rock Hudson.

The Iron Man had not even finished shooting when Howard Hughes loaned out Harlow again. *The Public Enemy* was based on John Bright's novel, *Beer And Blood*, and was promoted by Warner Brothers as, 'An accurate depiction of criminal life amongst certain sections of society, as opposed to the glorification of the criminals themselves.' It was directed by William Wellman (1896–1975), who excelled at action movies. His aviation blockbuster, *Wings*, had won the very first Academy Award in 1927. Immediately after *The Public Enemy* he would make *Night Nurse* with Barbara Stanwick and Clark Gable, though the part pencilled in for Harlow would go to Joan Blondell, who also appears here, because in Wellman's opinion Blondell 'acted rings' around her. Harlow had filmed her first scene when she was recalled by George Hill to re-shoot a whole section of *The Secret Six* where she had fluffed her lines. For Harlow, filming virtually around the clock presented no problem: she was in the public eye, and loved working. What she did not know at the time was that, while still paying her $200 a week, Hughes was raking in his customary $2,000 a week from three different studios.

The film, which took just four weeks to shoot, opens with a Prohibition montage of illicit beer parlours and police raids, into which is introduced a group of children which include Tom Powers and his best friend Matt, youngsters for which poverty, violence and corruption go hand in glove. William Wellman had originally cast Edward Woods in the central role of Tom – the 'meanest boy in town', who spits a lot – with relative newcomer James Cagney as Matt, but after viewing the rushes for their first scene as adults, and after witnessing Cagney in a strop after a night on the tiles, swapped them around. Therefore in this opening scene the children's roles are reversed, confusing audiences – Tom's sister subsequently becoming Matt's sister! Cagney was also a kind of anodyne to the usual thugs and hoodlums invariably depicted as big, brawny types – hence the 6 foot 1 inch Clark Gable's early roles being essentially extensions of himself. Cagney (1899–1986) was small, wiry and possessed of a machine-gun rattle diction, and also full of himself on and off the screen. He hailed from New York's Lower East Side, and had learned from an early age how to take care of himself. In casting him, Wellman set a precedent: Cagney, and the likes of Edward G. Robinson and Humphrey Bogart would spend almost their whole careers playing hard-edged, diminutive tough-guys, frequently much more convincingly than their heftier colleagues. Few characters have proved more odious and frightening, for example, than Cagney's Marty 'The Gimp' Snyder, Ruth Etting's psychotic husband opposite Doris Day's Ruth Etting in *Love Me Or Leave Me*. As for Woods (1903–89), Warner Brothers promised him a major role for stepping down in Cagney's favour – only to fire him when his contract expired. Henceforth he would be relegated to so-called Z-movies and cameos – such as the bellhop, opposite Harlow, in *Dinner At Eight*. In 1938 he bowed out of the movies altogether, while Cagney of course went on to reach the dizzy heights of fame.

The scenario, meanwhile, shifts to Tom's dysfunctional family – his weakling mother, his brutal cop father whose idea of dealing with his delinquent son is to take the razor strop to him. The Powers' only saving grace is their older son, Mike (Donald Cook), who because of his abhorrence of crime is branded an outcast and sissy by Tom. Needless to say, Tom and Matt soon get involved

with crime – petty stuff at first, then, as adults, they are hired as
heavies by local bootlegger Paddy Ryan (Robert Emmett
O'Connor). What Tom lacks in stature he more than compensates
for in ruthlessness, even towards the best friend he constantly
derides. While Mike enlists for the marines, Tom conceals the
source of his formidable income from his mother – she naively
thinks he is involved with politics.

Tossed into this mêlée is a curious little scene where Tom goes
to be measured for his first suit. The then archetypal gay, lisping,
limp-wristed tailor (Tyrell Davis, 1902–70, who forged a career out
of playing so-called 'sissies') quite obviously fancies him, and Tom
is not too dismissive of his advances. Pointing *inside* his waistband
he says, 'Don't forget, plenty of room in there!' The camp tailor
squeezes his bicep, 'Sir, *there's* where you need the room – *such* a
muscle!' To which the tough guy replies, 'Make it snappy or you're
gonna find out what it's for!'

Cut to a speakeasy, where a pair of 'taxi girls' (Joan Blondell,
Mae Clarke) have been let down by their partners, slumped out
over the table. 'A couple of lightweights,' one says. 'Yeah, flat tyres,'
the other quips – the term being Hollywood slang in those days for
a man unable to sustain an erection. Matt ends up with Maisie
(Blondell) while the Clarke character, Kitty, becomes Tom's
mistress, this term a clear indication that she has a husband
somewhere.

As the friends sink further into their tangled web of crime, so the
scenario grows increasingly more violent. They become involved
with mobster Nails Nathan, and start racketeering beer – the
customers are given a choice, to buy from them or suffer the
consequences. Mike comes home from the war, decorated but
shell-shocked, and finally tells his mother how Tom has acquired
his fortune by way of 'beer and blood' – once he has smashed the
family beer barrel to smithereens. Tom explodes at this, for in his
eyes Mike is just as much a killer as he is: 'Your hands ain't so
clean. You kill and like it. You didn't get them medals for holding

hands with them Germans!' In a subsequent scene, Cagney mocked Donald Cook for 'poncing around' and demanded that he hit him for real. Cook did this, and knocked out one of his teeth! Such was Cagney's professionalism, however, that he played out the scene and this was canned in a single take. Then in the next and most famous sequence in the film, we see Kitty getting the brunt of Tom's temper at the breakfast table. After she has nagged him once too often, he snarls, 'I wish you was a wishing well so that I could tie a bucket to you and sink you!' – then pushes the grapefruit he is about to eat into her face! Both Cagney and Mae Clarke later confessed that this scene was not in the script, but that they improvised it to judge the reaction of the film crew. William Wellman insisted that it stay put.

Tom walks out on Kitty, and in the next scene is driving through town with Matt when he stops the car and picks up good-time girl Gwen – Harlow making her first appearance, 47 minutes into the film. To say she looks rough around the edges is an understatement – she's dressed like the cheapest whore and has the street written all over her bloated, over-made-up face. This is Harlow at her very worst, and entirely superfluous to the proceedings – any starlet could have played the part with equal or better conviction. 'I'm not accustomed to riding with strangers,' she whines, though obviously she is anybody's so long as the price is right. Her accent and mannerisms defy description. First she is Joan Crawford, next a poor man's Mae West. And as Matt decides to make an honest woman of Maisie, so Gwen becomes Tom's moll. In the next scene, looking much better in diamonds and furs but acting just as atrociously, we see them dancing – Harlow almost as tall as Cagney and making him look rather silly.

Before Matt's wedding can take place, the boys have a job to do: old enemy Putty Nose (Leslie Fenton) is back in town, and it is payback time. The execution scene progresses beyond camp when the mobster falls to his knees and begs for his life to be spared – then rushes to the piano to croon, 'Lizzy Jones, big and fat. Slipped on the ice and broke her –', the 'twat' in the popular ditty censored by the explosion from the gun. Cut to Tom and Gwen, in her boudoir. Harlow by now looks ravishing, Cagney like a befuddled old lecher. He wants sex, which she is reluctant to provide until he talks of breaking up with her. Reading between the sparsely camouflaged lines, she suspects that because he spends so much time with men, he may be gay, a scene which was edited for 1931 audiences.

After the previews the film was cut from 96 to 83 minutes on account of this, the copious violence, and the scene with the tailor – also a sequence with the real-life character Bugs Moran was removed on the insistence of the Hays office because he was still alive. 'Do you want things to be different, to please your boyfriends?' Gwen asks, before removing Tom's hat and holding his head to her ample bosom. 'Oh, Tommy, I could love you to death,' she croons, seconds before his 'honour' is saved by the doorbell. It is one of his men, announcing that Nails is dead, thrown from his horse. Off they go to the stables, where Tom pays over the odds for the horse – and shoots it.

The carnage reaches its zenith when Tom and Matt's enemies roll into town. Matt is gunned down in the street: Tom is seriously wounded while machine-gunning his friend's killers. 'I ain't so tough,' he moans, as he staggers out into the rain. He survives, only to be kidnapped from the hospital by friends of the men he just butchered. Then the film ends as it started – the phonograph playing 'I'm Forever Blowing Bubbles'. Tom's mother gets a call to say that he is coming home. And in an unintentionally hilarious scene, the door opens and his still-bandaged corpse tumbles into the room. What has happened to Gwen is not explained – as with Harlow's alter-ego in *Hell's Angels*, no one really cares. Then Warner Brothers flash their moral dictum across the screen: 'The end of Tom Powers is the end of every hoodlum. The public enemy is not a man, nor is it a character – it is a problem that sooner or later WE, the public, must solve.'

The Public Enemy made an overnight star of James Cagney, but did little to further Harlow's career other than to hammer home the fact that she was an 'easy lay'. The following year, the film would be Oscar-nominated for Best Screenplay. Such was its popularity that one New York cinema played it 24 hours a day, non stop, for two seasons. Women's and religious groups, on the other hand, condemned it for its graphic scenes of sex and violence. There was outrage when it emerged that, to add an element of realism to Matt's murder scene, William Wellman had insisted that real bullets be fired at the actors, but sprayed against the wall above their heads. The stuntman firing the Tommy-gun misjudged his aim, and had it not been for a sheer stroke of luck that Cagney tripped and fell over the kerb, he would have been killed.

Harlow appears to have set a precedent for mediocre reviews. 'The acting throughout is interesting, with the exception of Jean Harlow, who essays the role of the gangster's mistress,' observed the *New York Times*. The critic from the *New York Herald Tribune* praised the 'grim directness, Zola-esque power and chilling credibility' of the film, but added, 'Miss Jean Harlow completely ruins the scene in which an attempt is made to show the comparative values of shooting and loving in the animal mind of our amiable hero.'

The major point of contention was, as has already been explained, her pronunciation. Mama Jean, after meeting Clara Bow at a party, was so shocked by her Brooklyn 'honk' that she decided that, from now on, her daughter would speak with an 'English aristocracy' accent. Unfortunately, the voice coach she dispatched her to was no better spoken than Bow, and her wasted efforts on Harlow are never more evident than in *The Public Enemy*. 'Her interpretation of whatever she is supposed to be defies adequate description,' Irving Shulman observes in *Harlow*, 'She claims to come from Texas, but her diction runs the gamut of pronunciation from Woolworth counter clerk to what she imagined would be proper for a woman loaded with diamonds and kept at the Ritz.' And Shulman could not resist repeating what a friend had told Harlow's agent, 'Tits are tits, Arthur. But the best of them can't talk. And if Harlow did have a talking tit, people wouldn't expect it to win an elocution contest.'

Once shooting wrapped, Harlow was whisked off to New York – for a rest, the press were told, before she started her next movie. The truth was, Marino Bello had several shady business deals going on here, and just as Mama Jean did not trust him whenever she was not constantly by his side, so she did not relish the idea of leaving her daughter behind to risk falling victim to the corruption that she claimed was taking over the movie business. In New York, Harlow had a brief affair with bandleader and all-round entertainer Harry Richman (1895–1972), a man so utterly full of himself, and whose reviews had been almost as bad as her own. One critic had quipped of his most recent film, *Puttin' On The Ritz*, 'A songwriter drinks and goes blind, and after seeing this you'll want to do the same.' Richman had started out as Mae West's pianist, and had a penchant for brassy blondes – or rather the publicity they attracted. Harlow enjoyed spending time with him, and is said to have seriously considered his marriage proposal – at which point Marino Bello sent in one of his heavies to 'have a chat', whence Richman made a hasty exit from his stepdaughter's life.

Returning to New York, Mama Jean and Bello elected to have it out with Howard Hughes once and for all. In paying her just 10 per cent of what he was raking in from the studios, she said, he was ripping her off, and this had to stop. Either he should release Harlow from her contract, or put her into a film. Hughes gave the impression that he was submitting to their demands – no doubt threats, on Bello's part. Would they be happy if he offered Harlow a part in his new gangster movie, *Scarface*, to be directed by Howard Hawks, and starring Paul Muni and real-life gangster associate, George Raft. This was supposed to be loosely based on the life of Al Capone, whose name Hughes changed to Tony Camonte. In an exercise in wishful thinking, two endings were filmed – one where Camonte gets his comeuppance from a rival mob, the other of him being found guilty by a jury, and hanged. Mama Jean acquiesced, and the deal was signed. Then Hughes pulled his dirtiest trick so far. Harlow's part in the film was a cameo – and she was uncredited because, Hughes declared – her co-stars considered her *so* bad an actress that they did not want their names appearing alongside hers in the credits!

Harlow received some support in her battle with Hughes from producer Sam Goldwyn, who sent his representative to Caddo with an offer to buy out her contract for an unspecified sum. When Hughes showed him the door, he sent along United Artists' chairman Joseph Schenck – an unpopular man known in the trade as Joe Skunk. Goldwyn was casting *The Greeks Had A Word For It*, based on the stageplay by Zoe Akins, and wanted to offer Harlow the part of Schatzi, one of a trio of would-be socialites who feign being rich to attract sugar daddies. Schenck accused Hughes of exploiting his star, and offered $4,000 to take her off his hands. The deal was almost clinched, but Schenck withdrew when Warner Brothers' Daryl F. Zanuck, who had cringed at her performance in *The Public Enemy*, was asked why *he* had not put in a bid for her, taking into consideration the revenue she had earned for his studio – and replied that she was by far the worst actress that he had ever seen, and that William Wellman had lost count of the number of takes there had been before she had got it right. The part of Schatzi was given to Joan Blondell and, fearing a backlash from moralists who know only too well that 'it' was a substitute word for 'sex', the film's title changed to *The Greeks Have A Word For Them*. Thirty years later it would more famously be remade as *How To Marry A Millionaire*, with Marilyn Monroe.

Fox saved the day by loaning Harlow for *Goldie*, a sex comedy which was filmed in just 15 days. It was notable in that it was the first Hollywood movie to feature the word 'tramp', which was of course directed at her. The story centres around Spike (Warren Hymer), a ship's second mate who finds a book filled with women's names and addresses. He dates them one by one, discovers that each has been tattooed by a sadistic lover, and opts to find this man who 'brands' women and give him a pasting. When the culprit turns out to be loveable rogue Bill (Spencer Tracy), he befriends him instead. The two sail for Calais, where Spike falls for local strumpet Goldie (Harlow). Like every other Harlow character so far she is an opportunist, and Spike of course fails to heed Bill's warning that she is bad news. He finally sees through her charade once he gets her in the boudoir – Bill has been there first, and left his mark. 'She is a decorative person, but lacks the spark needed to make her shine as a personality,' carped the *New York Daily News*. The other critics were less complimentary.

Women did not know what to make of her. Moralists loathed her, but flocked to see her all the same to acquire ammunition to attack her with. The red-blooded males in the cinema audience used their hats to cover their laps. The critics squirmed and tried to find new ways of denouncing her. Studio bosses despaired, wondering what she would do next, what obscenity would come tripping out of her red-painted mouth – 'the lovely Jean's other vagina', as Tallulah Bankhead called it – but nevertheless appreciated the revenue she was bringing in, whether she could act or not. As her journalist friend Ben Maddox put it, 'Harlow's tits put asses on cinema seats, and the studios saw only the dollar signs.' If the so-called 'honourable majority' questioned her talents, the real-life mobsters were so convinced by her on-screen shenanigans that they adopted her as their unofficial mascot. In May 1931, *The Public Enemy* went on general release, and Howard Hughes – Harlow's employer, as per the terms of her contract, and not the studios – dispatched her on another tour of personal appearances solely with the intention of placating some of these shady characters. He even upped her salary to $300 a week. And of course, Mama Jean and Marino Bello tagged along for the ride.

First stop on the road was Chicago, the hub of the mobster world, where Harlow had been booked for a week at the massive

Oriental Theater. Basically, all she was expected to do was execute a little song and dance patter before the screening – mindless of the fact that she had been trained to do neither – and meet whichever celebrities happened to be in the house. She suffered terribly from stage fright, and to cope with this started drinking – not heavily, but enough for those sitting nearest the stage to notice. More often than not, one of these guests would drop something – a programme, or maybe a pen – so that she would have to bend down, from the hip of course, to pick it up and flash as much cleavage as she could without running the risk of getting arrested. The critics might have been merciless, were it not for Harlow's new friend – the most feared mobster of them all, Al Capone.

Harlow is believed to have met Capone (1899–1947) by way of one of Marino Bello's 'associates'. Just how involved with him she became is not known, though almost certainly the pair were never sexually embroiled. Capone was coming towards the end of his reign of terror, which had peaked with the St Valentine's Day Massacre in 1929. Though never successfully convicted of bootlegging and racketeering charges, the authorities would bring the curtain down on his activities shortly after he met Harlow, with an indictment for tax evasion. Harlow may have relished the thought of a wild affair with the most notorious criminal in America, but her role as a real life gangster's moll would be strictly reserved for Abner 'Longie' Zwillman, a thoroughly nasty piece of work who had recently served time in a state penitentiary for almost beating a black pimp to death – 'Just because he happened to be in the way.' On the other hand, he could be astonishingly charitable – offering a huge reward for the return of the Lindbergh baby in 1932, and later contributing $250,000 to the Newark Slums Redevelopment Project. Their meeting took place, courtesy of Al Capone, while Zwillman was visiting Chicago 'on business'.

Born in Newark's Jewish quarter, Zwillman (c.1900–59) was a founder member of the National Crime Syndicate, and one of the so-called 'Big Six' Mafia Ruling Commission, nicknamed 'Murder

Incorporated' – the others were Jake Shapiro, Louis Buchalte, Lucky Luciano, Meyer Lansky and Bugsy Siegel, names guaranteed to strike terror in the hearts of decent Americans everywhere. Forced to leave school after his father's death, Zwillman had helped support his mother and six siblings by selling fruit and vegetables in the neighbourhood, then moved on to selling illegal lottery tickets – firstly through local merchants then, as the competition intensified at the height of the Depression by hiring heavies to force competitors out of business. By 1920, he had been in almost total control of New Jersey's numbers racketeering. With the advent of Prohibition, Newark had become the epicentre for bootlegging, and Zwillman had begun smuggling whisky and other contraband across the Canadian border. He had invested much of his rapidly amassed fortune in gambling and prostitution rackets, besides opening several above-board restaurants and nightclubs. By the time of the Wall Street Crash, he is said to have been worth $2 million, though the collective assets of the Big Six are thought to have been 50 times this amount.

Zwillman introduced Harlow to the other members of the Big Six, their friends and associates. When one joked that he would not mind 'having a piece of the action', she obliged in a round about way – trimming her 'clitty bush' so that Zwillman could place a few strands in gold lockets, which he distributed by the score. Occasionally, these turn up in auctions, and even on ebay. When Mama Jean learned of Zwillman's connections with the movie industry, she did all she could to encourage his relationship with her daughter. And Marino Bello, of course, would have sold his soul to become part of the Zwillman gang, or at least play a role in the illicit liquor business – maybe own a speakeasy or two. This would never happen, though having Zwillman involved with his stepdaughter guaranteed him one important benefit – protection from federal agents who had had their eye on his own suspect operations for some time.

It was Zwillman who 'asked' Columbia Pictures' Harry Cohn to find Harlow a decent part in a film, and to offer Howard Hughes $5,000 for the privilege – and to insist that Hughes double Harlow's weekly salary. Cohn obliged, but Hughes refused to dig deeper into his pocket. Harlow would get $300 a week and not a penny more, he declared, because she was not worth paying any more. Zwillman uncharacteristically conceded defeat. He told Harlow that Hughes had upped her pay to $1,000 a week, and personally made good the shortfall. And to ensure that the film would be a good one – Harlow is believed to have never found out – Zwillman ploughed $500,000 of his ill-gotten gains into the project.

It was at this stage in the Harlow–Zwillman relationship that Mama Jean tried to intervene. Her daughter was getting in too deep, she said, with the wrong people. She of course had only been too happy until now for Harlow to be involved with a multi-millionaire, wealthier than Chuck McGrew had been, and perhaps even Howard Hughes himself, by now denounced by all and sundry involved with Harlow as a tightwad megalomaniac. Even the *New York Daily News* had commented during their review for *Goldie*, 'If Caddo Productions are still looking for a descriptive name for Jean, I would suggest the borrowed blonde, for since her sensational introduction in *Hell's Angels* she has been borrowed by one producing company after another in Hollywood.' What Mama Jean was really frightened of, of course, was Zwillman's glitzy lifestyle gaining more control over her daughter than she had.

Mama Jean consulted her fellow Christian Science practitioners. Though material possessions and fame were frowned upon by the religion, they more or less advised her to take all she could get – no doubt in the hope of a substantial donation for their invaluable advice – so she next approached Zwillman and asked him if his intentions were honourable. Zwillman insisted they were, but instead of buying Harlow the anticipated engagement ring, he gave her a $5,000 diamond and ruby charm bracelet. He also paid off her debts to manager Arthur Landau – to the tune of $10,000, mostly run up by Mama Jean and Marino Bello for cars, furniture and a *haute couture* wardrobe. One week later, the trio moved out of the tiny apartment they had been renting in Beverly Hills – into a furnished two-storey house on the more exclusive West Club Drive. Zwillman picked up the tab – and presented his sweetheart with a spanking new bright Cadillac, one that matched her favourite lipstick, to drive herself to her new home.

CHAPTER FOUR
Platinum Blonde

'No one expects a great lay to pay all the bills.'

Jean Harlow

'*She Was Gorgeous! He Was A Man! So The Other Girl Had To Wait!*' So screamed the tagline for *Platinum Blonde*, which began shooting in June 1931. It was a production that caused Columbia Pictures an almighty headache – entirely their own fault – long before the first scene had been canned. Based on the story by Harry E. Chandler and Douglas Churchill, its original title was *Gallagher*, with the action centring around a cocky young reporter of that name – played by 18-year-old Loretta Young, whose first screen appearance had been as an extra on Valentino's *The Sheik*. Harlow was for once assigned to a 'non-trollop' role (playing Anne), and the title change was effected by Frank Capra, on the up and a directorial power to be reckoned with.

Capra (1897–1991) was a feisty European, a veritable genius who devoted his entire career to championing the 'Ordinary Joe', the man in the street who through moral determination and an unswerving conscience always triumphs over adversity to beat the odds in feel-good movies. Born in Sicily, he had moved to California when young. In 1925, Mack Sennett had employed him to write gags for the clown, Harry Langdon, who had subsequently hired him as his personal director. Capra had just moved to Columbia, where he had teamed up in what would prove a phenomenally successful partnership with Robert Riskin (1897–1955), already an established playwright and married to *King Kong* star Fay Wray. Among their triumphs would be *The Miracle Woman, Lost Horizon,* and *It Happened One Night* with Clark Gable and Claudette Colbert.

Capra perceived no real potential in Loretta Young, already scathingly referred to as Saint Loretta because of the holier than thou stance she had adopted towards some colleagues. Loretta (1913–2000), who later appointed herself a clean-up merchant for the Catholic Church, would install holy water stoups at her Hollywood home, casually forgetting that she had seldom practised what she had preached to others. Her castigation of Harlow, accusing her of having no morals, was a classic case of the pot calling the kettle black. Just one year earlier, Loretta had eloped with 26-year-old actor Grant Withers, and their marriage had only recently been annulled – citing the non-Catholicism of the groom, of which she had of course been well aware before marrying him. The annulment took place a few days before shooting began on the Capra production, coinciding with the release of Withers' and Loretta's movie, the inappropriately titled *Too Young To Marry.*

Some years later, Bosley Crowther, the waspish-tongued make-or-break critic with the *New York Times,* would famously say of Loretta Young, 'Whatever it was that this actress never had, she still hasn't got.' She certainly does little to impress here, and after watching her in rehearsal, Frank Capra, in search of a gimmick, elected to change the film's title to *Platinum Blonde,* for no other reason than to capitalise on Harlow's distinguished locks. He was not, however, the one responsible for giving her the moniker, 'Platinum Blonde', which she would wear henceforth like a second skin. This honour, as previously explained, belonged to Kansas City journalist Frank Condon, who had coined the phrase when she had been promoting *Hell's Angels*. And for the rest of her life, Loretta Young would only recall Harlow with resentment.

The real acting competition here comes as Louise Closser Hale and Robert 'Bobby' Williams. Hale (1872–1933) was like Marie Dressler a delightful, matronly actress who died just as she was coming into her own. Born in Chicago, she had worked for many years as an actress, novelist and playwright, not hitting Hollywood until the age of 57. Perhaps her most famous role was the travelling landlady-brothel owner in *Shanghai Express* whose plum line, pronounced to Marlene Dietrich, was, 'I have a boarding house in Shanghai – Yorkshire pudding is my speciality!'

Unquestionably, a great tragedy of post-silents Hollywood was Bobby Williams, whom Harlow is thought to have enjoyed a fling with while making the film. Born in Morgantown, North Carolina, in 1897, as a child he had run away from home to join a travelling tent show, then performed on Mississippi river boats and with stock companies before reaching New York. Here, he had appeared many times on Broadway. Williams' acting career had almost ended in 1922 when a seven-year-old boy had dashed out in front of his car, sustaining fatal injuries. The actor had been arrested, but subsequently cleared of dangerous driving because the accident had not been his fault. The tragedy had put a strain on his first marriage, and a second marriage had proved short-lived when the tabloids – daring for the time – had outed his second wife, actress Alice Lake, as a lesbian. At the time of his involvement with Harlow, Williams was experiencing problems with his third marriage, to stage actress Nina Penn, though professionally he was on the verge of international fame. Williams had scored a triumph on Broadway in Donald Ogden Stewart's *Rebound* – the movie version, starring him, had just been released and had attracted rave reviews. He had been contracted to make *Lady With A Past*, opposite Constance Bennett, immediately after completing the

Capra film, but sadly his involvement never progressed beyond the rehearsal room. On 1 November 1931, the morning after attending the *Platinum Blonde* premiere, Williams was rushed into hospital suffering from appendicitis. In a repeat of what had happened five years earlier with Valentino, surgeons fought to save him, but failed. Peritonitis set in, and three days later he died, aged 34. Harlow was devastated.

The film opens in a noisy newsroom where reporters squabble over who should cover the so-called 'Schuyler Scandal'. Michael (Donald Dillaway), the son of the wealthy socialite clan, is being sued for breach of promise by the unseen Gloria, a girl of questionable repute who he has promised to marry, then dumped. Stew Smith (Williams) is the luckless hack assigned to the case and we first see him chatting to Gallagher (Loretta Young). So far as he is concerned, theirs is a platonic relationship, though she has other ideas.

At the Schuyler mansion, the family try to bribe Stew into not printing a story which will ruin them. He gives them his word not to publish, but goes ahead anyhow. 'I've met some rotters in my time,' scathes Michael's sister Anne (Harlow), 'but without a doubt you're the lowest excuse for a man I've ever had the misfortune to meet!' The way she says this only highlights the fact that she has the hots for him, though initially he tries not to reciprocate. 'She is queenly, and I know queens,' Stew tells Gallagher, pronouncing the first of the film's several in-house gay quips which at the time sailed right over the heads of the general public. He adds that in his book there are two kinds of women – brewery horses and thoroughbreds. Gallagher has yet to meet her love rival, but already she has assigned her to the former category, mirroring Loretta Young's own opinion of Jean Harlow. When Stew acquires Gloria's incriminating love letters and refuses Anne's offer to buy them back – he is a man with a conscience, a Capra character trademark, and tells her she cannot buy people like that – she shows her gratitude for his pulling her into line by asking him to lunch. Next they are kissing passionately in the garden, beautifully filmed through a curtain of water cascading from the fountain. Later, Anne tells Michael that Stew will be her experiment – he is the latest in a long line of men, a tramp who she will transform into a gentleman.

The couple elope, and Stew insists that marrying into money will not affect him: he and Anne will get a little place of their own, and they will live happily and on his meagre salary until he makes money from the play he is writing. His colleagues know this will never happen, croon 'Just A Gigolo', and forecast that from now on he will be under his rich wife's thumb. 'Anne Schuyler's in the *Blue Book*, and you're not even in the phone book,' one says, while another opines of their class difference, 'He's like a giraffe marrying a monkey, a rich wife's magnolia!' The Schuylers hate him, with the exception of Michael, who seems to have taken a shine to him. 'You're really not as bad as everyone thinks,' he says with a nudge and a wink, 'Come upstairs and I'll give you a little….' The pair bow repeatedly to one another, and Stew glances up at Michael as he enters his bedroom and pronounces, 'He can bend!' Needless to say, the Hays Office asked for this little tableau to be removed from the original print.

Gallagher, though distressed, pretends to feel happy for Stew – he has married a beautiful woman, whereas she considers herself 'just an old load of hay'. Still to meet Anne, in her capacity as official reporter for the event, she attends a society bash at the Schuyler mansion, and for the first time Stew realises he has married the wrong woman – until now he has never seen Gallagher in an elegant gown. Likewise, he now confesses that until now, he assumed that Gallagher was a man! All the same, he tries to salvage his marriage by trying to play the dominant role. When a rival reporter calls him 'Cinderella Man', he socks him one. This earns him respect among his colleagues, who write a piece headlined, 'Cinderella Man Grows Hair On His Chest.' This was the powers at Columbia having their say, just to inform audiences that Stew was not weak – in other words gay, seeing as his wife has just called him 'slowpoke' – in an age when even some leading doctors and psychologists believed that hirsute men could only be voraciously heterosexual.

The crunch comes when Stew refuses to accompany Anne to an all-night society function and she tells him, during a fight, that he has always been an embarrassment to her. He gets drunk, and invites all his old friends to the house – who in turn bring *their* friends, causing chaos but convincing him that for the past year he has been a bird trapped in a gilded cage. Instead of attending the party, Stew sits in his room with Gallagher, working on his play. Now, with her help, he changes the plot and bases his work on the stuffy family he lives with. Anne catches them together, assumes the worst, and he tells her he has had enough. 'This magnolia is leaving your sweet-smelling joint!' Stew moves out, sets up home with Gallagher, and finishes his play. The film ends with him admitting that he has loved her all the time, and asking her to marry him. He says that when he married Anne, he was too poor to give her a present, so he gives her one now – a divorce!

All in all, *Platinum Blonde* is a corker of a film, but one which for Thirties audiences was soon regarded as a tragi-comedy in view of the fact that three of its principal stars died before reaching their full potential. As a sharp-talking, wisecracking duo, and given a sparkling script by Robert Riskin, Harlow and Williams are every bit as effective as Lombard and Powell, Grant and Hepburn. The critics, praised only Williams – a mark of respect because he died while they were penning their reviews. 'Miss Harlow, as the society girl, is competent but not much more,' observed the *New York Herald Tribune*'s Richard Watts, while Regina Crewe of the *New York American* observed, 'For all her top billing, Jean Harlow has very little to do, and Loretta Young even less. To say they are competent to the picture is only a mild compliment.'

Platinum Blonde set a trend across America as women of all ages tried to emulate Jean Harlow, frequently with disastrous results. Her hair was no different now than when she had made *Hell's Angels* –

save that this had been more of a man's film. Asked if platinum was her natural colour, she claimed that it was – flashing her pubic hair, if the journalist happened to be an attractive man, to show that she was 'the same color all over'. Several of the movie magazines ran competitions to find other women in America with *exactly* the same colouring, their announcements coinciding with a statement leaked by Columbia's make-up department that, twice weekly, Harlow applied a paste to her scalp comprising equal parts of Lux soapflakes and neat peroxide to achieve the desired effect. Sales of these shot through the roof, as did visits to doctors' surgeries and hospital emergency rooms, while several wealthy Harlow fans attempted – and failed – to sue Columbia for giving them the idea in the first place! Platinum Blonde Clubs sprang up around the country, where well-heeled matrons with nothing better to do sipped gin, compared dyed locks, and discussed the latest Harlow snippet put out in syndicated gossip columns. In Los Angeles, an elocution school opened which guaranteed wannabe starlets that, after a month's tuition, they too could talk like Jean Harlow! Worse still, laminated 'coats' were sold under the counter – plastic-covered Edwin Bower Hesser postcards (which turn up regularly on Internet retail sights) which the horny Harlow admirer could wrap around his penis while pleasuring himself, and wipe clean after use!

A visitor to the *Platinum Blonde* set was Paul Bern, who Harlow had not seen since taking up with Abner Zwillman. Bern had persuaded Howard Hughes to loan her out to appear alongside Myrna Loy in *Freaks*, about to begin shooting with Tod Browning at the helm. Browning had directed Harlow in *The Iron Man*, and since the unprecedented success of *Dracula* had become obsessed with making a film which he claimed would change the prejudiced world's attitude towards disabled people, his theory being that where physical disabilities were concerned, beauty really was skin deep. Unfortunately, he did not go about this in a very sensitive way. '*Can A Full Grown Woman Truly Love A Midget?*' his first flyer wanted to know, until Bern and the similarly vertically challenged Arthur Landau objected, declaring that some critics might think Browning was referring to them. The director's compromise, however, could not have been more prejudiced:

We'll Make Her One Of Us!
From The Gibbering Mouths Of These Weird Creatures Came
This Frenzied Cry!
No Wonder She Cringed in Horror!
This Beautiful Woman Who Dared Toy With The Love Of
One Of Them!

Harlow had been pencilled in for the role of kind-hearted, sympathetic Venus, but when Myrna Loy rejected the part of the evil Cleopatra, Venus was given to Leila Hyams and Harlow asked to step into Loy's shoes. In the story, Cleopatra loves the strongman, Hercules, but marries the midget to steal his money, poisons him, and is found out. Subsequently, the other 'freaks' punish her by turning her into Feathered Hen – a horrendous chicken with a human head. In the original print, they also castrate Hercules, who becomes an operatic soprano! When Harlow turned up for a cast meeting and saw that, rather than calling on the make-up department, Browning had hired real deformed-disabled people (hermaphrodites, Siamese twins, limbless men and women, and microcephalics or pinheads), she was horrified and refused to have anything further to do with the production. The move almost ended her friendship with Paul Bern, who offered the part of Cleopatra to Russian actress Olga Baclanova. There were so many complaints about the finished film that the Hays Office slashed its original 90 minutes down to 63, then pulled the necessary strings to get it banned entirely, virtually ending Tod Browning's career overnight. The ban held good for another 30 years, whence the film was re-released, quickly acquiring 'counterculture' cult status.

Grateful that their friendship had been salvaged, Bern next sought to exploit the 'platinum explosion' by putting Harlow into

Blonde Baby, with Marie Prevost and former co-star Mae Clarke. Directed by William 'One Shot' Beaudine, this tells the story of Cassie Barnes (Harlow), who relocates to New York to share an apartment with friends Gladys (Clarke) and Dot (Prevost) – the former the mistress of a married man, and Dot the honest drudge who earns her crust addressing envelopes. For once, Harlow did not portray the slut – she becomes a department store model, and falls for lecherous tycoon Jerry Dexter (Walter Byron), only to discover that he has a wife. Morality prevails, however. Gladys commits suicide when her beau goes back to his wife. Dot marries her chauffeur lover, and when Cassie finds out about Jerry's wife and heads back to her old home, he acquires a divorce and follows her. Variations of the same story had been done before, and better. Halfway through the production, Columbia changed the film's title to *Three Wise Girls* so that it would not clash with *Platinum Blonde*, but this failed to make an impression at the box office. 'She does better than might be expected,' *Variety* observed of Harlow, 'but she fails to be convincing, and Mae Clarke takes the acting honors from her.'

By the time she made *Three Wise Girls*, Mae Clarke's five-year run as a successful leading lady was drawing to a close. Until the 1960s, when she retired from acting, she would be assigned mostly character roles in B-movies. As for Marie Prevost, her career was already on a downward spiral. This former Mack Sennett Bathing Beauty would prove a delayed casualty of the post-Talkies boom. Her Bronx twang came across as even more ear-splitting than Clara Bow's, and the critics were merciless. Like Bow, she hit the bottle with a vengeance and piled on the pounds, then, in a last desperate bid to salvage her career, embarked on a series of crash diets which resulted in near starvation. When she was found dead in 1937, her corpse partially devoured by her pet Chihuahua, the Hollywood coroner's department recorded one of the worst cases of malnutrition it had ever seen.

Scarcely allowing her time to pause for breath, and with gentle 'persuasion' from Abner Zwillman, Howard Hughes loaned Harlow to MGM for *The Beast Of The City*, with Walter Huston, and 11-year-old Mickey Rooney in an uncredited role. She did not get along with the strait-laced Huston (1884–1950), father of future director, John, describing him as 'an almighty pain in the ass', while he denounced her as 'an even bigger tramp than Joan Crawford' – Crawford had just signed to play Sadie Thompson opposite his sex-crazed preacher in Somerset Maugham's *Rain*. Now, Harlow was playing true to type – a hard-bitten gangster's moll. The tagline was, 'Beware The Hunters Who Stalk Their Prey Through City Jungles!', which Zwillman objected to, claiming that it was not realistic enough. By the time the playbills were commissioned, it had been amended to 'Huston, Harlow & A Hail Of Bullets'. Mama Jean complained about this, but only because her daughter's name had not been included first. Her protest was ignored because Huston was by far the bigger star.

In this little seen *film noir* set at the height of Prohibition, Huston played police captain Jim Fitzpatrick, whose failed attempts to catch mobster Sam Belmonte (Jean Hersholt) results in him being demoted and sent to another precinct. After nabbing a pair of robbers, however, he is promoted to Chief of Police and once more sets off on his quest. His efforts are thwarted by his crooked cop brother, Ed (Wallace Ford), who will do anything to push him through the ranks. When Ed is appointed to keep an eye on Belmonte's moll, Daisy Stevens (Harlow), he falls for her and starts taking bribes. Together, Ed and Daisy conspire to steal a shipment of money: foiled, they are indicted, but a terrorised jury delivers a not-guilty verdict. Fitzpatrick realises that the only way to bring these men to justice will be by way of a shoot-out. The good guys win, of course – the Hays Office would have it no other way. The gangsters die under a hail of bullets – Daisy too, as she is trying to escape.

It was by no means a brilliant film, but it had its moments. In a party scene, where Daisy enters with a tray of drinks, she pauses in front of a table where there is a photograph of Clark Gable. *The Beast Of The City* had been scripted by John Lee Mahin, who had just completed *Red Dust* for Gable; the latter had asked for Harlow as his leading lady. As with all Mahin scripts, the banter was sharp. 'Mind if I ask you some questions?' Ed asks Daisy, to which she responds, 'Sure, if you don't ask them in Yiddish!' The reviews were getting better, too. 'There is extra special work by Wallace Ford and Jean Harlow,' observed the *New York Daily News*, 'yep, the platinum blonde baby really acts in this one, and mighty well.' The *New York Times*' Mordaunt Hall, not an easy man to please, called her 'a distinct asset' to the film.

In December 1931, having completed seven films in 10 months, Harlow found herself managed – a temporary move, thank goodness – by Marino Bello, who had finally wormed his way into Abner Zwillman's good books. Between them, Bello and Zwillman put together a six-week promotional movie tour of America, subsequently extended to 12. Exactly who paid her $3,000-plus weekly salary is not clear. Howard Hughes is certainly on record as having offered her an $8,500 bonus, which she ungraciously declined upon learning that accepting this, as per the terms of the contract, would net him 50 per cent of the profits. As before, the tour opened in Kansas City, where Harlow subjected herself to a 'hair test' with a leading coiffeur to prove that platinum was her natural colour – to keep it shiny and in good condition, she now claimed she only washed it in 'common soap and water'. No one believed her. The 'shows' were very much as before. She would walk on to the stage, meet whichever personalities happened to be in town, and show as much of her cleavage as was legally allowed.

At the height of the tour Harlow was visiting up to 10 movie theatres a day, seven days a week, an exhausting schedule which saw her staggering off the stage in Pittsburgh on 27 December, and collapsing in her dressing room. A doctor was summoned, against Mama Jean's wishes: he diagnosed abdominal flu, and ordered complete rest. Mama Jean would not hear of this, and consulted the oracle – Mary Baker Eddy – whence it was diagnosed that the only cure for her daughter's condition would be more work. In Philadelphia, a few days later, Harlow collapsed again and begged Bello to allow her to return to Hollywood. He refused, and when Harlow called Zwillman, he threatened Bello with 'a fate worse than death' for pushing her too hard, and arranged for her future shows to be handled by Nils Thor Granlund, who was paid $600 a week for the privilege of attempting to turn Jean Harlow into an American Mistinguett. Granlund was also told to limit her appearances to one a day, two at the most, and to allow her as much rest as possible between shows.

Mistinguett (1875–1956) was for over 50 years the undisputed queen of the French music-hall. Though not particularly beautiful, and with a singing voice that would shatter the strongest nerves, La Miss, as she was known, was an agile dancer, even well into her seventies. What led to her popularity on both sides of the Atlantic was her unique personality and innate charisma – and her legendary temper. Mistinguett had played New York's Shubert Theater – Joan Crawford, then plain Lucille LeSueur, had danced in the chorus. Swedish born Nils Thor Granlund (1882–1957), an impresario who claimed that he could turn any sow's ear into a silk purse, had met Mistinguett but failed to ensnare her for one of his revues – after watching one of these, she had denounced it as 'a piece of shit'. Granlund, referred to as NTG (some claimed because the initials stood for 'Not Too Good'!), had started out in vaudeville, then worked in radio and as a boxing commentator. His forte, however, was hiring naive young woman for a pittance, with the promise that he would turn them into household names, while sleeping with as many of them as he could. By 1931 he was working as publicity chief for Marcus Loew's Theaters, MGM's parent company, and clearly perceived Harlow as the next notch on his bedpost.

The Jean Harlow Show opened at Brooklyn's huge Metropolitan Theater in January 1931, its first tableau a replica of Mistinguett's last show at the *Folies Bergère*, minus the feathers she was renowned for. Every light in the auditorium was extinguished, and a single spotlight trained on the curtains as these swung open to reveal a huge staircase. Even the music was Mistinguett's theme, 'Mon homme'. Then the spot travelled up the staircase to pick out Harlow, standing nervously at the top. What spoiled the magical moment was Granlund bawling at the top of his voice, 'This is Jean Harlow, folks, and she isn't here to steal your husbands, ladies, like she does in the movies!' And that was about it. Harlow descended the staircase as best she could – Mistinguett frequently did so faultlessly, with 15 pounds of feathers on her head – pouted at the front row, stooped to pick up flowers tossed on to the stage by Granlund employees, and tried not to let her breasts tumble out of the lowest cut gown most people had ever seen.

After the show, one of the visitors to Harlow's dressing room was the legendary showman, Florenz Ziegfeld, who offered her an undisclosed sum to appear in his latest venture. Between 1907 and 1931, Ziegfeld's *Follies* had ruled the New York vaudeville scene, but the last one of 1931 had seen poor attendances owing to the increasing popularity of radio – just as the movies would suffer, two decades from now, with the advent of television. Now, he was about to leap onto the bandwagon – the first *Follies Of The Air* had been scheduled for broadcast on 3 April (Ziegfeld died three months later) and Harlow was invited to share the bill with *Follies* stalwarts Helen Morgan, Eddie Cantor and Fanny Brice. Harlow declined the offer – there was no point, she said, of her being in a show where nobody could see her 'boobies' – and the next morning set off for Newark, New Jersey. Here, Abner Zwillman was waiting for her at the State Theater. Mindless of the scandal, she allowed the press to interview her in their suite at the Riviera Hotel.

The latter section of Harlow's tour coincided with the release of *The Beast Of The City*, and her first truly good reviews. As most of her personal appearances were in Loew's theatres, and with fans rioting to get sometimes even the slightest glimpse of her, company chairman Nick Schenck approached the head of MGM, Louis B. Mayer, with a view to succeeding where his brother, Joseph (Joe 'Skunk') had failed – in making Howard Hughes an offer 'he couldn't refuse' to buy out Harlow's contract. Mayer, whose family-values approach to movie making was only one step away from the Hays Office's paranoia for overt censorship, hit the roof. Harlow, he declared, was 'the filthiest woman to have ever set foot in Hollywood', and, 'a bigger tart even than Joan Crawford'.

Like all the Jewish movie moguls, Mayer (1885–1957) had triumphed over adversity to make it the top, and was wholly unyielding when it came to demanding his own way. Born in Minsk, Russia, he had emigrated to New Brunswick, aged three, with his family, and by the age of eight had been part-managing a scrapyard. In 1907 he had bought a house in Haverhill, Massachusetts, and turned it into one of the first Nickelodeon cinemas. Soon afterwards he had acquired a theatre chain in New England, and purchased the screen rights to *Birth Of A Nation* which, directed by D.W. Griffith, had proved a veritable hit around the world in 1915. That same year he had founded Metro Films and Louis B. Mayer Productions, and in 1924 had joined forces with Sam Goldwyn to form Metro-Goldwyn-Mayer. It was Mayer who consolidated the Hollywood Dream Factory and founded the star system, which sadly does not exist today. Mayer's big stars in 1931 were Garbo, Crawford, the Barrymores and Norma Shearer – married to MGM's 'Boy Wonder' producer, Irving Thalberg.

New York born Thalberg (1899–1936) had started out as secretary to Universal's Carl Laemmle, worked his way through the ranks to producer status, and had been instrumental in Mayer forming MGM, joining the team in 1923. Mayer had appointed him studio vice-president and, more than any of the other executives, relied on Thalberg's tact and experience. Yet despite his uncanny gift of turning everything he touched into gold, the two never really got along. Thalberg was the archetypal mama's boy, and suffered extremely delicate health on account of a heart defect.

Therefore he was allowed far too much of his own way. When Mayer told Thalberg in no uncertain terms that he would never have Jean Harlow anywhere near his studio, let alone offer her a contract – and when Thalberg bawled him out, siding with his friend Paul Bern that, irregardless of her lack of morals, she would earn their studio a fortune – Mayer cursed the air blue for a few days, but finally relented.

Next, Mayer had to deal with Howard Hughes and Mama Jean. The former, not surprisingly, proved a walkover when Paul Bern – who had previously offered $5,000 to buy out Harlow's contract, now upped the stakes to $30,000. As for Mama Jean, Bern waited until 3 March 1932, Harlow's 21st birthday when she legally became an adult. She was doing her show at Baltimore's Century Theater – Mama Jean and Marino Bello were out organising the backstage party – when the call was put through. Verbally over the telephone, she agreed to MGM's terms, and was told that her first job with MGM would be making a screen-test for *Red-Headed Woman*. Mayer offered her the regulation seven-year contract, starting out at $1,250 per week and increasing in annual instalments to a minimum $5,000 by the third year. What happened beyond then depended upon how well she did at the box office, but her salary was guaranteed *not* to go below this amount. She was also assigned the services of a chauffeur, personal maid, secretary and hairdresser, and unlimited usage of the studio's wardrobe department.

Based on the novel by Katharine Brush, MGM – with Thalberg pressurising Mayer into a project he loathed, finally convincing him that the controversy alone surrounding *Red-Headed Woman* would rake in a fortune – had originally hired F. Scott Fitzgerald to write the script. Thalberg had denounced this as too serious, and commissioned a rewrite from Anita Loos, demanding that where sexual content was concerned, the emphasis should be on comedy so as to get the production past the Hays Office. Loos (1893–1981) had been discovered by D.W. Griffith, and between 1915 and 1917 had scripted Douglas Fairbanks Sr's movies before moving to New

York to embark on a glittering career as a novelist. In 1925 she had published her most famous book, *Gentlemen Prefer Blondes*, filmed three years later with Ruth Taylor and Alice White, and again in 1953 with Marilyn Monroe and Jane Russell.

Thalberg spent several days with Will Hays, personally vetting the script. Hays' concern was that the central character, Lil Andrews (Harlow) – who someone describes as 'strictly on the level, like a flight of stairs' – was a sinner, and that his Code did not permit on-screen sinners to go unpunished. Thalberg was therefore asked if he might ask Anita Loos to amend the ending so that she could be killed off! Loos would not hear of such a thing: neither would he order Harlow to 'cover up' in the seduction scenes, for this would have been defeating the objective. Hays told him to expect trouble. Though the Hays Office could not actually ban a film, if they disapproved of a production vociferously – as had happened with *Freaks* – they could stir up enough of a fuss among moral and religious groups to force exhibitors into boycotting it.

Red-Headed Woman had already had its share of problems. French director Marcel de Sano had been hired, fired and replaced by Jack Conway (1887–1952) who had worked successfully with Joan Crawford and Clark Gable, and recently completed *Asene Lupin* with John and Lionel Barrymore. Conway had no difficulties casting the other leads. Like Anita Loos, Chester Morris (1901–70) had started out with D.W. Griffith. Typecast as psychopaths, he had triumphed in *Alibi* (1929), and again the following year as the convict in MGM's *The Big House*. Leila Hyams had replaced Harlow in *Freaks*. And providing as many wisecracks as Harlow was Una Merkel (1903–86) who a few years later would achieve immortality for the catfight with Marlene Dietrich in *Destry Rides Again*. Finally there was British actor Henry Stephenson and, in his second film role, a young, little known French actor named Charles Boyer.

In an exercise not dissimilar to the nationwide search for Scarlett O'Hara, a few years hence, though on a much smaller scale, Irving

Thalberg had pulled out all the stops to find the perfect Lil Andrews. However, whereas one of the hundreds of hopefuls who tested for Scarlett would have traded their souls to play the heroine of *Gone With The Wind*, few wanted to be involved with a part which Will Hays had publicly denounced as 'a common little tart' and 'an out-and-out harlot'. Thalberg's first choice had been Clara Bow, temporarily off the bottle and eager to make a comeback. When her agent suggested that Lil Andrews might prove the beginning *and* the end of her second career, she scuttled back into obscurity. Next, Thalberg approached Marlene Dietrich. 'Another whore part,' she told me in 1990, 'and in any case, I was committed to Joseph Von Sternberg and Paramount.' When Marlene rejected the part, so did several other Paramount stalwarts, including Colleen Moore. Thalberg tested Ann Sothern (then working under her real name, Harriet Lake) and Lillian Roth, who he had admired as the mysterious vamp in *Madam Satan*, still doing well at the box office two years after its release. Thus far, Roth had been his favourite, and when she turned it down, he began clutching at straws – testing the unlikeliest candidate imaginable for such a role, Ethel Merman, and in a moment's madness even considering Garbo.

By the time Harlow entered the equation, there was virtually nobody left to test, so when Bern reassured Thalberg that his protegée *was* Lil Andrews, the Boy Wonder was ready to listen. In the past, Bern had been spot on with his choices: Lila Lee, Mabel Normand, Joan Crawford, Barbara Lamarr and Clark Gable were lasting proof of his star-finding abilities. Yet it was only at this crucial stage, once Harlow had signed the contract – *without* being tested – that the question of her hair was broached. Harlow was famed for her platinum locks, and now she was expected to play a character with red hair – the way-off theory (which would hold good for some years) being that, just as homosexuals were thought of generally as lily-livered, effeminate degenerates, so redheads and whoredom went hand in glove. Firstly, Harlow flatly refused to dye her hair, once more claiming that platinum was her natural colour. Initially, she also refused to wear a wig, declaring that if MGM brought in an efficient cameraman – such as Lee Garmes, who had photographed Marlene Dietrich for *Morocco* – then, with the right combination of light and shade, in monochrome she could be *made* to look like a redhead. Thalberg would not compromise: she would flatten her platinum locks with paste, and wear a wig whether she approved or not!

After turning the air blue, on 19 March 1932 Harlow submitted to a test, for no other reason than to see which of the 20 wigs supplied by MGM's costume department would photograph best.

Shooting took place over a four-week period beginning on 20 April: Thalberg had already pencilled in the premiere for 25 June! Instead of Lee Garmes, MGM brought in Harold 'Hal' Rosson, who in the not too distant future would figure prominently in Harlow's life. Anita Loos visited the set every day, effecting last-minute changes to the script as Harlow's every movement was monitored by an 'official' from the Hays Office. She led everyone a merry dance as crew members and extras – male ones of course – looked for the slightest excuse to be waiting in her dressing room when she arrived, and not just to partake of the breakfast hamper she always brought with her to make her 'guys' feel at home. While the other stars hung their coats and hats on the pegs provided, and changed behind screens, Harlow shed every stitch in full view of everyone and *then* called for her dresser. And if the Hays Office official disapproved, he certainly was in no hurry to leave until she was fully clad again, or at least as fully clad as she would ever be for the morning's shooting.

Lil Andrews is a stenographer working for the Legendre Company, and a woman who gets what she wants. She sets her sights on happily married boss Bill (Chester Morris) because all she dreams about is becoming part of the local society set. Lil buys only the most expensive gowns, and in one scene asks the shop assistant if she can see through the dress she has tried on. 'I'm afraid I can,' comes the reply, to which Lil quips, 'I'll wear it!' In another scene, in glorious close-up, she snaps a garter containing Bill's photograph around her thigh and barks, 'It'll get me more hanging there than it will hanging on the wall!' Bill falls for her ruse, divorces his wife Irene (Leila Hyams) and marries his pretty opportunist – who subsequently fails to impress his posh friends because they loved Irene so much. Lil therefore shifts her attentions to coal tycoon Gaerste (Henry Stephenson) – only to fall for his chauffeur, Albert (Charles Boyer). Gaerste hires a private detective, who comes across a cache of 'compromising' photographs. Bill finds out about Lil's affairs, there is a row, and she shoots and wounds him. Freed from jail, she divorces Bill, who remarries Irene. The film ends with the protagonists meeting in Paris for the *Prix de l'Arc de Triomphe*. Lil's horse has won the race, and she is here to collect the prize with her bearded aristocrat sugar daddy – as the credits prepare to roll we see them being driven away by Albert who, we assume, still also keeps her bed warm on a night.

The film, the *Last Tango In Paris* of its day, caused a furore when released, with Thalberg having had to make 17 cuts before it was passed by the censor. In Britain, a campaign spearheaded by King George V saw it banned completely – not that this prevented him from commissioning a private copy. It was also banned in Germany, and given a 'restricted' release – in other words, screened only in what then passed for porno cinemas. And the more controversy it caused, the more audiences flocked to see it, the moralists so that they could slam out of the theatre the instant Harlow appeared in a low-cut gown which made it more than obvious that she was not wearing a bra. These people with their smaller than small lives were missing the point completely, of course, because she was *sending up* sex, not promoting it.

'*Red-Headed Woman* – red hot cinema!' exclaimed the *New York Daily News*' Irene Thirer. 'The ex-platinum Jean Harlow now sparkles as the titian siren, her emoting improved immeasurably along with the change in shade of her tresses. Svelte, slender and seductive, Harlow gives a splendid performance.' And the critic with the *New York Daily Mirror* observed, 'This shapely beauty gives a performance which will amaze you, out-Bowing the famed Bow as an exponent of elemental lure and crude man-baiting technique.'

Though she was still seeing Zwillman, two weeks into the shooting schedule, Harlow was Paul Bern's official date to *the* show business event of the year, the star-studded premiere of *Grand Hotel*, at Grauman's Theater. About 25,000 fans lined both sides of Hollywood Boulevard to cheer the arrival of the stars and guests of honour. Among the stars were Marlene Dietrich, on a rare public outing with her husband, Rudolph Sieber – the Gables, Irving Thalberg and Norma Shearer, Louis B. Mayer and his entire family along with the other MGM executives and theirs, Harry Warner and his rival team from Warner Brothers. The film's most important star, Greta Garbo, was conspicuous by her absence. Because of this, Harlow and Bern were largely ignored by the press, who were only interested in finding out why Garbo had not turned up, if she had really returned to Sweden in a huff, as one rumour suggested. 'She's frightened of large crowds,' director Edmund Goulding announced, 'but you may rest assured that she's here in spirit.'

Reporters *almost* got around to interviewing Harlow, when it was announced that Garbo *had* turned up, and a near riot erupted as hundreds of pressmen invaded the front of the stage – where 'Garbo' had suddenly materialised, looking somewhat larger than expected. This was her co-star, Wallace Beery, in an oversized gown and badly fitting blonde wig! And had the press got around to talking to Harlow, they might have learned that Paul Bern had just asked her to marry him.

CHAPTER FIVE

Who Killed Little Father Confessor?

For close on 80 years cynics, film buffs and fans have posed the question. Why did Jean Harlow marry Paul Bern? What did this young, vibrant, sexy, full-of-life enigma see in this middle-aged, balding man of dubious sexuality? The obvious answer seems to have been on account of Bern's money and position with MGM. Rumour still persisted, in 1932, that Norma Shearer had latched on to Irving Thalberg for exactly the same reason, though the detractors there had been proved wrong in one respect: time had shown them to be a blissfully happy, devoted couple.

Bern *did* have wealth, or so it was assumed at the time, and a great deal of clout with the studio. But unlike Thalberg, he had a shady reputation and within days of he and Harlow announcing their engagement, on 21 June 1932, the press began digging into his past. In the meantime, within 24 hours every major newspaper in the country carried their photograph on its front page – Harlow looking radiant as always, Bern looking old enough to be her father with a receding hairline and what appeared to be a big bruise down one side of his face. Did the uncredited caption provider for the *Los Angeles Record* know, or was he/she merely guessing that Bern was handy with his fists, when penning the sub-heading, 'Even

Hollywood's Flaming Platinum Blonde Can't Help Getting Hit When Cupid Goes Hunting'? Declaring that Hollywood was about to lose its 'father confessor' and most famous bachelor, the editorial concluded, 'Nobody in Hollywood can efficiently weep over their troubles except on Paul Bern's coat lapel. He has brought sympathy and helpfulness to more sorrowing souls than any other person I have ever known. He must sleep like a fireman with his boots by his bedside.'

Leading the scandalmongers and hiding under the mantel of respected journalist was Adela Rogers St Johns (1894–1988), William Randolph Hearst's ace reporter and by all accounts a nasty piece of work. Adela would later develop an unhealthy crush on Clark Gable, and neither confess nor deny that the baby she gave birth to was his. She had previously published several exclusives concerning Bern's relationship with Barbara La Marr, including his suicide bid when La Marr had rejected his rumoured marriage proposal. Bern had tried to drown himself by shoving his head down the toilet, and had got his head stuck, necessitating his butler summon a plumber to free him – a studio employee who had fed the story to Adela. Other hacks referred to Bern's 'fatherly' attachments to Joan Crawford and Clark Gable. Harlow defended her fiancé, claiming that he had never 'tried it on' with her because he had always behaved like the perfect gentleman – adding that he was so special, that this time she was 'saving herself' for her wedding night. She told her reporter friend, Ben Maddox, 'We listen to music and read books together. Paul likes me for my mind. He isn't pawing me all the time and talking fuck, fuck, fuck. Our friendship goes beyond that.'

The wedding took place on the evening of Saturday 2 July, at Bern's home on Club View Drive – with all the guests vetted by Mayer and Thalberg. Harlow wore a floor-length white satin gown, and flat shoes so that the five-foot-nothing Bern would appear the same height as her. She had been allowed to invite her mother and Marino Bello, naturally, Arthur Landau and Aunt Jetta, and that was all. Bern's brother Henry was there with his wife, as was his sister Fredericka Marcus. Other 'close friends' of the bride and groom were the Thalbergs, Clark and Ria Gable, David O. Selznick, best man John Gilbert, his fiancée Virginia Bruce – and most important of all, Bern's lawyer, Oscar Cummings, to witness the signing of the register just in case the likes of Adela Rogers St Johns dismissed the event as a publicity stunt.

The ceremony had been stage-managed by Louis B. Mayer, as part of his plans to put some distance between Joan Crawford and Clark Gable, similarly, between Joan and Bern. Some months before, while shooting *Possessed*, Joan and Gable had become passionately involved. The ubiquitous Adela Rogers St Johns had been the one to break the news, writing that Joan's marriage to Douglas Fairbanks Jr was beyond repair, and that she was hoping to marry Gable when they were both free to do so. Mayer had put Joan into *Rain*, filmed on Catalina Island, and halfway through the production she had miscarried what almost certainly had been Gable's child. Paul Bern had been there for her and, terrified that Joan might make a play for him – following a Ben Maddox story which professed the Gables' marriage to be stronger than ever – Mayer had packed Joan and Fairbanks off on a belated honeymoon to Europe. Though Mayer did not want Bern to marry Harlow either, he considered her the lesser of the two evils, and had already listened to the rumours that Bern may have been gay. And what better way to divert such attention from a man who was earning his studio a fortune than to have him marry the most voluptuous woman in Hollywood? Joan was in London, sitting in Noël Coward's living room, when she was shown the newspaper with the photographs of the wedding. Her words, according to Coward, were, 'That fucking trollop's stolen the nicest guy in Hollywood. It sure as hell won't last!' Her words would prophetically ring true.

There was no honeymoon. After the ceremony, the couple were driven to their new home, at 9820 Easton Drive, where a reception took place the following afternoon. The same guests were in attendance, along with resident hacks Louella Parsons and Hedda Hopper. No one wanted them there, but in 1930s Hollywood, these were the rules: Hedda and Louella had to report back that all was well with the newlyweds, but more importantly search for the slightest whiff of scandal, which as yet was not forthcoming.

In fact, all was far from well. Within 12 hours of the rice settling, according to Arthur Landau, Harlow was already discussing divorce proceedings. The rot had set in between the naive, childlike siren and the schizophrenic producer as Harlow learned the real reason behind Bern's 'gentlemanly' behaviour in the run-up towards their wedding. She certainly must have been aware of his earlier suicide attempt, which had been reported widely in the press. Whether Bern told her personally about his mother's suicide, or whether she found out from a third source is a matter for conjecture. Henrietta Levy appears to have suffered from mental illness most of her life, a condition which could not have been helped by having 18 children in rapid succession, only nine of which had survived, and the sudden death of her husband, in 1908, shortly after the family emigrated to New York. Henrietta had flung herself off an embankment in September 1920, aged 72, a few months before her son moved to Hollywood to work with Sam Goldwyn.

For once, Harlow could have done with her mother close at hand, but Mama Jean refused to be separated from Marino Bello, and Harlow had made it patently clear that she wanted him nowhere near her, now that she had someone else to 'protect' her. Therefore, while Bello warned Bern what would happen to him if he did not take good care of his 'Baby', Mama Jean effected a compromise. She asked Harlow for a small framed photograph, which she promised she would carry around with her so that she could 'watch over her in spirit' at all times.

Bern's psychosis, as previously explained, stemmed from an inability to have sex on account of his under-developed genitals – a penis which, on the rare occasions he achieved an erection, measured less than two inches. Writing for *Liberty* in December

1933, Adela Rogers St Johns would describe him as, 'Interested in abnormality and complexes, in inhibitions, perversions, suicide and death.' In her memoirs, Anita Loos gets straight to the point and calls him 'a German psycho'. In the summer of 1932, however, few people were aware of Bern's genital abnormality because, so far as is known, he had never attempted to have sex with any of his intimates – including Harlow, before or after their wedding. It may well be that *she* was not even interested in having sex with a man twice her age when there were so many perfect specimens at her beck and call, should she want them – that she was perfectly content, now that the ring was on her finger, with the warmth and security she felt she had. What she did not anticipate was her new husband's psychotic streak or his tendency towards mental and physical brutality.

Bern was an educated man. She considered herself 'just another kid from Kansas', but she was way above average intelligence – what would today be called streetwise. That she was willing to learn, as she mounted the society ladder, goes without saying. In her later interviews she displays a vocabulary which is both articulate and worldly. As Tallulah Bankhead once said of her, 'That girl sure knew her onions!'

Bern, however, was paranoid about one-upmanship. He had always moved in the very best circles and considered himself ultra-sophisticated. Which of course begs the pertinent question: if this was the case, why hook up with a girl whose reputation preceded her everywhere she went, and invariably only opened her mouth to put her foot in it? One of the answers to this is that he needed someone to lord it over. Bern was a control freak who constantly monitored his wife's gestures, who picked her up on her speech, loudly told her which cutlery to use at the crowded dinner table, how to address people without sticking out her breasts and blurting out, 'Hey, buster. How's it hanging?' He was also so insecure that he carried a loaded gun around with him most of the time, even to board meetings.

As Mrs Paul Bern, Harlow was promised only the most superlative scripts from now on, and her next venture was no exception. In 1926, in the wake of their triumphant *Flesh And The Devil*, Irving Thalberg had purchased the rights for *Red Dust*, based on Wilson Collison's stage play, for Greta Garbo and John Gilbert, then Hollywood's golden couple who could do no wrong. Their glorious reign had ended abruptly in the September of that year at the wedding of director King Vidor and actress Eleanor Boardman – intended as a double ceremony with Garbo and Gilbert. Garbo had done one of her infamous vanishing tricks and, in front of the hundreds of guests and press photographers Louis B. Mayer had marched up to Gilbert and bawled, 'What's the matter with you, Jack? What do you have to *marry* her for? Why don't you just fuck her and forget it?' Gilbert had socked Mayer in the jaw, and The Messiah had exacted his revenge the following year by deliberately sabotaging Gilbert's voice test, which had deemed him unsuitable for sound. His would be a long, agonised decline with just a clutch of decent films – *Queen Christina* with Garbo being by far the best – before his death from a heart attack, aged 40, in 1936.

The revised script for *Red Dust* was by John Lee Mahin (1902– 84), who had part-scripted *The Beast Of The City* and *Scarface*. When one reads the account of Gable's casting as Gilbert's replacement – by Mahin, director Victor Fleming and producer Hunt Stromberg – as told by his biographer, Lyn Tornabene, one might be excused for thinking that she attempts to conceal the fact that every man associated with the film was a screaming queen! Gable, Mahin and Stromberg are described as 'men's men and a half', while Fleming is a 'man's man and three-quarters'. Mahin, who did have a crush on Gable, recalled how he told Stromberg after watching one of his films, 'There's this guy – my God, he's got the eyes of a woman and the build of a bull. He is really going to be something!' Though Gable had the charisma – and the nerve – to seduce even the most reluctant of men during these formative years of his career, like every other male involved with *Red Dust* he was interested only in winning the lottery: getting Harlow into bed.

Harlow and Gable were made for each other, the perfect combination of earthy humour and unbridled sexuality. In *The Secret Six* he had shared her with Johnny Mack Brown, but in this and their four subsequent films he would have her all to himself, with electrifying results. They were also immensely compatible on a personal level. Ten years Harlow's senior, Gable hailed from Cadiz, Ohio. His mother had died while he was still a baby: his stepmother, Jenny, had helped nurture his innate artistic abilities, earning him the emnity of a despotic father who had denounced him as a 'sissy' for wanting to join the acting profession. For the rest of his life, Gable would strive to prove himself, quite unnecessarily, the archetypal *supermensch*. Yet on the other hand, like Harlow, he had taken whatever steps he had felt necessary to step up the Hollywood ladder. His first wife, acting coach Josephine Dillon, had been a lesbian and the marriage had never been consummated. His current wife, socialite Ria Langham, had provided for him financially and he had cheated on her relentlessly with both men and women. Harlow and Gable also shared a natural vulgarity which comes across well on the screen. He is the shrewd, cynical, pretend hard-bitten louse – in reality, just a big softy who hides his true feelings from the world, very much like Gable himself, who spent his whole life hiding behind a facade of enforced machismo instead of just being himself. She is never less than the busty, brassy, fun-loving doxy with a conscience whose every movement and utterance is pure magic, perpetrated with such seeming innocence that she gets away with everything, no matter how coarsely she behaves.

In *Red Dust*, set in Indochina, Harlow is Vantine, the wise-cracking tart with a heart who, on the run from the Saigon police, shows up at the rubber plantation managed by Denny Carson (Gable). He is ebullient and initially resentful of the siren who introduces herself as 'Polyanna The Glad Girl', telling her that she may only stay until the next boat docks. 'It's bad enough having to play around with them in Saigon, much less having one in your house,' he says of the other whores he has known, adding that he has been looking at her kind since his voice changed.

Denny is grumpy: production is down on account of it being 'red dust' season, a situation he hopes will be remedied when he gets his new surveyor, Willis (Gene Raymond). Meanwhile, his lack of hospitality and Vantine's coarse observations lead to physical attraction: he calls her Lily, she calls him Fred, nags about his boozing, hums 'Home Sweet Home' and *never* stops talking. For ever hitching up her skirt and flashing her thighs, she bathes in the outdoor vat which contains the men's drinking water and is surprised when Denny objects – avowing that any red-blooded male would *want* to drink the water all the more because she has been in it. Her language (for the day) is appalling, and even the parrot is berated when she cleans out his cage – 'What you been eating, cement?' And when Denny threatens to hit her, Vantine responds, 'You, and what man's army?' Which of course leads to the obvious, as the scene fades.

Willis arrives, accompanied by his pretty but standoffish wife, Barbara (Mary Astor). He is mild-mannered, while she is in direct contrast to Harlow's loveable slut, though Denny wants her just the same, and naturally the two women in his world do not get along. 'I wouldn't touch her with your best pair of rubber gloves,' Vantine tells him of her rival. When Willis catches a fever and Denny winds Barbara up the wrong way, she slaps him and this unleashes his animal instincts – when he kisses her, she appears to be having an orgasm. And no sooner has Willis recovered than he is dispatched on a jungle mission so that Denny can finish what he has started.

Denny has never had a *lady*. Similarly, Barbara is unaccustomed to this sort of thing, and feels obliged to come clean to her husband. Denny agrees, then follows him into the jungle, where they bond during a tiger shoot. Hearing how much Willis loves his wife, and of the plans they have made for the future, Denny cannot go through with it. He goes home, and when Vantine sees him looking glum, she barks, 'Is the burial private, or didn't ya bring the body home with ya?' – to which he responds in equally deadpan style, 'Where's ya git that kimona?' Then he realises that he must do the honourable thing and give Barbara up, that the woman he really wants is Vantine because they are the same class and temperament. They are getting into a spot of friendly wrestling-foreplay when Barbara walks in. Furious, she bawls out Denny and realises he has been stringing her along. To the delight of thousands of Gable fans he levels, 'I'm not a one-woman man – I never have been, and never will be. If you want to take your turn, all right, if it makes you feel any better!'

Barbara draws a gun and plugs him – not fatally – just as Willis arrives and Vantine jumps to her defence. 'You oughta be proud of her,' she tells the distraught husband, 'this bozo's been after her every minute, and tonight he breaks into her room and she shoots him. It's the only way any virtuous woman would with a beast like that!' Of course, her quick thinking has assured Vantine of having Denny all to herself. Her rival and her husband now eager to leave, Vantine cleans up Denny's wound and as the credits roll, we see him domesticated and lounging on his sickbed while she reads him a children's bedtime story!

Astonishingly, Harlow's and Gable's antics, even the bathing scene, got past the Hays Office censors. 'I never wear panties, so why should I put them on to take a bath in a barrel when nobody could see me?' she asked Victor Fleming – though he, the cameraman, Gable and every single technician on the lot ensured themselves an eyeful. Mary Astor's 'orgasm' was left in, when John Lee Mahin claimed her character's affection for Denny leaned more towards the maternal than the carnal – Astor was five years younger than Gable! The biggest fuss occurred in one scene when Gable removed his shirt and ripped it off in another, revealing not just his navel but that he was not wearing a vest. Shops across America reported a decline in the sales of men's undervests during the winter of 1932–3. Louis B. Mayer asked for these scenes to be shot again. Gable agreed to cover his navel, but the vest stayed off: MGM publicity chief Howard Strickling gave a statement to the effect that Gable was an outdoors type, and therefore tough enough not to need one.

And MGM ultimately realised, as had happened when they had teamed Gable and Crawford, that they had discovered another winning combination to the box-office jackpot. There would be four more Gable–Harlow movies, each one as successful as this. Twenty years later, Gable himself would star in the remake, *Mogambo*, with Ava Gardner and Grace Kelly. It would prove a good film, though still not a patch on the original. Even the former Harlow detractors loved it. 'The flagrantly blonde Miss Harlow, who hitherto has attracted but intermittent enthusiasm from this captions department, immediately becomes one of its favorites by her performance in *Red Dust*,' opined the usually caustic Richard Watts of the *New York Herald Tribune*. And making comparisons with another famous slut, immortalised by Somerset Maugham, *Time Magazine* observed, 'Her effortless vulgarity, humor and slovenliness made a noteworthy characterisation, as good in the genre as the late Jeanne Eagels' Sadie Thompson.'

Despite the enormous fun everyone appears to have had making it, *Red Dust* was blighted by a singular tragedy which, like the deaths of Marilyn Monroe, President Kennedy and Princess Diana may never be fully explained on account of the wildly conflicting stories, hearsay, possible cover-ups and speculation. Shooting on *Red Dust* was halted on Sunday 4 September 1932 for the Labor Day weekend. Instead of going home with Bern, Harlow had agreed to spend the night with Mama Jean and Marino Bello at Club View Drive. Bern had been invited to join them for dinner, but had declined. The next morning, his naked body was discovered face down in his dressing room in a pool of blood, drenched in Harlow's favourite Mitsouko perfume. He had a gunshot wound to the head, and the .38 pistol was still in his hand.

The *Los Angeles Times* would subsequently draw attention to life imitating art by comparing this scenario and the scene scripted by Valentino's wife, Natacha Rambova, in *What Price Beauty?* (1928) where the lead male character, weary of the artificialities of the film capital, stands in front of the mirror and puts a bullet into his brain. Bern's butler, John Carmichael, made the grim discovery – he claimed at 11.30am – and, in accordance with Hollywood's unwritten laws, contacted Louis B. Mayer's office. This enabled Mayer and MGM's chief of police, Whitey Hendry – the man responsible for getting stars off the hook, be it speeding fines, sex scandals or even murder – to check out the scenario and remove any 'unwanted' evidence. Within 30 minutes they were joined by Irving Thalberg and Norma Shearer, Howard Strickling and Virgil Apner, a studio stills photographer. It was Apner's shot of Bern's corpse, doubled up on the floor and with his genitals airbrushed out, that was subsequently wired around the world.

Mayer's first action upon arriving at Easton Drive was to seize what he assumed to be the suicide note with a view to destroying it. Bern had scribbled this on to a page of his address book, next to which there lay a second .38 pistol. Strickling advised him not to, declaring that without a suicide note, one or more persons close to Bern – he was obviously referring to Harlow – might be suspected of murder. The note read,

> Dearest dear. Unfortuately [sic] this is the only way to make good the frightful wrong I have done you and to wipe out my abject humiliation.
> I Love [sic] you. Paul.
> [PS] You understand that last night was only a comedy.

Why on this particular morning Bern's butler and his cook wife, Winifred, should have arrived at Easton House so late – why they were not there, when he is known to have regularly risen and breakfasted by 9am at the latest – was not explained, and was almost certainly a part of Mayer's plan to 'move on' the events of the day.

There was a short delay, Carmichael said, between discovering the body and calling Mayer because he had fainted at the gory sight, though in his subsequent statement the gardener Clifton Davis, denied this. Mayer and Thalberg ignored Davis' claim, however, because he was 'only a negro', which of course only proves what truly delightful people they really were. It was Mayer who called Mama Jean and informed her of Bern's death.

Whitey Hendry was among the group who headed for Club View Drive where Harlow – who had learned of the tragedy from her mother – was briefed on how to react when the regular police, and of course the press, arrived to inform her of her loss. Marino Bello, who Mayer suspected was not incapable of sending in one of his heavies to 'punish' Bern for taking his 'Baby' away from him – was ordered (and doubtless paid handsomely) to lie to the police about the fishing trip he had been on with Clark Gable. Gable was told to go along with the story, if he wanted to stay on the MGM payroll. The pair were told to say that they had left for the trip at around 3am, but there is every possibility that they set off much later than this, probably immediately after Whitey Hendry's initial examination of the death scene when Mayer had called Mama Jean. Joan Crawford later confessed that Gable had spent the night of 4 September with her, and that he had not left her house until dawn. Gable almost certainly had been kept in the dark by Bello – a man he could not stand. He was never questioned by the police, and claimed that the first he had learned of Bern's death was when he had seen news of it splashed across the newspapers later that evening.

The regular police were informed of Bern's death at around 3pm, between six and 12 hours after the trigger had been pulled. According to the police report, clearly fabricated, it was only at this stage that the 'suicide weapon' was found. One hour later, his body was transported to the Price & Daniel Morgue, at Sawtelle. By this time, the incident had been reported in the early editions, and a huge crowd had gathered outside 9820 Easton Drive, with ice-cream salesmen and hot-dog vendors jostling among the curious. According to the police report, clearly fabricated, it was only at this stage that the actual gun which had killed him was found, gripped in his right hand, underneath his body, and held fast by rigor mortis. Hendry, Mayer, Strickling, Thalberg *et al* had all assumed, they lied to the police, that the fatal weapon was the one lying on the table next to the address book. The gun was prised out of Bern's hand: five bullets remained in the six-cartridge chamber, and the police found the sixth bullet, which had passed through Bern's skull, embedded in the wall behind him. The question was posed that if Bern had been standing in front of the mirror, as Whitey Hendry had ascertained – his first *faux pas* – then why had the gun not dropped out of his hand when he had fired the fatal shot? No answer was given.

After viewing the body and turning on a few crocodile tears, Irving Thalberg and Norma Shearer drove to Club View Drive, arriving in time to see the police 'breaking the news' to Harlow of her husband's death. In a performance far better than anything she had done on the screen so far, she had a fit of hysterics, threatened to jump out of her bedroom window, collapsed, and was sedated by a studio doctor. This was studio perversion of justice at its most dire. The hysteria and collapse were but a charade, but the sedation was for real. Mayer had given specific instructions that she should *not* be allowed to be interviewed by the police, at whatever the cost. For the rest of her life, Harlow would never publicly refer to Paul Bern again, and hardly ever mention his name even to her closest friends.

Such cover-ups were nothing new in Hollywood. In 1923 Wallace Reid, who had become addicted to morphine after being injected by the drug following an on-set injury – in effect, so that he could continue working and save the studio from closing down for the day and everyone being sent home on full pay – had been declared 'diseased' by Will Hays and sectioned to a private sanatorium, where according to a later investigation he had been 'put to sleep'. Barbara La Marr, as already explained, had according to a concocted studio press release not died of a drugs overdose, but of 'rigorous dieting'. The under-aged girls which Charlie Chaplin had a great fondness for were always 'aged up' by the press in return for suitable pay-offs. Three years after Paul Bern's death, a drunken Busby Berkeley, Warner Brothers' ace director of musicals, would stagger out of a Hollywood party, drive several miles on the wrong side of the road and crash into an oncoming car, killing three of its occupants. By the time this reached the courts, several actors – who just happened to be on the studio payroll – swore under oath that Berkeley had left the party 'sober as a judge' and he was exonerated of all charges.

It was therefore evident, to those in the know, that Louis B. Mayer would put his own interests first – even if this meant personally perverting the course of justice – during the investigation into Paul Bern's demise. Over the next few days witnesses stepped forwards, vetted by Mayer or Thalberg and questioned beforehand, each giving their own insight into Bern's 'strange behaviour' in the days leading up to his death. His brother, Henry, flew in from New York. Asked by reporters at the airport if he had any explanation as to why Bern had committed suicide he said, 'Tension, almost unbearable tension. As for motives, I know none. Most of the motives suggested to me are completely untrue.' Pressed as to the nature of these motives, Henry refused to elaborate. Shrugging his shoulders, he walked away muttering, 'There was nothing wrong with Paul's financial position!' No one had ever suggested otherwise, and this little titbit of course added yet another slant to the mystery.

If these stories were to be believed, Bern had grown increasingly more psychotic with each new day, walking around in a trance or rushing about with his eyes staring out of their sockets, mumbling incoherently, and *always* with a gun in his pocket. Indeed, each time he had visited the house of an MGM employee, he had hung up his jacket and someone passing by the coat-rack had just happened to check if the gun was there. Adding to the speculation was the autopsy report which finally enlightened the world about Bern's 'deformity'. While Mayer spat out words like 'faggot' and 'fairy' in an age when small penises and 'deviants' were referred to in the same breath, all over America the less-educated reached for their dictionaries to find out what 'hermaphrodite' meant. This shocking revelation was counteracted by Henry Bern, who told reporters that his brother had had a normal-sized penis – *and* that there was a 'common-law wife' somewhere who, when the time was more appropriate, would come forward with enough evidence that he had known how to use it.

Clark Gable received a visit from Howard Strickling, a close friend, and was told to say nothing about the night/morning of Bern's death – not that he appears to have known anything. Marino Bello, when questioned by detectives, avowed that the Berns had been blissfully happy, and denied reports that he had been after getting his hands on the Easton Drive property. The gardener, Clifton Davis, swore – then later denied doing so – that he had heard Bern and Harlow having a massive row the night before: Harlow had wanted her husband to sign the place over to Mama Jean and Bello, in appreciation of all they had done for her, and he had hit the roof. Harlow had stormed out of the house, and soon afterwards a mysterious woman had driven up in a limousine. There were suggestions that money had exchanged hands between Mama Jean and the police, to prevent Harlow being questioned. This seems to have been the case, though the pay-off came from Louis B. Mayer. This fuelled the press into speculating that Harlow had something to hide – not least of all that *she* had killed Bern. This led to the District Attorney, Buron Fitts, actually applying for a murder indictment. Once again, The Messiah reached for his chequebook.

The inquest into Paul Bern's death took place on 8 September, the day before his funeral, at the Price & Daniel Morgue – with the corpse lying in the next room in an open casket, according to one tabloid 'so that folks could pop in and see that he was dead'. The 'guest list' was drawn up by Mayer, and the whole charade covered extensively by the *Los Angeles Examiner*. All had been instructed not to divulge that he, Thalberg, Strickling and Hendry had visited the house before the regular police. Harlow had been subpoenaed as star witness, but Mayer had overruled the coroner, Frank Nance. Her doctor, Robert Kennicott, provided a medical certificate declaring her unfit to testify. Attached to it was a note upon which he had scribbled, 'Miss Harlow has been under my care for a severe nervous collapse. Her appearance before a jury would gravely endanger her life.' The jury were told that she was under heavy sedation, and that MGM had appointed a nurse to sit in her room, just in case she woke up and tried to kill herself, such was her grief. Excuses were also made for Henry Bern, who everyone had expected to turn up with the mysterious 'common-law wife'. He was too tired, his own note explained, but was hoping for a satisfactory outcome by the end of the day.

Marino Bello, the first to take the stand, assured the court that the Berns' marriage had been sound, though despite this he could not work out in his own mind if Bern had killed himself or not. He denied that he had wanted his stepson-in-law to hand over the deeds to the Easton Drive house. The household staff had been debriefed by Louis B. Mayer and Howard Strickling. John and Winifred Carmichael denied ever hearing their employers argue, and Carmichael swore under oath that the detectives had arrived at around 1pm, two hours earlier than had actually happened. The gardener, Clifford Davis, who because of his colour had been compelled to enter the Price & Daniel Morgue via a side entrance, also changed his statement – he had most definitely *not* heard the couple arguing. Also, he omitted to mention the mystery woman in the limousine. Other witnesses attested to seeing the car, and to Bern's 'obsession' for travelling everywhere with a gun in his pocket. Irving Thalberg, the biggest hypocrite of them all who could turn on the waterworks at a moment's notice, told the court that Bern had suffered from severe depression and frequently spoken of suicide. Then, finally, there was the statement delivered by the coroner, Dr Frank Webb. After confirming that the deceased had not been suffering from venereal disease – the theory being that, if he had been, he could only have caught it off his wife – Dr Webb brought guffaws from the back of the room by announcing, when asked if Bern's genitals had been underdeveloped, 'I would say undersized. They were developed normally, sir, but undersized.' Whether Dr Webb was also in Mayer's pocket is not known, but not unlikely. The same may be said for the jury, who quickly delivered the verdict, 'Death by gunshot wound to the head, self-inflicted by the deceased, with suicidal intent, motive undetermined.'

Disturbing facts concerning Paul Bern's psychosis relating to his shortcomings in the boudoir, previously known only to his intimates, emerged after his death. Unable to have sex because of his genital abnormality, he had hoped that the sexually torrid Harlow might cure him of his impotence, despite the fact that physically he was attracted only to men. When he had failed to rise to the occasion on his wedding night, he had taken his frustration out on his bride, and beaten her senseless with a walking cane. In *Harlow*, Irving Shulman relates how she called Arthur Landau in the early hours of the morning, begging him to come and rescue her. Landau had recalled her injuries: 'Five long angry welts between the hips and shoulder blades. The welts were turning harsh blue, and the fourth welt above the kidneys was beaded with little blood blisters.' Harlow's agent concluded that he had called a doctor friend who had dressed the wounds so that she would not be in too much pain for the wedding reception later that day. Then, he had driven her back to Easton Drive, where they had found Bern in a drunken stupor, slumped naked on the floor – and subsequently discovered his 'secret'. And Harlow had stripped naked to reveal the full extent of her injuries – including bloody bite marks on her thighs and vaginal area (according to Landau, 'hymeneal rites' had taken place) – then screamed at her new husband, 'You're just a rotten awful fag with a dangle half the size of my pinkie!'

Some years later (and also in Irving Shulman's book), an amusing anecdote would offer one explanation for the 'comedy' referred to in Bern's supposed suicide note – that on the evening on 4 September he had arrived home with a strap-on, ejaculating dildo, complete with testicles, which he had put on before walking into Harlow's bedroom. Whether he had attempted to use this on her is not known, only that she had shrieked with laughter, which *may* have left him feeling 'abjectly humiliated', although when one reads Shulman's account of this, as relayed to Arthur Landau by Harlow herself, one has an inkling that Bern found the incident just as hilarious as she did:

> Above her own mirth she heard Paul laughing…strutting around the room, one hand on the dildo to hold it as if it were the staff of a proud flag…Paul began to gallop as if he were astride a horse and to utter crowing sounds in imitation of a cock…Now he held it with both hands as if it were a fishing rod, and as he pantomimed hooking a fish and fighting to land it, Jean's laughter cheered him on. He ran across the room to ram the dildo against the door and attempt an entrance into the keyhole, an effort which racked Jean with such hysteria that spasms of pain stabbed her from the back through to the chest.

Shulman goes on to say that, after all the giggling and madness, Harlow and Bern sat on the bed and wept together, then cut the dildo into pieces and flushed it down the toilet. He concludes, 'At last it was gone…and when Jean took Paul's hand and led him to the bed, he followed as a child might his mother.'

Despite the coroner's verdict, the case was not quite so clear cut. The press had followed up on the common-law wife referred to by Henry Bern, and put two and two together: they believed that she was almost certainly the mysterious woman seen leaving Bern's house by the gardener and the neighbours, the evening before his death. On 9 September, the day of his funeral, the *Los Angeles Times* ran a story under the heading, 'New Complications Add To Bern Death Mystery', and claimed that a 'Mrs Paul Bern' had been recently residing at New York's Algonquin Hotel.

The piece explained how she and Bern had been 'morally married', and a source there claimed that he had last visited her in October 1931. Henry Bern now broke his silence and named her as 48-year-old Dorothy Mellett (née Roddy), a bit-part actress who had worked under the name Dorothy Millette. According to Henry, she and his brother had 'cohabited' for around 10 years, firstly in Toronto, then moving around America before settling in Manhattan. Dorothy had been listed as Bern's legal wife in his naturalisation papers, dated 1917, and again three years later when he had drafted his will. In fact, in 1917 she had been married to someone else – a Lowell Millett – since 1907. Following his mother's suicide in 1920, Bern had had Dorothy committed to the Blythewood Sanatorium, in Connecticut – either because she had been truly insane, as Henry avowed, or more likely because, as his career moved from strength to strength, he had wanted her out of the way. One theory was that since being elevated to the position of 'one of Hollywood's top-notch Jewish elite', he was finding it embarrassing being 'married' to a Gentile.

Where Dorothy Millette was now, no one was sure. She had stayed at Blythewood just eight months before Bern had moved her to the Algonquin – famed for its Round Table chaired by such literary luminaries as Dorothy Parker and Willard Mack – where she had apparently lived as a recluse for 12 years. Bern's friends, colleagues and acquaintances had initially denied any knowledge of her existence, but now their memories appear to have been jogged – particularly when the Los Angeles District Attorney, Buron Fitts, told the press that he believed Bern had been murdered, and that Harlow was his number one suspect.

Louis B. Mayer had a lot of money invested in her, so now it was time for his 'boys' – Whitey Hendry and his team of unorthodox law enforcers – to do a little investigating of their own. Dorothy had last been heard of renting a room at the Plaza Hotel, San Francisco, but when the place was invaded by journalists, she was nowhere to be seen. One tabloid leaked the news that Harlow knew where she was – indeed, that she had travelled secretly to San Francisco to meet her. Detectives turned up at Club View Drive to interview her, but Mayer's nurse got to her first and put her under sedation. When witnesses started coming forwards claiming that they had seen Harlow in the city *and* in the foyer of the Plaza Hotel – and when newspaper clippings about the visit were found in the room Dorothy had occupied there – Whitey Hendry stepped into the breach: a spokesman came forward from the Mark Hopkins Hotel, who at first had denied any knowledge of her being there. Now he remembered. Harlow *had* stayed at his establishment with her parents on 18 August, and he distinctly remembered her telling him that she had been there exclusively to buy clothes! It was all rot, of course. There now seems little doubt that Harlow had gone to San Francisco to meet Dorothy Millette, and that if Marino Bello had been involved, it would not have been a social visit. She may have suspected that Bern was being blackmailed by this woman – alternatively, she may even have suspected him of the even more serious crime of bigamy if by some way she had learned about Dorothy's name being listed as his actual wife on his naturalisation papers and first will, for there was no record anywhere of his ever having been divorced. Then, the *Los Angeles Times* announced that it had 'substantial evidence' that Dorothy had been spotted on 6 December, boarding the *Delta King* riverboat headed for Sacramento. Heeding Henry Bern's mental illness theory, the authorities came to the conclusion that she had done so with the sole intent of committing suicide, and began searching the river for her body.

In the meantime, Harlow had Bern's funeral to contend with. The mixed-religion service took place in Inglewood Cemetery's Grace Chapel, and was presided over by Rabbi Magnin, who like the 52 invited (by Mayer and Thalberg) mourners, had to fight his way through a 2,000-strong crowd to get inside the building. The die-hard fans were merciless, climbing atop Harlow's car, autograph books at the ready. For the benefit of the press, the MGM chauffeur had been instructed to park well away from the chapel so that she could be photogaphed 'on the verge of collapse' and supported on either side by Marino Bello and Willis Goldbeck, a family friend and the co-scriptwriter of *Freaks*. Louis B. Mayer, embarrassed by the revelations concerning Bern's past and therefore secretly relieved that he was dead, had kept up the hypocrisy by commissioning $25,000 worth of flowers. Conspicuous by absence was Henry Bern, rumoured to be personally involved in the search for Dorothy Millette. The eulogy was read by former silents star Conrad Nagel – a devoted Christian Scientist who denounced the suicide theory as 'rot' because 'self-destruction' was not permitted by his church. Nagel had obviously overlooked the fact that not everyone in his ken was a devoted follower of the rantings of Mary Baker Eddy. Adding to the circus were the loudly expressed crocodile tears of Irving Thalberg, and what were almost certainly Harlow's sobs of guilt – she had, after all, been planning on divorcing her husband for cruelty, if Arthur Landau is to be believed. Who had made the decision to have the body cremated – Harlow, so that she would not have to face up to visiting his grave, or Mayer, in case some later newly discovered theory demanded disinterment – is not known. Whatever the reason, Mayer paid a studio technician to accompany it to the crematorium and actually *watch* it burning, just to ensure that Paul Bern was well and truly gone.

On 12 September, Harlow returned to the set of *Red Dust*. By this time the adverse publicity surrounding Paul Bern's shady past had begun working in her favour though the general public – then as now taking much of the sensationalist claptrap printed by the tabloids as gospel – were split 50-50 over whether she had actually put the gun to Bern's head and pulled the trigger. What the press were not told was that, for a few days, Louis B. Mayer had taken Harlow off the film – she had requested this, he planned announcing, out of grief and respect for her late husband. It was in fact the Hays Office, yet again confusing the actress with the part (though in this instance they were not far wrong) who deemed it inappropriate for a recently bereaved widow of a top Hollywood executive to be seen portraying 'a loose woman, cavorting in the jungle and taking nude baths in a barrel'. In one of the more foolish moves of his career, Mayer decided that it might be prudent to shoot all of Harlow's scenes with another actress, and offered the part to Tallulah Bankhead – 10 times more scandalous than a dozen Jean Harlows! The ruse backfired when Tallulah informed The Messiah that even she had scruples, as she explained in her autobiography:

> Would I care to replace Miss Harlow? I would not. To damn the radiant Jean for the misfortune of another would be one of the shabbiest acts of all time. I told Mr Mayer as much. I tossed in a survey of the background of some of his box office pets. He blanched. To distract me, he undertook to act out the circumstances of Paul Bern's death. He rose from his throne, became highly emotional, started to circle his desk, the better to ham up the scene. Purposely I misread his intentions. 'None of that now, Mr Mayer,' I said, 'stay on your side of the desk. I can visualize the scene. You don't have to demonstrate!'

Worse was to come, for when Mayer tried to force Tallulah's hand by threatening to expose her as 'a serial trollop who has seduced more Hollywood actors than most of us have hot dinners,' she called his bluff – hence the 'box-office pets' reference in her memoirs – venturing to inform the press of the names of six MGM *actresses* with whom she claimed she had been intimate, including

Garbo and Crawford. 'It would be 12 years before I'd face a motion picture camera again,' she concluded, 'but it gave me considerable satisfaction to deflate this Nero in my final gesture.'

Harlow's every move and non-scripted utterance on the *Red Dust* set was scrutinised. Hays Office spies hovered everywhere. Marino Bello never left her side for a moment – nothing to do with the story he fed to the press about wanting to care for his 'Baby'. For the same reason, Louis B. Mayer supplied her with a nurse who was instructed to sedate her, should she suddenly start talking about her late husband, or should a reporter suddenly turn up. The heat on the mock-jungle set was oppressive, and stank to high heaven. Clark Gable did his best to cheer her up, but was unable to try too hard in case his affection was mistaken for something more serious. Harlow's resilience while working under such tough, stressful conditions was noted by Ben Maddox, who observed in *Screen Book*, 'With her emotional and nervous system taut, at the breaking point, she never once gave in to a moment of weakness. The show went on.'

On 14 September 1932, 10 days after Paul Bern's death, Dorothy Millette's badly decomposed body was fished out of the Sacramento River, 30 miles southwest of the city, by two Japanese farmhands. The police concluded that, in a disturbed state of mind, she had jumped off the *Delta King* and been sucked under the boat by its paddle-wheel. Rumour also persisted that she had been pushed, probably by one of Bern's friends who blamed her for his death – or maybe on Louis B. Mayer's orders. Others would not have put it past Marino Bello to have her bumped off, just in case the 'wife' clause in Bern's naturalisation papers and first will held good, and Dorothy tried making a claim on his estate, robbing him of the house that Bern and Harlow had allegedly promised him.

Such was the confusion, still, that the public were willing to believe anything the tabloids threw at them. The police contacted Lowell Millett, but he refused to claim Dorothy's body, declaring that she had brought shame on his family, and that in any case he had divorced her years ago. For all he cared, Millett added, they could chuck her back into the river! In a very strange move – one which gave many the impression that she must have been guilty of something – Harlow paid for the funeral, and even had the name Dorothy Millette Bern inscribed on the gravestone. Her acknowledgement of Dorothy's status, however, backfired on her when lawyers for the dead woman's sisters and legal heirs, Mary Hartranft and Violet Hesser, declared that there was no difference in the eyes of the law between the terms 'wife' and 'common-law wife'. No one asked why these sisters had never visited Dorothy once at the sanatorium, at the Algonquin, or the Plaza Hotel – furthermore, that they had not come forwards when the San Francisco and Sacramento police had begged relatives to come forward with information that might help them with their search. All the press needed to know was that they were entitled to half of the estate of their late 'brother-in-law', which they estimated to be around $100,000 including the Easton Drive house.

These people soon changed their tune when they learned that there was nothing to inherit, and that instead of receiving a handsome hand-out, they might end up paying his debts on his behalf, should they persist with their claim. Suddenly, they were not so sure that Bern had married their sister after all, and they made a hasty exit. Bern had lied to Harlow about being a wealthy man, saddling her with debts totalling more than $50,000. MGM had paid him $80,000 a year, yet less than $500 remained in his bank account. The house he had shared with Harlow had been remortgaged to its full value of $60,000, and only days after Bern's death, Harlow received a bill for $10,000 that he had owed in unpaid taxes. How he had spent his vast salary was anybody's guess: again, the press came to a logical conclusion that someone must have been blackmailing him. Harlow's creditors swooped like vultures. She asked Mayer for a loan which he delighted in refusing – moreover, he sent her a bill for Whitey Hendry's services, including the 'protection' *he* had prescribed against her will! The house was repossessed and she moved in with Mama Jean and Marino Bello until she could work out what to do next. As before, agent Arthur Landau came to the rescue, loaning her the money to pay back every cent her husband had owed.

* * * *

And so to the burning question. Who killed Jean Harlow's husband? It is quite likely that the truth will never be known, but the following (in order of culpability) remain the chief suspects:

MARINO BELLO. On the face of it, the likeliest candidate. A shady, thoroughly unpleasant individual, insanely jealous of anyone who came within a mile of his stepdaughter. Bello had been instrumental in removing Chuck McGrew from her life. It is also virtually certain that he sexually abused her, or at least threatened and made lewd advances towards her. In his privileged position of 'father confessor', Bern would have been party to this information. His brother, Henry, later claimed that he had proof that Bello had given instructions for the killing, but never elaborated on this and may even have made the claim to draw attention away from himself – see below. If Bern had refused Harlow's request to sign over the deeds of the Easton Drive house to her mother and stepfather, then Bello could have got one step closer to acquiring the house by eliminating Bern, then menacing Harlow into signing the house over to her mother.

DOROTHY MILLETTE. The maligned former 'wife', who may or may not have been mentally unbalanced, and one of the two identities (the other being Harlow herself) of the woman in the limousine. If, as her sisters' lawyers claimed, there was no moral legal difference between the terms 'wife' and 'common-law wife', then it figures Dorothy too could have made a claim on Bern's estate. Even if this failed, she could have attempted to prove that his marriage to Harlow was invalid, by way of non-consummation. Obviously, as his partner for so many years she would have been well aware of his genital abnormality and inability to have sex, and would have been backed up in this by the autopsy report. Her mistake, if she killed him, was not seeing the note he had scribbled in his address book, though equally she could have seen this and interpreted it as an apology for the argument that is alleged to have taken place, the previous evening, between herself, Bern and Harlow.

Bern's depleted bank account very strongly suggests that he was being blackmailed by someone, and the likeliest candidate appears to have been Dorothy. David Stenn (*Bombshell*, pp 125–6) offers further evidence from butler John Carmichael's wife, who worked as Bern's cook, that Dorothy visited Easton Drive on the eve of his death: 'The next morning Carmichael found a woman's swimsuit by the pool. It was not Harlow's size, and it was still wet…and the mysterious swimsuit found by Winifred Carmichael matched both a bathing cap found in Millette's [San Francisco] hotel room and an empty container on the *Delta King*.' Stenn also cites an interview with Henry Hathaway, Bern's former protegé, wherein the director had visited Easton Drive on the eve of Bern's death, and been told by John Carmichael of the argument he had overheard between Bern, Harlow and Dorothy – in which Harlow had told her husband, before storming out of the house and heading for Mama Jean's place, 'Well, when you find out who you're married to, let me know.'

Hathaway further declared that he had seen Bern write the 'suicide' note, and that the 'comedy' and 'abject humiliation' within this referred to this unprecedented meeting between his two wives. 'He was going to send it to Harlow with flowers the next day, which is what he usually did,' Stenn quotes Hathaway as having said, 'but before he could, Dorothy Millette came back and shot him. Then she went to San Francisco and committed suicide. The studio covered the whole thing up. Better to impugn Paul's masculinity and make Harlow an innocent dupe than to have her party to bigamy.' This does not account for how the gun ended up in Bern's hand, though Dorothy could of course have put it there. So far as is known, the death scene was never fingerprinted – indeed, Whitey Hendry and his team very likely would have wiped the place clean before the regular police arrived. It all makes for sound sense.

HENRY BERN. Something of the family black sheep whose comments in the wake of his brother's death gives way to the maxim, 'Methinks he doth protest too much.' Henry was one of the few who knew about the insurance policy (see below), and its 'death by another person' clause which would not have prevented the company from paying out to the next of kin. Though he was not in Los Angeles at the time of Bern's death, like Marino Bello and Abner Zwillman, he had contacts who could have perpetrated the deed at his behest. As explained above, though he had *claimed* that his brother had a normal-sized penis and was capable of having sex when the autopsy report had declared otherwise, he would have had little difficulty proving Bern's marriage to Harlow could not be consummated, and with this rendered invalid, *he* would have been named next of kin. Since arriving in California, Henry had lied persistently to police and reporters that the couple had been happily married, when he had been party to some of their violent rows.

Henry is further believed to have been the only one aside from Bern to have been aware of Dorothy's whereabouts, which means that it is not outside the realms of possibility for them to have plotted together. One must also question why Henry never showed up at the inquest, unless he had something to hide which might be forced out of him while under cross-examination, or why he did not attend his brother's funeral, preferring to leave Los Angeles on the very day that Dorothy Millette's body was pulled out of the Sacramento River.

ABNER ZWILLMAN. The good-looking, red-blooded mobster who had been replaced in Harlow's affections – and her bed – by a man of extremely dubious sexuality, widely reputed to have been a hermaphrodite. Zwillman would naturally have been affronted by this, and may even have questioned his own sexual prowess. He is also on record as confessing to Bern's murder, though as he always had a tendency to boast, one should not read too much into this.

PAUL BERN. *May* have killed himself over the dildo incident when Harlow 'shrieked with laughter', though if Arthur Landau's story is to be believed, Bern found the episode just as hilarious as she did. More seriously, there was the subject of common-law marriage, illegal in California (as Rudolph Valentino had discovered to his detriment, a decade earlier), but not so in New York. It was a long shot, but Bern could have been indicted for bigamy. A solid reason for Bern not wishing to take his own life, however, relates to the $85,000 insurance policy he is known to have purchased on 1 September, four days before his death, which clearly defined that the policy would not be paid out in the event of suicide. On the other hand, he probably had not suspected that Dorothy Millette would turn up on his doorstep – if indeed such a confrontation took place – whence his state of mind during the evening of 4 September could have been completely different from when he acquired the policy.

JEAN HARLOW. The least likely suspect, but for a time at the top of District Attorney Buron Fitts' list. She could have been the woman in the limousine to whom Bern was alleged to have yelled, 'Get out of my life!' but this does not make her culpable of the crime. There is a faint possibility that she could have killed Bern as a 'crime of passion', particularly as he is known to have been physically violent towards her. Also, given her timidity and childlike naivety, one doubts she would have survived rigorous interrogation without breaking down and confessing, had she pulled the trigger – which of course may explain why Louis B. Mayer kept her sedated throughout the enquiry, to prevent her from having to answer awkward questions. In those days, backed by Mayer's millions, through the likes of Whitey Hendry being given *carte blanche*, and through sheer fear of reprisal, virtually any crime could be kept under wraps. Given her extreme honesty during interviews, however, if Harlow *had* been guilty, one sincerely doubts that she would have survived for another five years without letting something slip, no matter how inconsequential.

To sum up, therefore, taking into account the above facts, one comes to the conclusion: an 80 per cent chance of murder, a 20 per cent chance of suicide.

CHAPTER SIX
Dinner At Eight

'She has faith. It is this trust in the elemental goodness of people that has freed her from the petty entanglements of a movie career – which has, indeed, enabled her to survive tragedy.'
                    Ben Maddox, journalist, friend and lover, 1932

Ben Maddox had been right. The show had to go on because Harlow had nothing left but her work: no home of her own now that the Easton Drive house had been repossessed, a mother who smothered her with affection, a stepfather whose most profound wish had come true.

With Paul Bern gone, Marino Bello was back in control. His 'Baby' had been given back to him, and no sooner had the urn containing Bern's ashes been assigned to a storeroom at the Price & Daniel Morgue (where it remains to this day) than Bello began pestering her for sex. Only fear of Bello handing over the alleged Esser photographs prevented Harlow from reporting him to the authorities. The fact that Harlow did not call Bello's bluff suggests the photographs existed. Mama Jean would have turned a blind eye to Bello doing anything, even rape – she would never have risked giving up what she had striven for over the years by supporting her daughter against her husband. And of course, had Harlow taken the matter further, she would have fallen foul of Louis B. Mayer's stringent family-values policy – the fact that, no matter how vile a particular relative may be, one had no option but to grin and bear it, and treat him or her with respect whether they deserved it or not. What lovely parents these must have been! 'What kept Jean from so unnatural an act was the fear that Marino would enslave her sexually as he had Mama Jean,' Irving Shulman observes in *Harlow*, 'If she had not despised the man she might have gone to bed with her stepfather – she was a goddess, and therefore above mortal conventions – but enslavement to someone like Bello would have destroyed her.'

In an attempt to prove that, at just 22, she was still a desirable woman with a normal sexual appetite, Harlow took to importuning, driving off into the night in search of a man who might offer her what she had obviously been lacking since marrying Bern – and apparently without success. The reason she never 'scored', Arthur Landau said, was because each time a potential client approached her car he immediately recognised her, causing her to jam her foot down on the accelerator. The wife of one of these men had hired a private investigator to keep tabs on him, but her attempts at blackmailing her failed when Harlow told her to go ahead. She had reached such an all-time low that she did not care if her career ended or not. Landau handed the matter over to Whitey Hendry, and the woman never bothered her again.

It was on account of Ben Maddox and the more sympathetic journalists – people who had befriended her, and who believed in her – that Harlow's career survived. Had it been left to the likes of Hedda Hopper, Louella Parsons and Adela Rogers St Johns, all desperate to bring her down – she may well have followed the same self-destruct route taken by Barbara La Marr and Alma Rubens. Between enforced sedations, she had begun drinking heavily, and Louis B. Mayer's 'nurse' had done nothing to stop her. Mayer had been interested only in keeping her quiet and in getting her back to the *Red Dust* set as quickly as possible – while crossing his fingers that it would not all explode back in his face. On the strength of the scandal and out of sheer curiosity, he hoped, the public would flock to see the film. And if they decided to shanghai one of its stars into oblivion afterwards, so what? MGM still had Garbo, Shearer – and by the skin of their teeth on account of *their* improprieties, Crawford and Gable. What Mayer may not have realised was so far as the public was concerned, Paul Bern had been but a backroom figure they had seen only in the press – most Americans had never heard of him until that Labor Day weekend – whereas Jean Harlow, like Joan Crawford, had always been one of them – living proof that any one of them, with the right amount of luck and looks, could get where she was now.

In visiting her on the set of *Red Dust* and by exercising his power in refusing to leave until he had spoken to her, Ben Maddox had painted her as the victim. Then, and for the rest of his life, he would remain tight-lipped about their lengthy conversations in her dressing room – reporting to his readers only that she was a sad, lonely woman who deserved to be given a fair go.

Ben Maddox, born in Missouri in 1902, was a hugely influential freelance reporter who used sex as a means of acquiring his scoops. A muscular, good-looking six-footer, his trick was to interview subjects over lunch or dinner – almost always at their homes, where there was less danger of his coming unstuck – and, once they had fallen for his seemingly limitless charms, offer himself as dessert. As a cub reporter, one of his earliest conquests back in 1923 had been Rudolph Valentino. 'I allowed him to ride my favourite steed around Falcon Lair, and afterwards he rode me,' Rudy wrote in his diary after Maddox's first visit to his hillside mansion. Three years later, he had been one of the eight pallbearer-lovers at his funeral. When Maddox had visited the *Red Dust* set, however, he had been more interested in cheering Harlow up than in seducing her – and in any case, there had been a more lucrative prize on offer: the equally manly Clark Gable. A few months later, they would begin a passionate affair which would last until Gable met the great love of his life, Carole Lombard.

Some of Maddox's notes and spiked interviews make for interesting reading. In 1933, within the space of one week he bedded Anita Page, Sidney Fox, Marian Marsh and Sylvia Sydney – the latter in the back of his car in broad daylight – when the editor of *Silver Screen* commissioned him to pen a feature about 'Hollywood's bachelor maidens'. The general opinion was that all four were lesbians, but in the arms of this man, for obvious reasons referred to by Tallulah Bankhead as 'Big Ben', they turned into red-blooded tigresses. 'Every actress has her own opinions,' Maddox wrote, 'so I started to learn the facts as they appear to some of our charmers who so far have said NO to altar calls.' For his piece, Maddox refused to interview Barbara Stanwyck, dismissing her as 'too unglamorous', though he later 'lunched' with her husband, Robert Taylor. At around this time, Maddox was also 'the meat in the sandwich' during a weekend-long interview with lovers Cary Grant and Randolph Scott.

Maddox would have an on-off affair with Harlow, which came about one afternoon when they got into a silly argument at her house – for once she had the place all to herself – over which of them was the most attractive. 'This being red-hot on celluloid and good clean fun in person annoyed me,' Maddox told the readers of *Screen Book*, 'I deliberately steered clear until, finally, I started to think maybe I was wrong.' When Maddox told Harlow that, though he would always respect her as a friend, he would never find her attractive because she was 'just a sexless, phony blonde', she slapped his face, called him 'a big shit with a chip the size of Kansas on his shoulder' – and within five minutes they were in bed. 'And that chip fell off my shoulder long before I left her house,' he concluded, without letting on what had really happened, 'I can resist anything but sincerity!'

Red Dust was released in October 1932, six weeks after Paul Bern's death. Clark Gable had been assigned to other projects, but though public opinion had shifted enormously in her favour with the suicide verdict, Harlow was still considered studio poison. Gable attempted to defend her by marching into Mayer's office and ordering him to give her a chance. The Messiah's reaction was to wave Gable over to the window and point to the sidewalk: there were dozens of tall, good-looking men out there, any one of which could be offered a contract and transformed into the next Gable. Mayer was also still getting complaints about Harlow from religious groups, and the Hays Office were pestering him to fire her – on the pretext that, concerning the Bern scandal, there was never smoke without fire. Mayer offered a compromise: Harlow would be put into another film, eventually, but first she would have to prove herself by sailing through a six-months' probationary good behaviour period.

Another rock at this difficult time was Arthur Landau who, not content with loaning Harlow money to pay off her debts, took the liberty of buying a one-acre plot of land, on her behalf, at 214 South Beverly Glen Boulevard, in Hollywood's Holmby Hills district. She had authorised him to put in a bid for the $10,000 plot before Bern's death, which suggests that she had been serious about divorcing him, but amid the confusion of the last month had forgotten about it. Landau had used his own money, and told her that if she wanted the land it was hers – the deeds were in his name, and she could pay him back when and how she wanted, there was no hurry.

Landau convinced her that the success of *Red-Headed Woman*, swiftly followed by that of *Red Dust*, more or less assured Harlow of a future with MGM. Unless he could find solid proof that she was guilty of 'moral turpitude', Louis B. Mayer would not be able to fire her without being dragged not just through the courts, but into the newspapers. No one knew about the kerb-crawling episodes, not even Mayer with his spies: so far as the fans were concerned, she had behaved with unswerving dignity throughout her ordeal. Mayer was compelled to make a statement when asked if he was prejudiced against one of his biggest stars: he had never hated Harlow, just her public and on-screen persona – which was rather like someone saying they liked apple pie, but not the taste of apples! And yes, Mayer affirmed, his 'daughter' would work again, but first she needed a decent respite period to mourn her 'beloved' husband.

This in mind, Harlow gave the go ahead for the builders to move in, leaving much of the planning to her agent – her only stipulations being that everything should be white, and that though she would live in the property, once constructed it would be handed over to her parents! Completed in just 10 weeks, the house was a mish-mash of styles: a mock-Georgian facade with huge chimneys, flanked by tall trees, and with a 'Frenchified' interior. Later there would be a pool in which Harlow swam naked every morning, his-and-hers dressing rooms and a brick barbecue, and a lily pond with mock-medieval bridge. As befitting a 'lady of the manor', a garage would be commissioned to house her cars: a V-12 Cadillac and a Pierce Arrow Tourer. The actual building work set her back over $50,000, but she spent half as much again – inspired by her bedroom in the soon-to-be-made *Dinner At Eight* – on interior furnishings which included antique furniture, rare porcelain, mink headboards, gold fittings in the bathrooms, and even toilet seats covered with ermine. 'If a lady's gotta take a dump, she might as well sit all nice and comfortable,' she told reporters. Harlow was also one of the first Hollywood stars to have a walk-in refrigerator.

Harlow's house was 'officially opened' on Christmas Eve 1932 by Marino Bello, who ostentatiously carried Mama Jean over the threshold as members of the press watched in amazement. For MGM this was an important exercise in loyalty – one of Mayer's 'children' doing what he always did himself, putting his family first. No one saw through the hypocrisy, not even Hedda and Louella, who naturally had to be there to report the happy occasion. Hedda later informed her readers of Mama Jean's housewarming gift for her man: a five-carat diamond ring – though not that she had charged this to her daughter's account. And no sooner had the press left than Bello turned on his stepdaughter and accused her of being mean because she had asked permission to have the mirrored master bedroom for herself! The arch cretin, he marked out his territory by buying Harlow a bedpan so that she would not need to use the en-suite bathroom, which he had claimed for himself – any excuse to walk through her bedroom whenever he felt like it.

Ben Maddox was Harlow's escort at Louis B. Mayer's Christmas party that year to which absolutely everyone was invited, attendance being compulsory – according to Maddox's announcement in *Modern Screen*, 'Unless your name is Garbo, W.C. Fields, or God.' The 12-hour bash always kicked off with a long, boring speech from Mayer himself, thanking everyone for all their hard work of the past year, then leaving at once as a sign for the fun to begin. Though stingy with his employees the rest of the time, Mayer always pushed the boat out at the festive season. His bootlegger contacts provided a seemingly endless supply of booze, there was not a Hays Office spy to be seen, and stag-films were screened all night in backrooms where clothing was optional. Guests could have sex with whoever they liked, so long as it was with a member of the opposite sex. Needless to say, most of the major stars left their spouses at home, and it must have been intriguing for them to see Maddox there, knowing that he had 'had' so many of them. Some of the guests wore fancy dress: Clark Gable, costumed as a preacher, turned up with trapeze artiste Marion Davies – their characters in *Polly Of The Circus*. Harlow and Maddox went as themselves, she well aware that whatever costume she put on, someone would suggest that she was only wearing it for some ulterior motive.

This year, instead of leaving with Mayer, Irving Thalberg and Norma Shearer stayed until the end of the party, and got very drunk. The next morning, Thalberg awoke with a fever, and on 28 December he suffered a near fatal heart attack. Among his first visitors was Harlow, who turned up with Clark and Ria Gable, only to have Norma slam the door in their faces. The press were informed that Thalberg was suffering from nothing more serious than the flu. Even so, with his increasingly fragile health, this could easily have carried him off, and the hacks began scribbling their obituaries. Later it emerged that even the all-important Boy Wonder had had to supply Louis B. Mayer with a doctor's certificate to assure him he had not been pulling a fast one, whence Mayer announced that he personally would be stepping into Thalberg's shoes. By February, he was pronounced strong enough to travel for a rest cure at a clinic in Bad Neuheim, Germany. Norma and a retinue of lackeys accompanied him, and the press were informed that he would be overseas for at least three months. But Thalberg made the trip very much against his will. His theory had always been that, if he was going to drop dead at any moment, then he might as well work as hard as possible while awaiting the inevitable.

Mayer now set about delegating his extraordinarily heavy workload among his executives: Hunt Stromberg, Harry Rapf, Walter Wanger and Mayer's son-in-law, David O. Selznick. Handling the affairs of some of Thalberg's biggest stars, including Harlow and Gable, would be Eddie Mannix (1891–1963), a shady character now known to have been involved with mobsters and organised crime. In 1938 he would be accused of murdering his adulterous first wife, Bernice, by fixing a high-speed car crash to make it look like an accident. When the inquest into this re-opened two decades later, Mannix would also be accused of complicity in Paul Bern's death, besides that of television's *Superman* actor, George Reeves, who had an affair with Mannix's second wife. The story, much-fictionalised, reached the big screen with *Hollywood-land* in 2006.

It was Mannix who suggested Harlow for *Hollywood Party*, scored by Rodger and Hart, an enjoyable slice of hokum starring Jimmy Durante, Laurel & Hardy and future *Mexican Spitfire*

As the gangster's moll opposite James Cagney in *Public Enemy* (1931). The film's violent scenes saw it banned for many years.

'Where'd ya git that kimona?' With Gable in *Red Dust* (1932).

As Lola Burns in *Bombshell* (1933). The film was based on her experiences and problems with her own disfunctional family.

With second husband Paul Bern, 'Hollywood's Little Father Confessor', just weeks before his mysterious death.

With Gable in *Hold Your Man* (1933). He says, 'Wait till you see how I grow on you!' She responds, 'Yeah . . . like a carbunkle!'

With 'old windbag' Wallace Beery in *Dinner At Eight* (1934). They started off hating each other but became close friends.

Harlow's last completed film, *Personal Property* (1937), with Robert Taylor, arguably her most handsome co-star.

God, she was gorgeous.

actress, Lupe Velez. With the emphasis as usual placed on his enormous hooter, Durante played The Great Schnarzan, a jungle movie star whose films are bombing at the box office because his lions are anaemic. Needing to buy more from the tetchy Baron Munchausen (Jack Pearl), he throws a lavish party in an attempt to get him in a bargaining mood to which are invited several top Hollywood stars. And in the midst of the ensuing confusion, Walt Disney tosses in a Technicolor Mickey Mouse cartoon! Harlow's was a cameo role. Mannix wanted to ease her back into the movies gently, he said. She was hired to play a switchboard operator who warbles a little ditty, 'Prayer', but according to the story which emerged proved so 'tone-deaf' that the producer, Harry Rapf, fired her. This was unforgivably mean of him: the other now forgotten singers in the production are so dire, Harlow could not possibly have been any worse. 'Prayer' was subsequently revamped, given new lyrics – 'The Bad In Every Man' – and added to the soundtrack of Clark Gable's new film, *Manhattan Melodrama*. Later it became 'Blue Moon', entering the executive repertoires of Doris Day and Jane Froman.

Harlow reacted badly to rejection, particularly when Rapf referred to her as 'the Jewish widow'. Grabbing a pair of scissors, as a form of 'penance' in keeping with this religion she hacked off her famous platinum locks – not too severely, but enough to almost cause Louis B. Mayer to have a heart attack when the news was relayed to him. What happened next was mercifully kept out of the press by Whitey Hendry. Wearing cheap clothes and a five-and-ten-cents store wig so that nobody would recognise her this time, Harlow took the train to San Bernadino – why she chose here was never explained – and promptly took to the sidewalks of the city's red-light district – the difference being that she was the one paying anyone who might have her. According to Arthur Landau, Harlow looked so rough that she picked up just one customer – a travelling soap salesman with whom she spent the weekend in a tawdry hotel.

On 9 March 1933, Louis B. Mayer announced that sweeping

changes were to be made to his empire, to take effect immediately. This was the Depression, and with poverty across America at an all-time high and cinema audiences dwindling, MGM's stars had 'volunteered' to set an example and help the economy by working for the next two months on half pay. Secretly, they had been told that anyone refusing to comply would be fired! Most of the big names were too terrified of Mayer to stand up to him – though Garbo threatened to go back to Sweden and never return. To be on the safe side, Mayer kept her on full pay. Joan Crawford bawled him out, yelling, 'Mr Mayer, I only wish the ground would open up and swallow your sorry ass!'

The next day, this almost happened when, at 5.55pm, Long Beach was hit by an earthquake. Not far from the epicentre, at Culver City, Paramount were shooting *International City* with W.C. Fields and Bela Lugosi. While the crew and cast fled for their lives, the cameras were left rolling, inadvertently capturing an earthquake on celluloid for the very first time. Though the film sets were relatively unharmed, Long Beach was virtually destroyed, and 120 people lost their lives. Joan Crawford was not the only one to regret that The Messiah was not one of them.

Meanwhile, satisfied that Harlow had passed her good behaviour test – and with a good deal of touching up, that her famous hair was ready for public consumption – Eddie Mannix talked Mayer into putting her into *Dinner At Eight* in what would be the most illustrious line-up since *Grand Hotel*: Marie Dressler, Wallace Beery, John and Lionel Barrymore, Billie Burke and Madge Evans were but a few, so meticulously cast they could almost have been playing themselves. Indeed, in an act of pure selfishness, Mayer injected a good deal of pre-Method into the proceedings by hiring playwright Donald Ogden Stewart for a last-minute script revision. Stewart (1894–1980), a member of the Algonquin Round Table, had had hits on Broadway, and would pick up an Oscar for *The Philadelphia Story*, though his career would later be blighted when he was suspected of Communism during the McCarthy witch-hunt. Mayer gave Stewart free reign to investigate each of the main stars' personal lives. His script is sparkling and resplendent with witty one-liners, but he refused to compromise the actors' feelings when re-adapting their lines to touch on their every sore point: alcoholism, serial adultery, dodgy dealings, illness, wife-bashing and even terminal illness.

Produced by David O. Selznick and directed by George Cukor, *Dinner At Eight* was based on the stageplay by George S. Kaufman and Edna Ferber, and scripted by Frances Marion and Herman Mankiewicz. Though not as good as *Grand Hotel*, it followed the same blockbuster tradition in that all of its stars were promoted as of equal status – naturally this resulted in personality clashes. Harlow was delighted that Clark Gable had been cast in the relatively minor role of Park Lane doctor Wayne Talbot, but just as shooting was about to get underway, Louis B. Mayer announced that Gable had been dropped after considering the part beneath his status, and that he had been replaced by Edmund Lowe. The truth is, Gable refused to work with George Cukor, a close friend of former silents star William Haines, a man who knew all about Gable's secretive gay past. Harlow got along famously with Marie Dressler, a tragi-comic genius who like Louise Closser Hale (also in the film) had worked for many years on the legitimate stage, and arrived in Hollywood way too late. As had happened while making *The Secret Six*, Harlow found Beery to be 'a royal pain in the ass', yet she still socialised with him away from the set, which suggests that there was less to their so-called enmity than met the eye.

In his later all-female (including the animals!) masterpiece, *The Women*, George Cukor would superimpose each actress's face over the animal she was compared with in the plot. Here, he superimposes their faces on the dinner plates. The scenario, as with *Grand Hotel* a series of vignettes, opens with homely shipping magnate Oliver Jordan (the equally homely Lionel Barrymore) and his snooty wife, Millicent (the genuinely snooty Florenz Ziegfeld widow, Billie Burke). She is planning a soiree in honour of Lord and Lady Ferncliffe, the richest couple in England, and hopes that entertaining them will elevate her to the top of the society ladder in time for the wedding next month of her daughter, Paula (Madge Evans). Oliver remains indifferent: his business is going down the sluice because mystery buyers are snapping up his stock, though he peps up when he learns that his old flame Carlotta Vance (Marie Dressler) is back in town, and that Millicent has added her name to the guest list. Then he insists on inviting mismatched couple Dan and Kitty Packard (Harlow, Beery), whom Millicent cannot stand: 'You're joking! Ask that common little woman into my house? And that noisy, vulgar man? He smells Oklahoma!' What Oliver does not know is that it is Dan who is buying up his stock, and what no one knows is that Oliver has a heart condition – as had Lionel Barrymore.

Carlotta arrives at the Jordan house, swanning in like the proverbial battleship. 'Oliver, *ducky!*' she booms. He tells her how marvellous she looks – though she did not know it (Mayer and Donald Ogden Stewart did, as will be explained), Dressler was dying, which makes her lines now and later in the film, all the more poignant. From this moment on, Dressler dominates every scene she is in as the imperious but loveable has-been ham who still thinks she is God's gift to the acting fraternity. Cut to Kitty, decked out like a queen in her 'ten shades of white' boudoir, a breath of fresh air after the overbearing Millicent – scoffing chocolates in bed and bawling out her bumbling nurse, when she is no less articulate herself. Kitty has a 'cold' and is waiting for the doctor – her love, Wayne Talbot (Edmund Lowe) – though when he arrives (giving Kitty (Harlow) the chance to leap out of bed and display to cinema audiences that she does not favour underwear beneath her clinging satin robe), Wayne is not as enthusiastic as when last time he saw her because he realises that he still loves his wife. She (Karen Morley) knows about his serial womanising (though with Lowe it was with men), and forgives him for it. 'That slug never wants to meet any refined people,' Kitty says of braggard

Dan when he vows not to attend the dinner. Then she tells him that he must, otherwise she will expose him as a crook, to which he growls, 'Go lay an egg!' He yields, but only because the Ferncliffes will be there to help him with his scheme to buy up what little of Oliver's stock is left, and ruin him.

Millicent panics when a guest cancels – so unfeeling of him to contract pneumonia and ruin her big occasion! She therefore invites Larry Renault (John Barrymore), the once famous actor, now burned out and unemployable. 'In his photographs he has the most heavenly profile', someone says, enabling fact to blend with fiction. Barrymore (1882–1942), known as The Great Profile (an appellation persistently repeated throughout the film, along with the actor's insistence to be filmed in profile as much as possible), was arguably the greatest dramatic actor of his generation. Now, he was coming to the end of a magnificent career – compelled to read his lines from cue cards, it is believed because of the onset of premature cardio-vascular dementia. Like the real Barrymore (thus far in 1933) Larry has been married three times, seeks solace from his demons by way of the bottle, and has an eye for women much younger than himself – here, 19-year-old Paula Jordan. The fact that Barrymore, at 51, was 28 years Madge Evans' senior caused MGM more problems with the Hays Office than Harlow's lack of undergarments.

There is a last-minute dilemma when the Ferncliffes call to say they cannot make it. Carlotta tries to cancel too. Wheezing into the Jordan's house she pants, 'May I have a whisky and soda? You don't mind, do you? Millicent, really, I'm just *dying*!' Then she cracks that she is exhausted because she has lunched with four lawyers on the 88th floor: 'A cloud floated right into my soup plate!' Cut to Dan and Kitty having a row in her boudoir with Donald Ogden Stewart perhaps injecting too much of the real Harlow/Beery/Mama Jean into the situation, albeit with hilarious results – one of the funniest sketches either of them ever did. 'I've told you a million times not to talk to me when I'm doing my lashes,' she screams, when he bursts in to inform her that they are moving to Washington for him to fulfil his political ambitions. She is not having this, and gives him her opinion of politicians' wives: 'A lot of sour-faced frumps with last year's clothes on. Pinning medals on girl scouts and pouring tea for the DARs and rolling Easter eggs on the White House lawn!' He reminds her that he is the boss, that she will do as she is told unless she wants a hiding. She reminds him that his first wife died because he bossed her around, that this will not happen to her. Then the home truths start flying:

> KITTY: You're not gonna step on my face to get where you want to go, you old windbag!
> DAN: Listen, you little piece of scum, you. I've got a good notion to drop you right back where I picked you up, in the check room of the Hottentot Club, or whatever the dirty joint was.
> KITTY: Oh no, you won't –
> DAN: And then you can go back to that sweet-smelling family of yours, back to the railroad tracks of Passaic. And get this. If that snivelling, money-grabbing, whining old mother of yours comes fooling around my offices any more, I'm giving orders to have her thrown down those sixty flights of stairs, so help me!

Dan soon withdraws his threat, however, when Kitty threatens to tell the folks in Washington about his double-dealing. 'Politics,' she scoffs, 'you couldn't get into politics. You couldn't get in anywhere. You couldn't even get into the men's room at the Astor!' Cut to Larry Renault, also getting a few home truths from his manager: 'You're a corpse, and you know it. Go get yourself buried!' Larry decides his fate, and drunkenly staggers to the mirror. Mayer and Stewart had wanted him to pull a gun and 'do a Bern', but this would never have got past the censor – so he switches on the gas tap instead.

Then to the finale. As the band plays 'Chante pour moi, violons', the guests arrive. Carlotta has brought her dog. When this was filmed, the dog was called Mussolini, but on account of the increasingly volatile political situation in Italy, Mayer decided that he would be renamed Tarzan, and asked Marie Dressler to overdub her lines, though the viewer can still read her lips – which was why the film was banned in Italy. Carlotta breaks Paula's heart by informing her of Larry's suicide: more heartlessness from the scriptwriter when he has the dreadfully ill-looking old trouper pronounce, 'And nothing could be done. That's the unfortunate thing about death. It's so terribly – final.' Then Oliver suffers a heart attack upstairs and, prostrate on his sickbed, confesses to Millicent that they are broke, making her suddenly realise that there are more important things in life than her silly dinner party. They will economise, and be happy – and Dan, who was out to ruin Oliver, now heeds Kitty's threats and vows to help him out. And as the guests enter the dining room we have the immortal scene when Harlow waylays Dressler, the one scene which always shows up in retrospectives of their careers:

KITTY: I was reading a book the other day…
CARLOTTA: (stopped in her tracks) *Reading a book?*
KITTY: Yes, it's all about civilisation or something. A nutty kind of book. You know, the guy says that machinery is going to take the place of every profession?
CARLOTTA: (eyeing her up and down) Oh, my dear. That's something *you* need never worry about!

While Marie Dressler carried the picture from start to finish – she and Harlow only meet in the closing scene – and while audiences flocked to see if John Barrymore could still hold it together, the critics were all for Harlow, whose acting abilities and comic timing had really sharpened up in this past year. 'Harlow is magnificent,' wrote the *New York Daily Mirror*'s Bland Johaneson. 'By long odds the best thing she has done to date,' proclaimed *Variety*. And the *New York Herald*'s stuffy Richard Watts, who had never liked her, now submitted to defeat: 'It seems to me that Miss Harlow, an increasingly delightful actress with each picture, plays the guttersnipe of a wife who battles with Mr Beery, her vulgar husband, and makes love to Edmund Lowe, her amorous doctor, with such high spirits, comic gaiety and shrewd knowledge – or perhaps instinct – that among a congress of stars doing their best, she is quite the hit of the evening.'

It was during the production of *Dinner At Eight* that Louis B. Mayer's esteem plunged to an all-time low, even in the eyes of his friends. Inasmuch as he had sabotaged John Gilbert's career to assuage his own greed, so now he played a disgracefully dirty trick on 64-year-old Marie Dressler, MGM's biggest box-office draw after Garbo and adored by all who knew her. When Dressler was taken ill on the set, Mayer pretended to care and had her examined by his personal physician. Incurable cancer was diagnosed, but Mayer kept the news from her to keep her working and the money coming in. When she found out the truth from her own doctor, after collapsing again, Mayer took her into his office, 'sympathised' with her condition, and imposed a three-hour working day so as not to over tire her. Then he promised her a $100,000 bonus – so long as she promised to hang on until the end of the year and complete the trio of films he had lined up for her. Marie finished them in tremendous pain (she would die in July 1934), only to have Mayer go back on his word and pay her just $10,000 – telling friends that there was little sense in paying her more, seeing as she would not live long enough to enjoy it.

Without allowing Harlow's feet time to touch the ground, Mayer teamed her with Clark Gable once more and rushed her into *Hold Your Man*, which began shooting in April 1933. As good-time girl Ruby Adams, she even got top billing. As had happened with *Red Dust*, Hays Office spies infiltrated the lot, this time to ensure that Harlow and Gable were behaving themselves. They were, with each other. Gable and Ben Maddox were more or less able to conduct their 'buddies' routine right under everyone's noses – locking the dressing room door at lunch time on the pretext that they were sharing a bottle of illicit liquor and playing cards. Harlow, who in common with Joan Crawford and Carole Lombard already had the reputation of being a 'Tinsel Town fag-hag', may have known about their affair, as it is very strange that she never showed the remotest amorous interest in Gable, as happened with his other leading ladies. Arch-dragon Bette Davis later claimed that this was because of Gable's acute halitosis, but that was her just being bitter – a more likely explanation is that she did not want to come between him and Maddox, or get involved in a dispute with Joan Crawford, who was also seeing Gable.

With a fine script by Anita Loos, superb photography by Hal Rosson, and completed in just three weeks, Harlow and Gable were in cracking form. Gable played 'Lucky' Eddie Hall, a conman-hustler from Flatbush who barges into Ruby's apartment while pursued by cops. She is taking a bath. Instantly attracted to him, she get him to strip to the waist, cover himself in soap-suds and jump into the tub, where he pretends to be her very camp husband. In anticipation of services rendered, she searches his pockets and lifts $10 of the money he conned from his last victim, telling him she has been around. While his trousers are drying he struts around in a robe, examining the photographs on the wall – trophies of the men who have been here. When the whore next door drops in to borrow a cup of gin to drown her sorrows (a popular theory then being that drinking gin in the bath enabled a pregnant woman to self-abort), Eddie escapes and they meet again in the next scene: she has been stalking him, and finds him in his favourite speakeasy.

Tonight, Ruby is with regular flame Al (Stuart Erwin), who wants her to come off the game and go away with him. Right now, however, she is interested only in dancing with Eddie who growls, 'Listen, sweetmeat. How about you and me getting together? Wait till you see how I grow on you!' To which she responds, 'Yeah, I can imagine. Like a carbuncle!' Next day she drops in at his place, still pretending to play hard to get, but knowing that she wants him. 'I got two rules I always stick to,' she levels when he gets fresh, 'keep away from couches, and stay on your feet!' And when she sashays off to the bathroom, one sees that she is naked under her clinging Adrian gown. Enter Gypsy (Dorothy Burgess), Eddie's sozzled bit of rough who is none too pleased to find this dyed-haired harlot. 'Who's she?' she slurs, slapping Ruby across the face. 'The Queen of Sheba,' Ruby drawls, socking her in the jaw. Eddie puts on a record. It is their favourite tune, the one they danced to: shades of Sophie Tucker as Harlow herself sings 'Be Sure To Hold Your Man' in a pleasing contralto, suggesting that she had been dropped from *Hollywood Party* for no other reason than spite.

Now, Ruby and Eddie are an item, but he has to spoil it by pulling a job – one that gets him 90 days in the slammer. Upon his release, in an attempt to draw him closer and keep him on the straight and narrow, she makes up the story that she has been pestered by laundry owner Aubrey Mitchell (Paul Hurst). Far from making Eddie jealous, this gives him and his partner in crime Slim (Garry Owen) an idea: Mitchell, a married man, will be 'caught in the act' with Ruby and, pretending to be her brother, Eddie will blackmail him. The ruse goes wrong when a drunken Mitchell gets too rough. Eddie hits him, then whisks Ruby off to the borough hall to buy a marriage licence. But before the wedding takes place, Mitchell is found dead – he banged his head against the wall. Eddie scarpers, leaving Ruby to take the rap.

Sent to the reformatory for two years, she shares a dormitory with a bunch of working girls who all know Eddie – every Christmas he sends all the 'tramps' money. One of these is Gypsy, who has been locked up for drinking. 'What's the matter, Queenie? Did your boyfriend kick you off your throne?' she bawls, before Ruby chins her again and pronounces one the plum lines of that year's movie season, 'You know, you wouldn't be a bad-looking dame if it wasn't for your face!'

Put to work in the sewing room, Ruby discovers she is pregnant – though the Hays Office insisted that her condition was referred to only by way of innuendo. Al comes to see her: the child is not his, but he will marry her anyway. She however wants only one man, and when Gypsy is released she sees the error of her ways and brings Eddie to her on visiting day – her reward from Ruby being a kiss on the mouth which astonishingly, like the one delivered by Marlene Dietrich two years earlier in *Morocco*, got past the censor. Aided by another prisoner, Lily Mae (Theresa Harris), she and Eddie are wed in the reformatory chapel by Lily Mae's preacher father (George Reed) only minutes before the police arrive and drag him away. Now pardoned, Ruby goes off to have her baby. Eddie serves his time, a reduced sentence because his lawyer proved Mitchell's death to have been an accident – and the action jumps forwards three years where, in a too-rushed ending, he is reunited with his wife and son, ready to start a new life now that the forgiving Al has given him a job.

Harlow made a good friend while shooting *Hold Your Man*. Dorothy Burgess (1907–61) was another 'victim of circumstance' whose tracks had recently been covered by Whitey Hendry. A niece of the actress Fay Bainter, Burgess had appeared on Broadway, and in 1928 had starred in the first 'outdoor Talkie', *In Old Arizona*. A few days before the Christmas of 1932 and driving alone, she had crashed her car into another vehicle, killing 17-year-old Louise Manfredi. Though not an important star in the MGM firmament, she was engaged to Clarence Brown, Garbo's favourite director who in the last few years had received several Oscar nominations. Louis B. Mayer had sent Burgess to a San Francisco sanatorium while the accident was being investigated: the $25,000 compensation demanded by Louise Manfredi's family had been reduced to $5,000 – paid by Mayer personally – and Burgess permitted to pick up the threads of her career. Her character's name in *Hold Your Man*, Gypsy Angecon, tickled Harlow, who could speak French – it translated as 'angel asshole'.

Interesting too is the inclusion in the film, reputedly at Harlow's and Gable's insistence, of black actors who in these early years of the Talkies are not typecast as lackeys, slaves or maids. Theresa Harris (1909–85) was a delightful all-round entertainer who had played one of the legionnaires' camp followers in *Morocco*. Later she would star opposite Bette Davis in *Jezebel*. George Reed (1866–1952) was the son of slaves whose most accomplished role so far had been that of escaped slave Jim in the silent version of *Huckleberry Finn* (1923). Later he would be a regular in MGM's *Dr Kildare* series.

The film was released in July 1933, before *Dinner At Eight*, and was a huge hit, suitably lining MGM's coffers at the very height of the Depression. Costing $250,000 to make, a mere drop in the ocean compared with the other film's $2 million-plus, it grossed over $1 million during its first season. It attracted good reviews, mostly, though some critics considered those scenes following Ruby's incarceration in the reformatory not in keeping with the film's zippy, wisecracking first half. It was as if the Hays Office had ignored the sexual situations for once, but stepped in at the last minute to ensure that Gable whisked Harlow off to the altar, no matter how improbably. 'Miss Harlow is good at the beginning, excelling as she does in these hard-boiled types,' observed the *New York Herald Tribune*, 'But later, in the subdued poor-caught-creature exhibit, she seemed miscast. Frank S. Nugent of the *New York Times* agreed: 'The sudden transition from hard-boiled, wisecracking romance to sentimental penitence provides a jolt.'

Harlow was over the moon to have been applauded for two films on the trot. Also, she had another cause for celebration: one year after Paul Bern's death, she had a new, regular man in her life.

CHAPTER SEVEN

The Prizefighter, The Lady And The Cameraman

'There's only Loretta and the dogs that do a single thing for me. All the rest of you are just out for what you can get, and I'm getting pretty tired of being a golden goose, or whatever ya call it!' Harlow, aka Lola Burns, to her grasping relatives in Bombshell

Born in Omaha, Nebraska, in 1909, the heavyweight boxer Max Baer was the son of a Jewish hog butcher, something which never failed to tickle Harlow. He accredited his formidable strength and physique (6 feet 2 inches, 210 pounds) to his 'training' as a youth, when he had sledgehammer-slaughtered pigs and cattle to death with a single blow. Baer had turned professional in 1929, and the following year had lost his temper in the ring and KOd his opponent, Francisco Camilli, who died the following day. The incident had earned Baer a 'killer' reputation, and done much to further his career. In 1932 he had hit Ernie Schaaf after the bell, and five months later Schaaf had died after taking a jab from the great Primo Carnera – which the tabloids had attributed to Schaaf's earlier beating from Baer. In fact, the actual cause of death was meningitis.

Baer had gone on to win 72 of his 84 fights, 53 by KO. His greatest triumph, however, came in 1933, just as the political climate was darkening in Europe. Baer's opponent at the Yankee Stadium was Max Schmeling (1905–2005), Hitler's favourite fighter and the symbol of all that was supposedly perfect of the Aryan race. Baer riled the German by sporting shorts emblazoned with the Star of David (though after the war it emerged that Schmeling had actually saved the lives of two Jewish children, while still serving his country), and pummelled him through 10 rounds until the referee stopped the fight. Henceforth, Baer would be known as 'The Jews' Boxer'.

Max Baer's manager, Ancil Hoffman, wanted him to jump onto the bandwagon and become part of the Hollywood scene. Johnny Mack Brown had made a remarkably successful transition from the baseball pitch to action movies. Swimming champion Johnny Weissmuller had recently triumphed in the first of the *Tarzan* series. With this in mind, Hoffman negotiated a deal with Louis B. Mayer to make his acting debut in *The Prizefighter And The Lady*. There was no screen test, Baer was offered a non-negotiable $3,000 a week, and John Lee Mahin was hired to write the script centring around the boxer's own life – or as near as Hollywood would allow, which turned out to be around 20 per cent factual. Asked to choose his own leading lady, Baer asked for his estranged actress wife, Dorothy Dunbar. Mayer deemed this unacceptable: Dunbar was a 'society trollop' who had worked her way through five husbands. The reason why she had not acted since 1927, he added, was because she was no good. Baer was asked to choose again, and picked Jean Harlow, then shooting *Hold Your Man*. When Arthur Landau requested that Harlow's salary, still fixed at $1,500 a week, be raised to match that of this non-actor, Mayer showed him the door.

The Prizefighter And The Lady, directed by Howard Hawks, tells the story of bartender and serial womaniser Steve Morgan, discovered and trained by the Professor (Walter Huston). After winning his first big fight, he marries Belle Mercer – they meet after her car narrowly misses knocking him down in the road. In the course of the film he fights Primo Carnera, playing himself, while Jack Dempsey acts as referee. This being Hollywood and mostly make believe, Steve is not permitted to lose the bout – in a strange twist of irony, by the time of the film's release Carnera would be crowned heavyweight champion of the world, a title he lost to Baer the following year. The film would subsequently be banned in Nazi Germany, not because Baer was Jewish, but because he had thrashed Max Schmeling.

John Lee Mahin introduced Harlow to this incorrigible *ubermensch*, and it was love at first sight. In her opinion, being a 'boxer's squeeze' carried the same clout as the privileged role of gangster's moll. Within hours of their meeting, Baer had bedded her, and Harlow ignored Mayer's warning to stay away from Baer, socially, because he was still married, though only just. She read the script, and told Arthur Landau that she could not wait to begin shooting. It was at this stage that Marino Bello waded in, and turned everything on its head.

Never one to miss out on making a fast buck, and claiming that he had been behind Harlow's phenomenally successful stage appearances, Bello hit on the idea of putting Max Baer on the vaudeville circuit as a way of promoting the forthcoming film. At first, Baer was enthusiastic. Both Carnera and Dempsey had worked the theatres with huge success, and the hype had never deflected from their big fights. What Baer was not willing to put up with, however, was Bello's demands that he sack his manager and have *him* manage his boxing career as well on the premise that with his connections (that is, the underworld), Bello could guarantee him bigger fees. Baer's loyalty prevailed towards Ancil Hoffman, who had got him off a manslaughter rap after Francisco Camilli's death – Bello was sent packing.

According to one story circulating in the tabloids at the time, Louis B. Mayer is said to have offered Baer money to 'discreetly punch the Sicilian bum's lights out.' Bello's reaction towards being thwarted was to forbid his stepdaughter from ever seeing the boxer again. Quite how he did this is not known, though he may have still had something up his sleeve – as had happened with the Hesser photographs – which could have resulted in Mayer being forced to fire her for breaking the 'moral turpitude' clause in her contract. Yet again this displays Harlow's fear of this despicable man. Neither is it known how Bello and Mama Jean persuaded the usually unstoppable Mayer to drop her from the film. Within days of Max Baer exiting her life, the part of Belle Mercer was assigned to Myrna Loy.

Losing out on *The Prizefighter And The Lady* was effectively a blessing in disguise. Shooting wrapped on *Hold Your Man*, and Mayer immediately put Harlow into *Bombshell*, based on an unproduced play by Caroline Francke and Mark Crane. Scripted by John Lee Mahin and Jules Furthman, in its first draft it leaned heavily – again as far as Hollywood dared – on the Clara Bow story. As already explained, there was a history of mental illness in Clara's family, and she too is thought to have been suffering – like John Barrymore/Larry Renault in *Dinner At Eight* – from premature cardio-vascular dementia. Mayer and producer Hunt Stromberg had been scratching their heads for a while, wondering how they would get such a story past the censor, and not be sued by the 'It' girl, who in this movie becomes the 'If' girl.

Harlow's removal from the boxing film enabled Mayer to consult Mahin with a review to revising his script, and weave the scenario around one of the most dysfunctional families in Hollywood – Jean Harlow and the Bellos. Mahin then took the liberty of throwing in a few recognisable characters – including Stromberg – changing their names, naturally, to create what was then the ultimate spoof on the studio system. MGM becomes the Monarch Studios, run by a kindly Gentile (the exact opposite of Mayer on both counts) called H.E. Gillette. This was Mahin really taking his peers for a ride: 'gillette' was Hollywood slang for a bisexual man, a 'blade which cut both ways'. Clara Bow's Great Danes, renowned for making her home reek because they were not house-trained and she never cleaned up after them – were replaced by a trio of Old English sheepdogs and a goldfish named Fanny. For Howard Strickling, we have double-crossing publicity man Space Hanlon (Lee Tracy). And as Harlow's character's greedy family, standing in for the Bellos we have her horrendous father and brother.

Shooting got underway in August 1933, a few days before the premiere of *Dinner At Eight*. This film is important because it tells the real Jean Harlow story better than any Hollywood biopic ever could. In *Bombshell*, Harlow bursts onto the screen – literally, emerging from an exploding bomb. She is movie siren Lola Burns, the former beauty queen revered by fans from all walks of life. We see her face on magazines everywhere, fans emulate her, merchandisers market Lola Burns make-up and stockings. We see her on-screen, kissing Gable. Then we cut to her mansion: the servants are called Crawford and Loretta, her reprobate father (Frank Morgan) who answers all her interview questions on her behalf while she is present, and the secretary reminds us that the boss does not favour underwear. Lola is awakened for a dawn studio call by her sympathetic black maid, Loretta (the wonderful Louise Beavers). 'Gee, what a business,' she moans, 'you might as well run a milk-round!' Today, the Hays Office has ordered her to re-shoot the infamous nude scene in *Red Dust*, and this puts her in a bad mood. 'Don't think I'm gonna get in that rain barrel if the water's as cold as it was last time,' she snarls. 'A polar bear would have died in it!'

On the set, Lola's fickle temperament is brought to the fore by her father turning up asking for money for his wayward son, a middle-aged man who stalks her throughout the picture claiming to be her estranged husband, and the coterie of yes-men, chief of which is Hanlon who thinks nothing of keeping his stars in the limelight by feeding fake scandals to the press. 'Lola Burns is a family slogan,' he tells her. 'Strong men take one look at your picture, go home and kiss their wives for the first time in 10 years. You're an international tonic, you're a boon, a re-population in a world thinned out by war and famine!'

Such praise however does not stop her from thinking him a creep, though she is unable to resist his slimy charm. Tonight, he wants to take her to the Cocoanut Grove, but she is already being taken here by an Italian marquis, Hugo (Ivan Lebedeff). 'Tell him you've got klieg-eyes,' he says, a cruel reference to the injury Harlow suffered while shooting *Hell's Angels*. Hanlon knows that Hugo is a gold-digger who has other women, and argues his corner: 'Listen, sugar. I know I'm no prize out of a crackerjack box, but at least I don't allow a procession of dames to lead me around by the nose!' – bringing the tarty response, 'That's because somebody forgot to put a ring in it!'

Hanlon later gets even by having Hugo arrested as an illegal immigrant, and by having this on the front page of the newspapers *before* the arrest takes place. Now, from Hugo's point of view the love of his life is a 'cheap common little peasant' while he is a 'patent-leather peanut vendor'. Lola knows that Hanlon is behind the scam, and wants to get him fired, changing her mind when he says that if this happens he will just go away 'like Gable did in *Susan Lenox* with all those sailors and women' and never return. Lola, to a certain extent like Harlow herself, has always hated her sex-bomb image and out of gratitude for saving his job Hanlon promises to find her the 'homely' roles which thus far have evaded her. He begins by setting her up for an interview with *Ladies Home Journal*, where the unfortunately named dumpy matron Mrs Titcomb – whose husband died in search of fatherhood, in other words, while having sex – makes her realise that only one thing is lacking in her life: a baby. This brings the comment from Hanlon, 'You think I want my bombshell turned into a rubber nipple?'

Lola's first thought is to find a husband, and she plumps for manager Jim Brogan (Pat O'Brien) – they used to be an item. He however does not want children, so she heads for the local orphanage. The way Harlow interacts with the child she chooses makes one feel sad that she never had children of her own: indeed, motherhood would have completely changed her life, and its outcome would almost certainly have been less tragic because so many people have confessed that she had so much love to give, but hardly received any herself. But even wealthy movie stars have to be assessed, and in the next scene, once she has sorted out the nursery, she is visited by two fuddy-duddy matrons who will decide if she is suitable mother material. All goes well until her wayward brother turns up with his doxy girlfriend, followed by an irate Hugo who blames Lola for getting him thrown into jail, and Hanlon with a bevy of press photographers. In a hilarious scene, an all-out brawl erupts wherein the house is wrecked. Harlow's plum line comes when the goldfish bowl is smashed and she rescues her pet, dropping it into the water jug which father drinks from. 'Pops,' she exclaims, 'you swallowed my Fanny!' What is astonishing is that the Bellos, who escorted Harlow to and from the studio most days, did not appear to have a clue that they were being sent up in the next scene, and one only wishes that Harlow could have stood up to them the way Lola stands up to her money-grabbing relatives here in what the scriptwriters termed allegorical wishful thinking:

Get away from me, all of you. You're nothing but a pack of leeches....Where does my money go? I never see any of it....I've only stood it because it's the only home and family I've got. But I'm getting sick of it, you understand? There's only Loretta and the dogs that ever do a single thing for me here. All the rest of you are just out for what you can get, and I'm getting pretty tired of being a golden goose or whatever you call it....I'm through, with the business, with everybody. You can get another 'if' girl, a 'but' girl, or a 'how-when-and-where' girl. I'm clearing out. You can all stay here in this half-paid-for car barn and get somebody else to pull the apple-cart. *I'm* going where ladies and gentlemen hang their hats to get some peace and quiet. And if any of you try to interfere with me, I'll complain to the authorities!

Accompanied by Loretta and the dogs, Lola heads for Palm Springs, pursued by Hanlon and the sham stalker husband. When the latter accosts her while horseriding in the desert, she is rescued by wealthy, dashing would-be poet Gifford Middleton (Franchot Tone) who claims that he has never even heard of Lola Burns and speaks like he has swallowed a dictionary. In next to no time they are an item and discussing marriage. 'You're like Diana riding,' he oozes. 'You're some slim, lovely Amazon riding proudly in her captor's wake!' Later he tells her, 'Your hair is like a field of silver daisies. I'd like to run barefoot through you hair. Your mouth is like a gardenia opening to the sun!' To which she barks back, 'Not even Norma Shearer or Helen Hayes in their nicest pictures were ever spoken to like that!' The problems start when he introduces her to his distinguished, snooty parents (C. Aubrey Smith, Mary Forbes), and when Lola's father and brother turn up. There is no way that the Middleton's good name will be besmirched by allowing their son to marry a scarlet woman. The wedding is called off and Lola returns to the studio, but not before telling these people what she thinks of them:

> Gifford's a sap, that's what he is. I'd give him away with a spray of horse-radish. I wouldn't be caught dead with him in a duckboat. And if you're a lady and *they're* gentlemen, I'm Amy Semple-McHutton on a raft. You can take your Bostons and your bloodlines and your Bunker Hills and stuff a codfish with them. And then you know what you can do with your codfish!

The 'Amy Semple-McHutton' was John Lee Mahin's lampooning of 'bullshit religions' such as Christian Science and Evangelism – Aimee Semple McPherson had founded the Foursquare Gospel

Church, currently the rage in America, though like Mary Baker Eddy she did not always practise what she preached. Then, back at the studio, Lola sees Hanlon with the 'family' he introduced her to – actually a bunch of hammy actors, including the man who has masqueraded as her stalker husband, who Space Hanlon hired to make her realise that she belongs to her fans, and not any man in particular.

Harlow played Lola Burns as if she had invented screwball, and this reflected in the reviews. Mae West, Dietrich and Garbo were blatantly though not offensively sexual, but Harlow played the good-time girl with such innate wit and charm, she could now rest assured that her 'doxy' days were behind her. 'Miss Harlow reveals again that gift for an amalgamation of sophisticated sex comedy with curiously honest innocence which is the secret of her individuality,' foe-turned-fan Richard Watts wrote in the *New York Herald Tribune*. 'There can be no doubt now that she is a distinguished performer.' And Mordaunt Hall of the *New York Times* admired another aspect of her on-screen alter-ego: 'For the greater part of the time she is the fiery platinum blonde, but when she hopes to be entrusted with an infant she, as Lola, assumes a strangely quiet and sympathetic mood.'

Making the film earned Harlow the enmity of Joan Crawford. Previously, Joan had merely disliked her, a kind of professional rivalry – now she positively loathed her, and made no secret of the fact. One of the reasons for this – the others would come later – was Franchot Tone. The son of the president of the New York Carborundum Company, Franchot (1905–68), like his character in *Bombshell*, had been raised with a whole set of silver spoons in his mouth. He had rebelled against family tradition by becoming an actor, working in stock companies and on Broadway before coming to Hollywood – on his own terms, telling studio bosses that if they 'treated him like shit' the way they did everybody else, then after 12 months he would be on the next train back to New York. Franchot's first Hollywood film was *The Wiser Sex*, with Claudette

Colbert and Ross Alexander. He had fallen for the dashing
Alexander (who in 1937 would take his own life) and was living
with him, though the press reported him to be 'going steady' with
Joan Crawford, who after months of deliberating had just divorced
Douglas Fairbanks Jr. She and Franchot had already made two
films together: *Today We Live* and *Dancing Lady*. Astonishingly,
the gossip columnists had not picked up on the Tone–Alexander
romance. For one thing, they were too busy writing about his
political activist mother Gertrude's very open relationship with the
writer Dorothy Thompson. For another, *only* a red-blooded
heterosexual would get within a mile of the man-eating Joan. Little
did they know! While Joan tolerated her husband-to-be's
homosexuality (they would marry in October 1935), she refused to
turn a blind eye to the rumours that he was also sleeping with
Harlow and Bette Davis, his co-star in *Ex-Lady* – sparking off a
bitter feud with Bette which would drag on for the rest of Joan's life
and be brought to the screen in *What Ever Happened To Baby
Jane?*, and with Harlow until she died.

Franchot, in turn, now began getting aggravation from Clark
Gable, who had also starred in *Dancing Lady*, and currently in one
of his 'fag-hating' periods. Gable marched into Howard Strickling's
office and demanded to know why both Joan and Harlow had asked
for 'that fucking fairy Tone' and not himself to be in their next
pictures (*Sadie McKee* and *The Girl From Missouri*). Word of this
reached Franchot, who threatened to have it out with Gable and
tear him apart! To look at him, one would not imagine Franchot to
have had an aggressive bone in his body, but as a youth he had
been expelled from at least one private school for unruly behaviour,
and since arriving in Hollywood he had developed a reputation for
drunken brawling. It was however Franchot's knowledge of Gable's
own gay past that prevented these two from thrashing it out and,
surprisingly, within a few months they would set aside their
differences and become good friends.

These rumours – Harlow–Gable, Harlow–Baer, Harlow–Tone –

precipitated Louis B. Mayer into calling an emergency meeting with his executives, and of course, Mama Jean and Marino Bello were asked to sit in. The Platinum Blonde's behaviour was whirling out of control and something needed to be done about her with the utmost urgency. A few years before, Mayer would not have thought twice about firing her, but now she was almost on the same level as Garbo and Crawford – earning a fraction of their salaries – when it came to bringing in revenue for the studio for Mayer to let her go on a 'technicality'.

It did not take long for the group to reach a decision: if Harlow could not find herself a man who was not married, a 'killer', or a mobster, then they would find one for her and she would have no say in the matter if she wanted to keep on working. Again, the mind boggles as to why this young woman – so fiercely independent, brazen and outspoken in her films – could have been so easily led and forced into anything, including almost certainly having sex with her stepfather, without offering the slightest protest.

Fortunately for now – though her victory would prove Pyrrhic – for once Harlow *did* meet these masochists at their own game. The locations for *Bombshell* were in Tucson, Arizona, and coincided with the first anniversary of Paul Bern's death on 5 September. Naturally she was feeling low, and with no one to talk with – Mama Jean had stayed in Hollywood, and Max Baer was attempting a reunion with his wife which would fail and see her filing for divorce by the end of the month – Harlow found herself seeking solace among her favourite people: the cast and crew, and in particular cameraman Hal Rosson.

Harold 'Hal' Rosson (1895–1988) had started out in 1912 as an extra at Vitagraph's New York studios. Famous players had subsequently hired him as a factotum, and two years later he had relocated to Hollywood to work for Metro. Following a two-year stint with the US Army, he had been employed by William Randolph Hearst as assistant cameraman on Marion Davies' *The Dark Star*. In 1920, Mary Pickford had poached him from Davies to shoot films for her actor brother, Jack. In a long career Rosson would receive five Oscar nominations, but it is for his association with Jean Harlow that he will be best remembered.

There is no evidence to suggest that Harlow had ever nurtured feelings for Hal Rosson in the 18 months she had known him, nor he her, which suggests that her next move must only have been precipitated by her suddenly being made aware of Mayer's and the Bellos' machinations. Later it was claimed that she had leaned heavily on the cameraman for emotional support against her demons, and that she had allowed psychological weakness to rule her head – as she had with every man in her life since Chuck McGrew. The reason *she* proposed to him was almost certainly to get one over on Mama Jean and Mayer, because it all happened so quickly. Harlow asked Rosson to marry her on the evening of 17 September 1933. He accepted without hesitation, and one hour later they boarded a chartered two-seater plane to Yuma, without even bothering to call ahead to warn the then tiny airport that they were on their way. Money exchanged hands and the airport manager, Joe Redondo, drove the couple and the pilot, Allen Russell, into the town where at 4.30am the wedding ceremony was conducted by a Judge Freeman, with Redondo and Russell standing in as witnesses. Judge Freeman later told the *Los Angeles Herald* over the phone, 'Miss Harlow wore a dark blue travelling suit, but no hat. She may also have worn a fur – I was too nervous to notice much.' Then, once Harlow had cabled Howard Strickling with the happy tidings, the little party returned to the airport for the long, bumpy flight home.

The press had a field day, and raked up all the old scandals. What was it about Jean Harlow and older, unattractive men? Paul Bern had been over 20 years her senior, Rosson was 16 years older – in those days somewhat controversial. Both husbands were employees of MGM, afforded the seal of approval of Mayer and Thalberg (or so reporters were told). Both were on the small side – Rosson stood 5 feet 5 inches – 'with receding hairlines and funny little moustaches,' observed Louella Parsons. But while Bern had had tremendous hang-ups about his sexuality and equipment – something which had only come to light after his death – Rosson was renowned all over Hollywood for his legendary appendage, the fact that 'big things really do come with small packages'. This little titbit had been bandied around by his first wife, Ziegfeld girl Nina Netts, whom he had married in 1928 and divorced three years later – and by jealous rivals, who scathingly referred to him as 'The Dong'.

The likes of Hedda and Louella, of course, jumped to the obvious conclusion about the hastily executed wedding – Harlow could only have been pregnant. Over the next two months her figure would be scrutinised, but when no telltale bump was forthcoming, the hacks assumed that MGM must have paid Rosson to marry her, just to bring her back down to earth after her numerous escapades. Such a notion was not implausible, which may explain why he had said yes to Harlow's proposal without even thinking of what he might have been letting himself in for. 'Ours is the one Hollywood marriage that will last,' she told Ben Maddox, repeating what she had supposedly said in Howard Strickling's faked statement. Maddox was one of the bevy of reporters waiting on the lawn at Beverly Glen when the newlyweds returned home, none of whom believed Harlow's opening comment that she and Rosson had been planning the event for months. 'We've been friends for two years,' she piped. 'We only decided last night to elope to Yuma and get married because we were both so busy with our film work. I just can't imagine how all of you found out. After all, it *was* an elopement!' Gallantly, the assorted press went along with the ruse.

Between taking the call from Yuma and the Rossons' return to Hollywood, Howard Strickling had handed Harlow's 'exclusive statement' – in other words, written by himself – to the press. The *Los Angeles Examiner* was the first to run this on 19 September, along with the previously scripted speech delivered by the couple on the tarmac at Burbank's United Airport:

HARLOW: (to a female reporter she said was giving her husband the eye) Hal is MY man!
ROSSON: I'd admired Jean for years. For months, I've loved her. And now she is mine!
HARLOW: We are happy –
ROSSON: And we will stay happy for always!
HARLOW: I believe I've reached the point where I know what I want. Hal's the finest, kindest, most sincere and honorable man I've ever known. The difference in our years won't matter. I've always known people older than myself. He's just old enough to be my mentor. I respect him, so I'll always heed his advice. I know that ours is one Hollywood marriage that will last. I will try to be the ideal wife –
ROSSON: Which she is already!

Next, Harlow had to face Louis B. Mayer. According to Arthur Landau, Mayer had hit the roof – firstly because he had wanted to meet the Rossons at Burbank and pretend to welcome them home with open arms – secondly because Harlow, like Garbo, had proved that she had a mind of her own. 'What's the matter with that stupid *shiksa* of yours,' Landau quoted Mayer as having yelled. 'Didn't I personally give her an order not to get married again without first getting my permission? There aren't enough Christians in the world that she has to go around marrying Jewish boys?' Mayer was racist, homophobe, bigot and megalomaniac all rolled up in one decidedly unpleasant package. He loathed blacks, homosexuals, adulterers and mixed-religion marriages, in that order. In fact, Rosson was not Jewish, and Harlow resented Mayer referring to her as *shiksa*, an offensive Yiddish word for a non-Jewish woman. However, when he summoned her to his office to explain herself, she sent a message back: as a new bride, she had better things to do to occupy her time.

In the meantime, Howard Strickling set about penning Hal Rosson's 'biography'. Most of Harlow's fans had never heard of him

– the screen credits' extent of the movie stars' names rarely figured in their interests, and so long as Harlow looked drop-dead gorgeous in every scene, few were interested in who had photographed her. Strickling 'let slip' one of his star's best-kept secrets – she had not been born Harlean Carpenter, but *Carpentier*. There was a French connection! Additionally, she owed her artistic abilities – which not so long before, Strickling himself had dismissed as 'virtually non-existent' – to being a direct descendant of Edgar Allan Poe! Neither fact was true, of course, but it made for good copy. Now, the gullible public were told that Rosson was so good at his craft that Gloria Swanson, his biggest fan, would never set foot in front of a camera unless he was behind it. Some cinematographers – though Strickling was cautious not to name them – were so in awe of his technique that they had studied him for years and still failed to emulate his unique lighting and shading techniques. Directors who wished to remain anonymous had even fired cinematographers because they had failed to match up to Rosson's impeccable standards. More truthful were the revelations of his family connections: his brothers, Richard and Arthur, were both directors and his sister, Helene, was an actress – though nobody could remember what she had appeared in. Another sister, Gladys, had been Cecil B. DeMille's personal assistant.

Harlow's wedding enabled her to 'even the score' – for a little while – with Joan Crawford, who had forecast (accurately, as it would happen) that she and Rosson would be divorced within the year. Among the journalists waiting at Beverly Glen was one of Joan's closest friends, Dorothy Manners, who worked for *Photoplay*. The two had met in 1926, after which Manners had described herself as 'Miss Crawford's lady-in-waiting'. A few days after Joan's wedding to Douglas Fairbanks Jr in 1929, Manners had been the only journalist invited to lunch with the newlyweds at New York's Roosevelt Hotel, after which she had sworn her loyalty to 'Queen Joan' by keeping her informed about the private and professional lives of her three bitterest rivals: Bette Davis, Norma Shearer and Harlow. The fact that Harlow had called Manners from Yuma and invited her to the wedding reception rankled Joan, who on that same day had booked a lunch appointment with Manners, to formerly introduce her to Franchot Tone. Now, Joan sent a messenger to Beverly Glen: Manners could be her friend or Harlow's, but never a friend of both. Making her excuses, Manners left, giving everyone the impression that she and Harlow had had a row over some exclusive that the journalist was about to print. Another of Joan's friends asked along that afternoon was Alma Whitaker, a highly respected freelancer hired to cover the event for the *Los Angeles Times*. Joan had asked Whitaker to glean whatever gossip she could about Hal Rosson, and to subsequently try explaining to the world why Harlow had the knack of always choosing the wrong man. She certainly did not beat about the bush in her piece which went out on 24 September:

> It's all very well, but when a glamorous Jean Harlow, arch siren – who pretty well has her pick of the sex – chooses Hal Rosson 'for better or worse, till death do them part', we want to know how he did it! He's no Apollo. His best friends wouldn't call him a ladykiller, but he obviously reeks of lure. So tell us, lovely Jean, what it is that won you?.... 'The physical means nothing to me,' she said 'if you love a person, he or she immediately becomes beautiful. I know *exactly* what won my heart. It's Hal's exquisite loyalty of friendship, his vast capacity for loyalty. Then there's his divine sense of humor! However *do* people get through life without humor?....I could never do anything but respect him highly, though it is I who am likely to have a hard time living up to *him*!'

Harlow was furious, first claiming that she had spoken to Whitaker in confidence – then, when the *Los Angeles Times* refused to print a retraction, declaring that she had not spoken to her at all. Now, the whole world knew of her tendency to seek out older men who were unattractive, and it would appear for reasons which had nothing to do with love. Worse still, word was now out that here was one 'arch siren' who was *not* interested in sex. She threatened to sue the newspaper, but backed down when reminded that she had said many more things which Whitaker could have repeated, had she chosen to do so. Next, Harlow threatened to seek out Joan Crawford and scratch her eyes out. Then suddenly she found herself with other matters to deal with, far more pressing.

Immediately after Harlow's wedding, the Bellos had stepped in to protect their investment, enabling Hal Rosson to feel the full force of his new in-laws' hold over his wife. And again, one may only be amazed at how much these people could get away with. On 20 September, Mama Jean and Marino Bello acquired the deeds to Beverly Glen. The next day, their lawyers visited Rosson and coerced him into signing a post-nuptial agreement which would prevent him from making any claim on Harlow's assets and money – not *if* they divorced, but *when*. They had not done this with Chuck McGrew because he had been loaded – or with Paul Bern, whom they had assumed to be. Rosson, they declared, was but a lowly cameraman. His response to this was to move out of the big white house and into a suite at the Chateau Marmont complex, with Harlow picking up the tab. The press were told that this was his idea of a belated honeymoon – the couple needed time on their own, and once Harlow had supervised the editing of *Bombshell* (this was cut and edited in a record three days) she would be joining him. She did, on 29 September, 11 days after the wedding – but instead of moving in with him, she rented the adjoining apartment. That evening, she and Rosson attended the *Bombshell* premiere as if nothing had happened, and Harlow left her hand and footprints in the cement outside Grauman's Chinese Theater.

For the first time since taking over the handling of her affairs, Arthur Landau missed a Harlow premiere. What makes for interesting reading is the letter (quoted by Irving Shulman) that Mama Jean dispatched to him in New York, the next day, part of which reads,

Bombshell was a SENSATION, a WOW, a SUCCESS and what an evening. The wires poured in here and Hunt Stromberg sent the Baby a huge box of roses with this note, 'To my favorite actress for a perfect performance. Love, Hunt.' Which made the Baby cry with gratitude....We are so grateful and happy for the Baby. LB [Mayer] sat in front of us and when he and Mannix came in they did not even speak to the Baby, ONLY nodded. When it was over and the audience went WILD, LB stopped at the Baby's side and started to explode, caught himself and said, 'God, Tracy has great lines!'....Not even, 'Jean, your work was nice.'...CAN you imagine such a fool as to think he could intimidate three people like us with such childish tactics? Really, those people must think we are of very limited intelligence and of very lowly birth to accept such childish tactics. BUT Pops [Mama Jean's affectionate term for Landau] if I had anything to do with the situation I would make that gentleman pay in blood for the insult.

Then Mama Jean concludes,

Yesterday the Baby finished the concrete at the CHINESE and we are so proud to have her name among the biggest in the industry. I have only met Miss Dressler once, but Pops will you please tell her I am a really devoted fan of Dressler the great actress? I adore her!

The missive is important in that it reveals the true extent of Jean Bello's delusions of grandeur – the fact that she had placed herself on a pedestal and truly believed that everyone cared for, loved and respected her, when the truth is that few people, in particular Marie Dressler, could stand her. And for a supposedly intelligent woman, not to mention the fact that she was one of the most popular movie stars in America, how could Harlow tolerate being treated so obviously like a backward child? Surely being called Baby *all* of the time – never Harlean or Jean – by her parents must have irritated the hell out of her? Or was she really so naive as to believe that their machinations were perpetrated with her best interests at heart, enough to have signed over her home to them? Yet their power over her during the next few days would almost cost her her life.

On 15 October 1933, Harlow and Hal Rosson were guests of honour at the Los Angeles Coliseum, for the University of Southern California–St Mary's football game. The couple met the team afterwards in the locker room, then headed for Beverly Glen, where the Bellos had organised a dinner party. The purpose of this was to give Harlow instructions on how to best give Louis B. Mayer a piece of her mind in the wake of his snubbing her at the *Bombshell* premiere. In fact, Mayer had 'made up' for his gaff by paying for the Rossons to have a belated honeymoon in Hawaii, to begin the following week. It mattered little that the gesture was completely false – as had been the case when he had financed Joan Crawford and Douglas Fairbanks Jr's trip to Europe to put distance between Joan and Clark Gable. The press had been informed of this 'most generous gift', and Harlow had expressed her gratitude, equally phoney, by way of a statement issued by Howard Strickling. She promised her mother that she would sort Mayer out – though she had no intention of even trying – and after the dinner, returned to the Chateau Marmont. Here, one hour later she collapsed with agonising stomach pains.

Hal Rosson was well versed in the MGM way of life so far as emergencies were concerned. Instead of summoning an ambulance, which any caring husband would have done, he called Howard Strickling, who contracted Louis B. Mayer, then Mama Jean. Mayer then telephoned Rosson, and gave him *permission* to fetch a doctor. The doctor diagnosed appendicitis, and Harlow was transported to the Good Samaritan Hospital. Mama Jean and Marino Bello arrived just as she was being prepared for surgery, and the former hit the roof. She and not Rosson was her daughter's legal guardian and next of kin, she declared, and therefore she was refusing permission for surgery because this was against her Christian Scientist beliefs: Harlow may be in great pain right now, she argued, but the power of prayer would alleviate this, and by morning she would be well enough to go home. Rosson, who appears to have been no less submissive than his wife, hovered in the background while surgeons argued that, without the operation, Harlow would almost certainly be dead by morning. For once, Bello was on the doctor's side – he telephoned Mayer, who like himself was interested only in protecting his investment. *He* was Harlow's guardian, he growled – she was *his* star, under contract to *his* studio. He would decide what was best for her, and if the hospital knew what was good for it, the operation would take place without further delay. Twenty minutes later, Harlow went under the knife.

Within an hour of the news hitting the early morning editions, the hospital and Arthur Landau were inundated with requests, among the hundreds of letters and get-well cards (though there was none from Mayer), for strands of Harlow's 'downstairs hair'. Again, the tabloids speculated and jumped to conclusions. Appendicitis was the oldest chestnut in the book. Actresses had used the condition to camouflage any number of hospitalisations – the ones for having abortions being the most common. Also, the suite to which she was taken was Room 826, traditionally used for patients recovering from terminations. Harlow would subsequently always ensure never to reveal her midriff in public: the only nude photographs of her taken after this time are tastefully done, and show nothing of her nether regions where the scar might have been. What *is* known (as disclosed by David Stenn in *Bombshell*, among others) is that, whatever operation she underwent, surgeons found traces of venereal disease, which suggests that they must have 'travelled' further down than her appendix. Also, she stayed in hospital longer than was usual for a regular, uncomplicated appendectomy – 15 days, until 30 October –

and would have stayed longer, had not Mama Jean signed the discharge papers.

The ambulance returned Harlow not to the Chateau Marmont, but to Beverly Glen, where Mama Jean had set up a clinic room so that she could nurse her daughter around the clock. To complete the picture, she had even bought a nurse's uniform. Needless to say, the honeymoon in Hawaii had been cancelled. Hal Rosson's brief reign as Harlow's mentor was over. The Bellos were in charge of 'Baby' once more.

CHAPTER EIGHT

Reckless

'Her altar and temple were a bed, thinking about her [was] a ritual, and there was nothing she could do about it. No studio anywhere would change her image. The public would not accept an alteration in its worship.'

Irving Shulman

Harlow's next film was announced: *The Age Of Larceny*, scripted by Anita Loos, and with Clark Gable pencilled in as her co-star. While she was recuperating at Beverly Glen, Marino Bello went to see Louis B. Mayer personally. MGM was not paying his stepdaughter what she was worth, he declared, and unless they upped her salary accordingly, she would not be returning to the studio.

This was the height of the Great Depression, where soup kitchens were seen in every town and city across America. Poverty was rife, box-office takings were rapidly dwindling – this also partially on account of the rising popularity of radio, a situation which would intensify even further, a generation later with the advent of television. Therefore while millions feared starvation, *Screen Book*'s Jay Vantol conducted a survey of who was earning and spending what in Hollywood, and the results were disturbing. Garbo, Marion Davies, Wallace Beery, Janet Gaynor and Norma Shearer were revealed to be shelling out over $100,000 each in income tax each year. Cowboy star Tom Mix was spending $12,000 a year just sending out replies to fan mail. Constance Bennett 'came clean', telling Vantol that she was economising – now she was spending *only* $20,000 a year on clothes, and she no longer kept a full-time nurse on salary just in case she got sick. Norma Shearer, the studio's favourite because she was married to the boss, was reported to be earning in excess of $100,000 a film. And at the height of her popularity, Garbo was raking in $250,000 a *week*. Even stars who had passed their sell-by date, such as Ann Harding, were netting $5,000 a week, less than big names Joan Crawford, Bette Davis and Myrna Loy. And at the opposite end of the scale came Harlow and Gable, earning huge profits for MGM yet still being paid a paltry $1,500 a week.

On the face of it, had it not been for Bello's own greed and Machiavellian workings, such a demand would not have been considered unreasonable. There is absolutely no question that Mayer and Thalberg were using Harlow – Crawford and Gable too – and being deliberately stingy because they disliked them. Bello demanded $5,000 a week to bring Harlow more in line with Joan Crawford, her nearest rival, but made the grave mistake of issuing an ultimatum: unless MGM agreed to the deal, his stepdaughter would go on strike. Harlow had no say in the matter, and on 13 November 1933 when she failed to report for work on *The Age Of Larceny* – now retitled *Eadie Was A Lady*, she was put on six months' suspension and the film was temporarily shelved. Mayer's outburst to Arthur Landau, before asking him to be on the lookout for another blonde actress so that Harlow could be sent back to Kansas, did not go unnoticed: 'Imagine a girl refusing to work for fifteen-hundred a week! And for what, for not having class!' Some journalists, in Mayer's pocket, accused her of being avaricious. Dorothy Manners, anxious to get back in her good books, did a take

on the Jay Vantol piece to display to Mayer just how mean she
thought he was – only to find herself barred from the MGM lot
until the mogul had calmed down, which did not look like being
in the foreseeable future. Harlow made matters worse by telling
Photoplay, 'Louis B. Mayer is the best friend any girl in the world
could have,' – while telling all and sundry that she could not wait
for him to drop dead.

On 29 November Harlow's paternal grandmother, Diana
Carpenter, did just that – three months after the death of her
husband – and Harlow, who only the day before had complained
of boredom, told reporters that work commitments would prevent
her from travelling back to Kansas City for the moment. The bad
press she received for this – particularly when she was seen playing
golf with seasoned professional and coach Leo Diegel on the actual
day of the funeral – by far outweighed anything that had happened
after Paul Bern's death. Here she was, MGM's 'golden girl',
brazenly refusing to uphold the studio's family-values policy – and
wearing white! The studio was inundated with hate mail. Louis B.
Mayer, the arch hypocrite who never stopped singing the praises of
his favourite 'daughter', was accused of being anti-Christian for not
allowing her to go to the funeral; to give him some credit, he did
offer excuses for her, putting out a statement that she was unable to
travel on account of her recent illness, and that playing golf was
therapy prescribed by her doctor to build up her strength. Then she
made matters infinitely worse by rushing off to San Francisco with
Rosson on what she called an 'appendix vacation'– a familiar term
to denote someone going to have an abortion. 'It's all the rage,' she
told Ben Maddox. 'All the big stars are having their appendix
removed – Claudette Colbert, Maureen O'Sullivan!' The cynics
among the gossip columnists were hard put not to substitute
'abortion' for appendectomy.

Besides golfing and swimming, Harlow spent much of her
suspension time getting photographed by George Hurrell. His
photograph of a scantily clad Harlow reclining on a polar bear

rug was one of his signature pieces. Hurrell (1904–92), who photographed every major Hollywood star, said of her, 'She was not frightened by the camera. She reacted to it, and in some strange way I was the third party – *they* [Harlow and the camera] were conspirators!'

Harlow, desperately in need of a friendly shoulder to cry on, saw a lot of the ever-dependable Ben Maddox at around this time. Louis B. Mayer had instructed her not to speak to the press, but she gave an extended interview to her friend which later appeared in *Screen Book* under the heading, 'The One Star Who Has No Enemies'. Reading between the lines of this today, of course, and studying other pieces he published at the time, it is pretty evident that the journalist was just as much in love with Harlow as he was with Gable. In 1934, much of this sailed over the heads of the general readership, and what made Mayer see red were the comments towards the end of the four-page spread:

> MADDOX: Okay, in my final endeavor to be stern with you, what advice do you have for newcomers, in view of the mistakes you might have made yourself?
> HARLOW: So far as the business end is concerned, I'd suggest they not sign a contract for more than a year. If a company wants you badly, they'll take you on that basis. Then, if you can click, you can profit on your rise.
> MADDOX: And, is there any one particular principle that you follow in your constant, everyday battle with Hollywood?
> HARLOW: Battle? I don't waste my precious hours in fighting! Gratitude, I'm convinced, is a good foundation for progress and success. *I* make every effort to reciprocate any interest shown in me!

Mayer contacted Maddox, and asked him to explain what right he had, coercing stars into making such potentially damaging statements. Maddox put the phone down on him – itself tantamount to an act of blasphemy in 1930s Hollywood, so Mayer called the editor of *Screen Book* and demanded that the journalist be fired. The editor refused, explaining that inasmuch as the dreaded duo, Hedda and Louella, were interested only in trying to ruin careers, Ben Maddox had done more than *any* Hollywood journalist to help the stars he befriended.

Meanwhile each night, alone in her mirrored bedroom, Harlow proved herself more intelligent than most people assumed by devising a novel. *Today Is Tonight* is an amalgamation of Harlow's most famous roles, her personal life and traumas, and the role she wanted to play more than any other – herself. Naturally, she did not sit down and write it herself. She confided the plot in her mother, who in turn told Marino Bello – who not surprisingly saw another way of making an easy buck. Harlow was asked to make notes and jot down anecdotes while Bello engaged a ghostwriter, Tony Beacon, to commit the work to paper for a measly $500.

Today Is Tonight centres around New York socialites Judy and Peter Lansdowne, whose marriage hits a snag when he is blinded in an accident, then loses all his money in the Wall Street Crash. Judy hits the bottle, and there are shades of Paul Bern and his mysterious suicide note when Peter tries to kill himself and she tells him, 'Cut the comedy!' She confesses to having had an affair with a boxer, and to save their marriage pretends to be a charity worker when she is actually starring in a stage production of *Lady Godiva*. Far from being disgusted with her when he finds out, Peter forgives her and they live happily ever after. The novel might have seen the light of day in Harlow's lifetime, had it not been for Marino Bello. Long before Tony Beacon had finished working on the script, Bello peddled the idea to every major studio in Hollywood *except* MGM. Louis B. Mayer hit back at this. Harlow was only on suspension – she was still on the studio's payroll, and unable to work for any other. Contractually, as the story purported to contain so many autobiographical details, selling it to another studio would have amounted to Harlow moonlighting, and the same rule applied to publication. Inasmuch as Mayer owned Harlow the actress until her contract expired, so too he owned the rights to any other talent she possessed! The book was completed, but it would not see the light of day for another 30 years.

In January 1934, Mayer summoned Harlow to court. The suspension still held good, but she could go some way to redeeming herself in his eyes, he told her, if she and other leading light, Robert Taylor, travelled to Washington as part of an MGM delegation for President Roosevelt's birthday ball to be held at the end of the month. Any other star treated so shabbily might have told Mayer where to get off, but Harlow complied. Her only condition was that Mayer pay for the Bellos to accompany her because she felt she could not cope on her own. There was no mention of her husband in the request. She caused a sensation visiting the Senate. Wearing a mink coat and jewel-encrusted turban, she was photographed with California's Democratic senator, William Gibbs McAdoo – and again with Bello, who she introduced as her 'beloved stepdaddy'. Outside the White House, she posed with Eleanor Roosevelt, and afterwards she and Taylor had a private audience with the President. And for the first time in her life, she claimed, for the Presidential Ball that evening she put on underwear.

In May, Mayer lifted Harlow's suspension and announced that he was raising her salary to $2,000 a week – still a pittance compared to what some of MGM's lesser-known leading ladies were getting. In what was an uncustomary benevolent gesture for him, he also paid her most recent tax bill – the $2,000 demand had arrived during her suspension.

Harlow celebrated her good fortune by announcing that she and Hal Rosson were divorcing, after just eight months of marriage. 'Just shows how wrong I was,' Joan Crawford said, 'I gave them a whole year!' Normally, such announcements were made by way of Hedda or Louella, if one wanted to stay on side. Harlow had a better idea: she delivered the tidings during the society wedding of actress Carmelita Geraghty to the scriptwriter Carey Wilson. Harlow was matron of honour, and Rosson was conspicuous by his absence. When asked where he was, she remarked casually to reporters how nice it was to be attending one wedding when that morning she had set the ball rolling to end her own. When this news reached Mayer, he had Rosson removed from *Eadie Was A Lady* and brought in Ray June, who became Harlow's favourite cameraman and stayed with her until the end. June (1895–1958) had begun his career as a Signal Corps photographer during World War I – his best work to date had been his anarchic cinematography in the Marx Brothers *Horse Feathers*, and most recently in Eddie Cantor's *Roman Scandals*.

As was to be expected, all the major columnists in town – with the exception of Ben Maddox, still a very close friend – wanted the lowdown on the marriage split, and again the battle royal was to be between Hedda and Louella over who would win the biggest scoop. In fact, Maddox was the first visitor to Beverly Glen, to comfort her as only he knew how and afterwards be rewarded with a brief statement:

> I regret more than I can say that my marriage with Hal Rosson did not work out. Believe me, this is no frivolous matter, but the only way out for both of us. We are uncongenial, and while there is no ill feeling between us, we realise that it is best for us to separate.

When Louella Parsons' spies informed her that Maddox's scoop was to appear two days later in *Screen Book*, the arch hack grabbed the phone and obtained one of her own, which she promised would not be printed until *Screen Book* had gone to press. Harlow should have known better than to trust her: the piece ended up on the front page of the next day's *Los Angeles Examiner*. One could almost imagine Louella fighting back the tears as she described how wistful and miserable Harlow had looked while the happy couple had been exchanging rings in the church, until it emerged that she had made this bit up – she had not been at the wedding, and had learned of Harlow's announcement only several hours after the event. Now, Louella reminded her readers for the umpteenth time about 'the unfortunate Bern affair', and repeated word for word what she claimed Harlow had told her alone:

> I've always felt that it sounds so silly when a husband and wife make up their minds to seek a divorce and then announce that now they will be better friends than ever and will probably see more of each other. Our marriage is finished. There will be no reconciliation, nor will we see each other every day. I will say, however, that Hal is a fine man. I regret more that I can say that our marriage has been such a failure. We simply were not meant for each other. There is NO other man or woman [involved].

The latter part of Harlow's statement was not true. The way she had stressed that no third parties were involved brought Louella and her rivals to the conclusion that there must have been another man in her life, and the tabloids speculated over his identity. She had been friends with Franchot Tone on the set of her new film; she had been seen dining with Max Baer, now divorced; and there was always Gable. In fact, she had been seeing Ben Maddox all the way through her marriage, and for a while now she had been secretly dating William Powell, though whether the relationship with Powell had yet progressed beyond the platonic is not known.

Like most of Harlow's men, Powell was old enough to have been her father. Like Paul Bern he was sophisticated, well educated and debonair, and sported – as had Hal Rosson – a trademark pencil-line moustache. Unlike Bern, Powell had no known sexual hang-ups, and he was the first man since Chuck McGrew to actually look like a gentleman and not a pervert or a thug. Unlike her other serious 'romances', he was the first to belong on her side of the show-business fence: indeed, he was just as accomplished in his field as she was, which only points towards the fact – given Powell's

track record with partners, and the track records of those partners –
that Harlow was already on to a hiding for nothing by becoming
involved with him.

William Horatio Powell had been born in Pittsburgh in July
1892, and had moved with his family to Kansas City in 1907. At the
time of Harlow's birth they had been living a few streets away from
the Carpenters. After high school, Powell had enrolled with the
American Academy of Dramatic Arts, in New York: two years later
after graduating from there he had worked with numerous
vaudeville and stock companies before trying his luck on
Broadway. He had appeared in his first film in 1922, playing
Moriarty to John Barrymore's Sherlock Holmes. His big break had
come in 1928, opposite the German actor Emil Jannings in *The
Last Command*, two years before Jannings made *The Blue Angel*
with Marlene Dietrich.

Though they must have bumped into each other as part of
Hollywood's social set, Harlow and 'Poppy', as she called him,
seem not to have clicked until she and Ben Maddox visited Clark
Gable on the set of *Manhattan Melodrama*, a few weeks before
announcing that she and Hal Rosson had decided to call it a day.
This film, also starring Myrna Loy, had been tailored around the
fading talents of 41-year-old Powell (who only a few years earlier
had been earning $6,000 a week) to gain himself and Loy publicity
for *The Thin Man*, about to be released. A huge success, this would
spawn another 13 couplings for the pair and land Powell an
extremely lucrative 10-film deal. Harlow caused massive disruption
with her daily trips to the set. When the technicians and extras wolf-
whistled she bared her breasts and, if feeling in a particularly
mischievous mood, hoisted her skirt to give them a flash of her
'platinum snatch'. For once, she did not care what the press said
about her. She had been honest when discussing her separation
from Rosson, vowing that there would be no going back. Powell too
was a free agent. In 1915 he had married Eileen Wilson, with
whom he had had a son – William Jr would commit suicide in

1968. Powell had divorced Wilson in 1930, but they were still on friendly terms – as indeed were he and second wife Carole Lombard, whom he had wed in 1931 and only recently divorced. In the near future they would star together in *My Man Godfrey*, one of the most successful 'social conscience' dramas of the 20th century.

It was at around this time that Harlow formed a close friendship with Kay Mulvey, who became some sort of soul sister while she was getting over the split from Hal Rosson. Slightly older than Harlow, and divorced with a small son, Mulvey had been appointed by Howard Strickling as MGM's 'official' magazine editor. As such, her duties were two-fold: writing articles in the style of Ben Maddox (but without the sexual involvement) in that these could make all the difference whether a star succeeded or not; and courting the broadsheets and classier magazines to achieve the same effect, effectively clearing controversial individuals such as Harlow and Dietrich away from the sensationalist hacks. With Harlow, of course, she was barking up the wrong tree – even if she had been asked to play a nun, the Platinum Blonde would have made the role orgasmic. What is interesting is that, during one of her visits to Mulvey's house at Playa del Rey, Harlow confided in her new friend that she had always wanted children, that she was now so desperate to have a family that she had considered adopting, as Lola Burns had wanted to do in *Bombshell*. Was she saying therefore, as the cynics had speculated during her recent hospitalisation, that she could not *have* children, that she had actually had a hysterectomy? Was this how the surgeons had discovered traces of venereal disease, not just by chance but because they had been looking for it? Or was she merely stating that adoption would have spared her the dilemma of having to take maternity leave from MGM at a time when her popularity was at its zenith?

Despite what Harlow had told Louella, in June there was a reconciliation of sorts when Hal Rosson contracted polio. The disease struck his upper torso, and he was quarantined at his sister Gladys' house while doctors deliberated over whether he would end up permanently disabled. Louis B. Mayer forbade Harlow from going anywhere near the place, and for once she heeded his advice – calling Rosson several times a day and telling journalists that if they did get back together again, it would be because she still loved him and not because he was ill. Mama Jean did visit, but she was not allowed inside the building. Instead, she hung around the porch reciting passages from Mary Baker Eddy, telling passers-by that 'Mr Harlow' would recover but only because she had willed this to happen. Four weeks later, Rosson was admitted to the Orthopaedic Hospital for physiotherapy, and at the end of August doctors gave him a clean bill of health. Having had enough of Harlow and her family, he left for London where he had been hired to work on a picture for Alexander Korda. Harlow was not there to wish him bon voyage: she was taking a break with William Powell at the Del Monte Lodge, 300 miles north of Los Angeles.

Also in August 1934, Harlow's new film premiered. At the time of its completion *Eadie Was A Lady* title's had been changed yet again to *Born To Be Kissed*. Now it was changed again on the instruction of Joseph Breen, Will Hays' Los Angeles-based assistant who had recently been appointed head of the new Production Code Administration (PCA), a body of moral crusaders who made the Hays Office appear tame. This had been formed at the end of 1933 in conjunction with the Catholic Legion of Decency (CLD), but Harlow had escaped their scrutiny until now because of her suspension. The PCA's purpose was to combat 'objectional content' in motion pictures, and it was the brainchild of John T. McNicholas, the Archbishop of Cincinnati whose mission from now on would be 'the prevention of massacre of the innocence of youth' – not that this prevented him and his team watching some 'items of filth' several times before condemning them. The movement had spread like wildfire, embracing not just Catholic puritans but those from other religions. By the end of 1934 the

CLD would have changed its name to the National League of Decency (NLD).

Basically, the good Archbishop decided, there were four 'actress whores' in Hollywood: Dietrich, Garbo, Mae West and Harlow. Among the films already singled out for condemnation that year were *Queen Christina* (Garbo wearing man's clothes), *The Scarlet Empress* (Dietrich, aka Catherine the Great, seducing a young soldier), *all* of Mae West's productions, Clark Gable's *Men In White* (where a woman dies on the operating table while having an abortion), and *The Public Enemy*, which MGM had just re-released. *Born To Be Kissed*, the NLD announced, was a dirty title for any film, least of all one with Jean Harlow in it. Therefore it became *The Girl From Missouri*. This, Louis B. Mayer told the press, was where his 'favourite daughter' originated from.

In *The Girl From Missouri*, Harlow is inadvertently speaking for most of her would-be successors when she pronounces, 'Two years in the spotlight if you make it – and when that's over you're nothing but a has-been for the rest of your life!' Here, she more than convincingly plays Eadie Chapman, who gives every impression of being a good-time girl when actually all she wants is to remain '100 per cent pure' until some lucky millionaire slips a wedding ring on her finger. Forced to work at Mrs Chapman's Hotspot – her mother's dancing joint where, courtesy of her lecherous stepfather there is only one way a girl will end up – she escapes to New York with her rough-diamond best friend Kitty (Patsy Kelly). Here they get work in a chorus line, and end up among the troupe hired for a stag party hosted by businessman Frank Cousins (Lewis Stone). These girls are a decidedly brassy bunch. 'We're gonna have so much fun spitting in this sink,' one says of a fancy apartment chock-a-block with antiques, while Kitty observes that if these men wanted ladies, they would be home with their wives. Later she pipes, 'I'm no lady. I'm just an old-fashioned home girl like Mae West!' Cousins' friends are however 'not ladies' men', which in 1930s Hollywood was a polite way of announcing that most of them are gay.

Despite the surrounding opulence, it soon emerges that Cousins is almost broke and the bash is for the benefit of millionaire banker T.R. Paige (Lionel Barrymore), who Cousins hopes will bail him out. 'I kinda like the butler,' Kitty says, to which Eadie retorts, 'Well, it's just as easy to like a millionaire!' Paige however is no pushover: he remembers the time when he was in a fix, and Cousins refused to help. Rejected, Cousins realises that there is only one way out of his dilemma. First he engages in a friendly banter with Eadie, half-jokingly proposing to her and giving her his ruby cuff-links to have fashioned into an engagement ring – then promptly blowing his brains out while the band plays 'Ain't Misbehaving'.

Having saved Eadie from arrest by relieving her of the cuff-links when the police arrive to search her, and after loaning her money to tide her over until she finds a decent job, Paige heads for Palm Beach, with Eadie in tow, convinced that he is the millionaire she wants, despite the fact that he is more than twice her age. She finds him on his yacht with his half-naked bachelor friends – one is getting a massage, and he keeps tapping the masseur to take his hand off his thigh. This scene was edited out of some prints of the film. By now, Eadie has met Paige's dashing playboy son, Tom (Franchot Tone); he is looking for her to be his next easy lay. The two become lovers and he gives her a diamond bracelet which she returns. She loves him, she says, and there is nothing wrong with him that a wedding ring will not fix. However, there is to be no funny business, she says, because she is a virgin – audiences loved this, coming from Harlow. Her put-down, too, when he coaxes her into his bedroom and locks the door, is pure Harlow gold:

You're pretty clever, aren't you? Shoving me around just because I haven't got a Park Avenue accent and a family to stick up for me and make a holler. I'm not afraid of you, you and your diamond bracelets. A lot of guys think they can buy you for a good meal, but it's all the same thing. I've been in spots like this before and I can take care of myself....I haven't had any education. I look like a hussy-tussy. Nobody ever cared two hoots whether I amount to anything or not. But *I* care!...I love you, Tom. You can make me cheap and common like a million others. But, gee, I wish you wouldn't!

Tom is crazy about Eadie, and wants to marry her, though he feels he cannot do this without his father's blessing. Paige Sr has just been appointed US delegate for International Disarmament, and such is Tom's urgency that he fetches him from the platform after he has just delivered his inaugural speech. This leads to the blink-and-miss 'hard-on' scene which had the censor in a tizzy and saw the scene removed (but recently restored): the young official who shows Tom into his father's ante-chamber wears tight trousers, and is in an obvious state of arousal. The old man acquiesces, albeit that he has a hidden agenda to remove this 'scheming little gold-digger' from his son's life once and for all, though Eadie has recently revised her opinion of Tom – she is so in love with him that she would still marry him if he were poor.

    On the eve of her wedding, Paige Sr sneaks a man into her room, then has her caught out by the vice-squad, who arrest her for stealing Cousins' jewels and throw her into jail. Tom visits her, and initially refuses to believe that his father has set her up. Paige Sr almost gets away with it: he and Tom are about to set sail for England, to attend a conference, when a would-be suitor pays Eadie's bail. She turns the tables on him by hiding in his stateroom on the ship – emerging in just her underwear just as he is giving a statement to the press. This brings a final drunken Harlow outburst to Kitty, the former maneater who appears to have turned over a new leaf, 'What's being good got ya? A pain in the neck. What's love? A lot of baloney. There's only one thing a man ever gives a woman, and that's dough!'

    Tom refuses to believe that his bride-to-be is a scarlet woman. He tosses her over his shoulder and, to sober her up, dumps her under the shower – creating another problem for the Hays Office because, soaking wet, it becomes more than obvious that Harlow is wearing no bra. Even so, the scene stayed in the picture, the censor of the opinion that, while a semi-erect penis and one man stroking another man's thigh was strictly taboo, Harlow's pin-pointed nipples poking through flimsy satin we perfectly acceptable. And if audiences could believe the final scene in *The Girl From Missouri*, they could believe anything. The *only* reason why Eadie was in his stateroom, Paige Sr tells reporters, was because this now decent girl had just married his son – precipitating a dash to the registry office!

The Hays Office and the NLD made such a fuss over the film's 'torrid and prurient content' that critics watching *The Girl From Missouri* were disappointed *not* to see audiences stomping out of cinemas in disgust. 'This increasingly astonishing young actress plays her role with such engaging freshness that it is no wonder that even the New York censors gleefully passed the work celebrating her exploits,' observed the *New York Herald Tribune*'s Richard Watts. And, applauding the film as 'noisily defiant, rip-snorting and raucous in parts', *Photoplay* concluded, 'Though the lines play pretty safe, it is fast and furious adult fare.'

Harlow fought against Irving Thalberg's decision to put her into *A Woman Called Cheap* – the title alone, she said, was insulting, but what really offended her was that the screenplay was based on a tragic episode in the turbulent life of Cincinatti-born torch singer Libby Holman (1906–71). The two had met while Harlow had been working the vaudeville circuit, and though never close friends they had enjoyed a certain rapport since then, meeting occasionally for dinners or at parties.

Harlow and Libby shared a common bond: an appalling taste in men. The daughter of a wealthy Jewish family swindled of $1 million by her uncle, Libby had begun her stage career in 1924. Complex does not even begin to describe this attractive, olive-skinned, doe-eyed tigress with a penchant for drink and drugs benders, black women, and neurasthenic bisexuals such as the actor Montgomery Clift, and her two husbands. The best known of these was Zachary Smith Reynolds, the 21-year-old heir to the Camel tobacco emporium who had been found dead of a gunshot wound in July 1932. Reynolds' family had trumped up a murder charge, accusing Libby of actually pulling the trigger, but it had emerged during the trial that Reynolds, a notorious drunk, had killed himself because he had been virtually impotent with his wife and terrified of this becoming public knowledge. Libby had inherited his fortune, and two months after the trial had given birth to a son, Christopher – sadly, he would die in a climbing accident in 1950, aged just 18. The Holman–Reynolds story, a woeful pastiche of self-loathing if there ever was one, would be remade as *Written On The Wind* in 1956: the protagonists were played by Lauren Bacall and Robert Stack, with Rock Hudson playing their best friend. The Harlow–William Powell–Franchot Tone version was to be a musical – Harlow's first and last, if her aborted appearance in *Hollywood Party* is to be discounted.

The comparisons between Zachary Smith Reynolds and Paul Bern could not have been more blatant: today, no reputable studio would get away with such callous behaviour, making one of its top stars relive the most harrowing time of her life, and it was only because of these similarities – and because she knew that Harlow had no way of rejecting the role – that Libby Holman did not sue MGM. Three years later, Franchot Tone would also deplore being forced into the film when his lover, Ross Alexander, shot himself after being hounded over his homosexuality by Warner Brothers and co-star Bette Davis. The only difference between Bern and Reynolds was that the latter had been able to 'get it up' for the many men in his life, but hardly ever for his wife – who in any case had never really been sexually interested in him, but in her aviatrix lover, Louise Carpenter. When Thalberg sent Harlow the script, she read just two pages and tossed it into the trash can. It was director Victor Fleming and William Powell who persuaded her to calm down, by which time the title had been changed to *Reckless*.

Even so, Harlow tried to worm her way out of the part, squaring up to Thalberg and telling him that the terms of her contract could not demand that she sing and dance. If he wanted vaudeville, she declared, then he would have to look elsewhere and find her another movie. The Boy Wonder had an answer for this: he had already hired Virginia Merrill to dub her voice, and Betty Halsey to double for her legs in the dance sequences. And yet when the crunch came, Harlow insisted on doing much of this stuff herself. In the Trocadero scene with Allan Jones, she sings most of the title track composed by Jerome Kern (with Merrill adding the high notes) and does all of the dancing. 'The show belongs to Miss Harlow, who, with lines and situations tossed like flowers at her feet, acquits herself quite nobly, even when presumed [upon] to sing,' Regina Crewe wrote in the *New York American*. The critic with the *New York Times* however did not agree: 'MGM has taken the screen's liveliest comedienne, and chased her through a stale and profitless meringue of backstage routines and high society amor.' Irving Shulman denounced it too, opining in *Harlow*, 'The public was still behind Harlow as the ideal pillowmate, and as long as her dialogue was loaded with sex, sex, sex, that was all that mattered. Singing was best left to the birds and Jeanette MacDonald.' The film would prove Harlow's only flop with MGM.

Well-heeled megalomaniac Bob Harrison (Franchot Tone) is so infatuated with musical comedy star Mona Leslie (Harlow) that he buys up all the seats for one of her Broadway performances just so he can watch her alone. Unaware that her agent Ned Riley (William Powell) is madly in love with her, Mona allows Bob to take her out and he subsequently jilts his fiancée, Josephine (Rosalind Russell) and elopes with Mona. When Josephine marries someone else, Bob confesses at the wedding that he only agreed to marry Mona because she coerced him into it – and subsequently kills himself. Mona and Ned find themselves at the centre of a massive scandal. She gives birth to Bob's baby, which his father claims until she relinquishes the fortune he left her. In the meantime, Ned has staged Mona's new review, which starts off disastrously. The first-night audience boo her until she gives as good as she gets, defending herself against the gossips and receiving a standing ovation. The film ends with Ned asking her to be his wife.

Much as she loved working with William Powell and Franchot Tone, Harlow hated this film more than any other since *Hell's Angels* – not just because of the storyline, but because much of the time she was feeling unwell. She seems to have been suffering from the kidney condition which would get progressively worse, almost certainly brought on by the beating Paul Bern had given her on their wedding night. While Mayer and Thalberg could not have cared less – their thoroughly heartless treatment of Marie Dressler, who had died the previous July, was proof of how much they truly respected their stars – both Powell and Arthur Landau urged her to see a specialist about the pains she was experiencing in her lower back, but she refused. She also had tremendous problems with her hair. The peroxide concoctions she rubbed into her scalp sometimes twice weekly had taken their toll: her hair had become so brittle that it was snapping off at the ends when she brushed it. MGM, of course, were interested only in preserving her trademark locks, and when informed that specialist treatment would take up to a month before starting to show any effect, Mayer sent her to the studio's leading stylist, Sydney Guillaroff, who had 'coiffured' her for *Red-Headed Woman,* and she was provided with a wig for her close-ups in *Reckless.*

Harlow cheered up no end when informed that her next picture would be *China Seas*, with Clark Gable. Shooting was to begin at the end of March, once she had got her divorce out of the way. Louis B. Mayer – and her friends – advised her to stick to the most common grounds for Hollywood divorces: irreconcilable differences. Harlow was having none of this, and as there was no evidence that Hal Rosson had ever cheated on her, nor she him, she plumped for mental cruelty. Louella Parsons broke the news, and there were long queues outside the courthouse, into which had been admitted just about every journalist in town. Some had heard the rumours about Bern beating her – all knew of his shortcomings in the boudoir – so they were expecting some very hot story involving physical violence. Harlow dressed soberly for the occasion: a black crepe dress which covered her ample assets, a brown sable wrap, and the dark glasses she still wore from time to time since making *Hell's Angels*. Rosson had wired his apologies from Alexander Korda's office in London. When asked by Justice Elliott Craig if her husband had abused her in any way, Harlow shook her head and, from a prepared statement, read aloud her take on mental cruelty:

> Harold read in bed until the late hours, much to the detriment of my art as an actress. The next day, after losing out on my sleep, I was unable to play my role to the best of my ability. He was jealous of my friends, my time and my position, of everything I had. He belittled my profession and I never knew how to take him. He was so sarcastic. It got so bad, his jealousy and sarcasm, that it affected my health and work. I could stand it no longer, so we parted.

Harlow added that Rosson had been rude to her parents – bringing more mirth from the press, some of whom believed after having had first-hand experience with the Bellos that he had not been rude enough. But his bad behaviour had peaked, she added, when he had refused to attend the Wilson–Geraghty wedding, causing everyone to speculate that there had been problems with her own marriage. When Justice Craig asked if she was seeking alimony, Harlow concluded that she was 'too much a lady' to suggest where he should stick this. The divorce was granted, to be made final in March 1936.

While waiting for the studio call, Harlow spent two weeks in seclusion at Beverly Glen. When Marino Bello tried to take advantage of her being a free agent once more, she brought in a team of interior decorators to transform her mirrored boudoir into a 'dream room' – one within which she could get a good night's sleep without him walking in and pawing her. She had the lock changed on the door, and the windows fitted with deadlocks and 'non-see-through' net curtains – Bello had apparently taken to climbing a ladder and perving on her while she was asleep. She could not throw him out of the house, of course, because in a moment's madness she had signed the place over to him and her mother. Bello merely shrugged his shoulders and concentrated on his other 'baby' – the yacht he had recently purchased with her money.

China Seas, directed by Tay Garnett, was an action-packed Thalberg production with two of its stars, Wallace Beery and Rosalind Russell, earning more than Harlow and Gable, who received top billing. For over a year, Ben Maddox had been campaigning for MGM to up Gable's salary, his pleas falling on deaf ears. Maddox visited the set most days: no longer sexually involved with Harlow since her marriage to Hal Rosson, his affair with Gable was still going strong, though the pair had almost been outed by Dorothy Manners. To cover their tracks, Maddox had penned a piece sub-headed 'Mr & Mrs Gable Could Not Be Happier!', which he syndicated across the country.

The film was scripted by Jules Furthman, who had just scripted *Shanghai Express* for Marlene Dietrich – there are similarities between the two, as indeed there are with *Red Dust*. Dietrich had got away with playing a prostitute working in the Orient who falls for a European, because *she* had not been Oriental. Furthman's original scenario had been black-pencilled by the Hays Office's anti-mixed-race policy, and by Gable himself. Disgraceful as this might seem today, the story of a white sea captain who gets his Chinese wife pregnant was, in the Thirties, perceived as indecent. In the remake no marriage takes place, there is no pregnancy, and she becomes China Doll, another Harlow floosie. There is a regurgitation of the Harlow–Astor *Red Dust* scenario – the genteel English lady versus the this time elegantly costumed bit of rough –

with the inclusion of wealthy widow Rosalind Russell. And supplying the obligatory element of menace was Harlow's old adversary, Wallace Beery. Although they were now friends, she still claimed that kissing him would have been less preferable than shoving her head between the jaws of a starving lion!

'Miss Harlow makes the tropical trollop gay and courageous and loyal,' was how the *New York Herald*'s Richard Watts described the heroine of *China Seas*, 'which is no small feat, because in less capable hands the girl might have seemed an unpleasantly vindictive virago.' Dolly 'China Doll' Portland shows up unexpectedly on board the ship captained by old flame Alan Gaskell (Gable) when this docks in Hong Kong, en route to Singapore with a secret $250,000 stash of gold bullion. Gaskell, grumpy and hungover, finds her in his bathroom. 'It's China Doll, the gal that drives men wild, just showering the dew-drops off the body beautiful,' she whines from behind the door. He asks her to leave, and she suspects that he is involved with the 'hunk of caviar', the Russian princess she saw him with earlier.

GASKELL: You and I are friends. We've had a lot of fun together, and as far as I'm concerned you're number one girl in the Archepelago. But I don't remember making any vows to you, nor do I recall asking for any!
DOLLY: Don't you get polite with me. When you start talking with your high hat on I know you mean it, and it scares me.

Dolly says that she has a job to go to in Singapore. Then they kiss hungrily, and he decides that she is staying. Enter Third Officer Tom Davids (Lewis Stone), who knows these waters like the back of his hand and has been the sole survivor of a pirate attack – and double-dealer James MacArdle (Wallace Beery), who also has a history with Dolly, and wants her to share his ill-gotten fortune. In *Shanghai Express*, Dietrich had purred, 'It took more than one man to change my name to Shanghai Lily.' Here it is a more strident,

> DOLLY: There ain't enough dough in all Asia to make me change the way I feel about one guy.
> MACARDLE: Well, whenever you get tired of running around with an Airedale and you want to run around with a St Bernard, let me know.
> DOLLY: Sure, if I ever get lost in the Alps, I'll whistle for you!

Gaskell's is one of the few vessels not to have been attacked by pirates, but shortly before embarking he apprehends would-be Chinese marauders who board the ship dressed as women. Then, adding to the complications, a last-minute passenger is his former lover, the recently widowed Sybil Barclay – Rosalind Russell speaking much better King's English than the supposedly English Gaskell. This was Gable stubbornly refusing to speak with any accent but his own, as would happen in his next film, *Mutiny On The Bounty*, in which he played 'Cockermouth-by-way-of-Ohio' anti-hero, Fletcher Christian. In the next scene, we see him in his bathroom again – where Dolly pops in to borrow a book. Gable had wanted to play the scene bare-chested, as he had in *Red Dust*, but this film would be going out on general release towards winter, and MGM had received enough complaints then from the manufacturers of undervests that Gable was 'doing them out of business'. Mayer thus issued the instruction, unusual for a seafaring drama, 'No naked male flesh.' (Harlow more than made up for this during a break from shooting when a snooty female reporter sniped that her dress was so low cut, she could almost see her navel. Dropping the front of her dress and exposing just-iced breasts, and without anyone else batting an eyelid – they were used to it – she strolled up to the refreshments trolley and calmly asked for a cup of coffee.) 'Have you ever seen an English river?' Gaskell asks for no particular reason. 'No,' she tells him, 'I'm dumb at geography just like I am at everything else.'

Next, while the passengers and crew talk about pirates in such a way that we know they will inevitably turn up, we see Dolly with her maid – the truly magnificent Hattie McDaniel who has the best putdown in the film. When Dolly asks while dressing for dinner, 'Isabelle, would you say that I looked like a lady?', the response is a blatantly honest, 'No, Miss Dolly. I been with you too long to insult you that way!' At the captain's table, Gaskell flirts with Sybil and calls Dolly a 'professional entertainer', while Dolly and MacArdle tense the atmosphere with coarse talk. Afterwards, Gaskell tells her to keep away from him, though we instinctively know this will not happen. They are soiled goods – 'A girl's got to do what she can with what's around,' she says of her involvements with ruffians in the past. They have always fought by moonlight, and made up when it rains – and a typhoon is looming on the horizon. This hits the ship and Dolly is reported missing, presumed washed overboard – in fact she and MacArdle are playing cards below deck and getting sloshed. She wins and he passes out, leaving her to take the money he owes her from his wallet. Also there is half of a £100 note, marked with Chinese letters. Aware that pirates use these as their signature, keeping the other half themselves, Dolly realises that MacArdle is in league with them.

Meanwhile, the storm reaches its zenith and *China Seas* takes on the feel of a Marx Brothers' madcap extravaganza: Davids cowers in the shadows as water is hurled onto the set and a steamroller breaks loose, rolling back and forth on the top deck, killing indiscriminately. Dolly gets drenched – this necessitated Harlow removing her wig, so that for a few seconds her hair is shorter and a slightly different colour. She tries to explain MacArdle's plot to Gaskell, but after sending his men on a wild goose chase looking for her, he is too angry to listen. Twenty years later, Gable would repeat this rip off from *Red Dust* to Ava Gardner in its remake, *Mogambo*:

DOLLY: I only came here for one thing –
GASKELL: I'm quite aware of that. You're always waiting for

a sailor to comfort him. Only a woman like you can comfort a man who's too tired or too drunk to care who it is.

DOLLY: Well, you've been begging for it, and now you're gonna get it. You won't be so high and mighty when I get through with you. You just wait, I'll fix you. You'll be lower than a coolie. You'll be lower than Davids. You'll come crawling to me on your knees!

This last hysterical if not high-camp outburst amused the *New York Times*' André Sennwald, who observed, 'Miss Harlow's exit after the captain refuses to listen to her will have to go on record as one of the season's major examples of etiquette.'

The pirates attack. Gaskell knows that it is an inside job because they are using his guns. He suspects Dolly and MacArdle because he saw him coming out of her cabin. 'He came to borrow a hot water bottle for one of his pigs,' she offers lamely. Gaskell has taken precautions, removing the gold and hiding it in the steamroller. Then a near-fatally injured Davids makes up for his earlier cowardice and saves the day, falling into the pirates' junk with a bag of explosives and blowing them to bits. Gaskell bawls Dolly out and she confesses that she stole the key for the armoury because of his antagonism towards her when she tried to explain what MacArdle was up to. 'When a woman can love a man right down to her fingernails, she can hate him the same way,' she drawls, before MacArdle takes the easy way out, overdosing on seasickness pills. The ship docks in Singapore and, having said goodbye to Sybil, Gaskell finally realises, as had happened with Vantine in *Red Dust*, that he has loved this wisecracking slut all along and that he will marry her once she gets out of jail for her part in the raid. As she is innocent, we suspect that he will not have to wait too long.

Two major changes were effected in Harlow's life within weeks of *China Seas* wrapping. In the first, Mama Jean finally saw sense and divorced Marino Bello: the yacht, the underground connections, and a string of mistresses were but the tip of the iceberg so far as his dodgy dealings were concerned. The divorce came about as a result of Harlow appearing on the cover of the 19 August edition of *Time* magazine, posed in an antique, velvet-covered chair (Irving Shulman called it her throne of love), wearing a silk negligee and ostrich feather boa, and holding a mirror. 'Fine Feathers Make Fans', the headline proclaimed. Founded in 1923, *Time* was at that stage something of a sexist, anti-show-business institution: just 30 women had featured on the covers so far of its 600-plus issues, and but a dozen movie stars including Chaplin, The Marx Brothers and Ethel Barrymore. The accompanying feature contained all the usual anecdotes and definitions: blonde was beautiful, even if the owner of the said locks was a little on the seamy side – certainly so far as her movie roles were concerned.

Astonishingly, Harlow had not wanted such an honour. On 19 October 1931 she had appeared on the back cover of the magazine, plugging Lucky Strike cigarettes. Then, a review of *Red Dust* had seen her grabbing the telephone and threatening the editor with a fate worse than death – not content with hammering the film, the critic had described her as 'Harlot Harlow'. Louis B. Mayer, however, had the last say. He had pulled the strings to get one of his stars on the cover of *Time*, therefore she would smile and get on with it.

During the weeks between Harlow being assigned to the *Time* feature, and this going to press, a silly event made the tabloids and some of the syndicated columns. One Saturday evening, after a night on the town, a group of female Harlow fans from the University of Arkansas who had somehow managed to acquire Harlow's telephone number called her at home in the early hours of the morning. Needless to say, she refused to take the call – like anyone else she was entitled to privacy when not working – the result of which saw these former admirers turning into vicious vigilantes out to scupper her career. Their 'case', which in today's atmosphere of security paranoia would see such cranks being investigated by the police – was taken up by the local Theater Owners' Convention. Howard Strickling, forced to publicly condemn Harlow's 'unsociable' behaviour, was therefore obliged to force her to sign a statement, apologising for upsetting these lunatics. She did however draw the line when Louis B. Mayer suggested sending her out to Arkansas to meet up with them. If she refused to comply, Mayer threatened, then he would have her replaced on the *Time* cover by Crawford or Garbo – something which would not happen because the accompanying feature had already been written. Instead, she called the college, apologised to one of the women concerned but with her fingers crossed behind her back – then added that the last laugh was on her, for she had reversed the charges!

The *Time* feature was basically an extension of Howard Strickling's original hugely exaggerated biography of Harlow, now embellished by the various scandals she had survived (Paul Bern was heralded 'a motion pictures Christ'), and one or two items of hype which were so far-fetched, it is no small wonder the columnists did not tear her apart. Describing her as 'the foremost US embodiment of sex appeal,' the writer expected fans to believe that she had been discovered by Ben Lyon, while working as an extra on *Hell's Angels*, and that Lyon had suggested to Howard Hughes that he fire Greta Nissen and use Harlow instead. Also, unlike most of the other major Hollywood stars, she did not employ a chauffeur: if she was feeling too tired to drive herself to work, then Marino Bello would put on livery and hop into the limousine! There were also sarcastic attacks on Harlow's intelligence and innate, frequently cutting wit. The anecdote where she had met a society woman called Margot (supposedly the wife of former British prime minister Herbert Asquith) and called her 'Margott', only to be told, 'The last letter in my name is silent, unlike yours!' was suppressed – *Time* had already got away with calling her a harlot once. Therefore the magazine came up with another event, possibly invented, where at a party she had dropped one of her one-liners, and someone had casually remarked, 'Who did *you* hear say that?' – the fact that she was generally believed not to have been possessed of a brain, where in fact the opposite more than adequately applied. When Harlow received her 12 complimentary copies of the magazine, in front of reporters naturally, she walked into her garden, threw them into the incinerator and set them alight.

Much more seriously, *Time* had delved deeply into Mama Jean's Fedora-esque complex – echoing the story of the once beautiful star who, as middle age beckons and her looks start to fade, slinks into the shadows and allows her equally attractive daughter to replace her, successfully fooling not just the public but those closest to her. Mama Jean, like the mothers of Judy Garland, Maria Callas and Montgomery Clift, would make life hell for their offspring because, through them, they were seeking to achieve their own unfulfilled dreams. With Harlow (as with Callas) this complex was expanded by the fact that, when interviewed, she invariably spoke in the third person as if she had actually stepped into her mother's shoes. For the first time, Harlow's fans were let in on the secret of just how much she was being manipulated by this woman – but worse still was the way Bello was exposed to have been exploiting the both of them.

A casual remark in the *Time* feature disclosing that Bello secretly owned gold mines was challenged by William Powell, arguably the only man in Harlow's life to have been interested in her for herself. Powell, aware that whatever assets Bello had were almost certainly financed by his stepdaughter, hired a private investigator to find out the truth. Bello had shown Harlow 'evidence' of a lucrative gold mine in South America, and she had been duped into handing over almost a quarter of her salary. The mine, of course, did not exist – all that Bello 'owned' here was a mistress. For Mama Jean, this was the last straw. Bello was kicked out of Beverly Glen. Within 24 hours, the locks were changed on all the doors and windows, and Bello's clothes and effects packed into suitcases and boxes and shoved in one of the outbuildings. Harlow personally went to see her bank manager with the instruction that his signature was to be no longer used to honour cheques and withdrawals from her account. Bello made a futile attempt to blackmail his wife into selling the house and paying him half of its value – around $300,000. Mama Jean stuck to her guns and refused: eventually he was paid just $22,000 to get out of her life, though like the proverbial bad penny he would turn up again from time to time. Louis B. Mayer was so pleased to be rid of this leech that he loaned her the money, which he deducted in instalments from Harlow's salary. A quickie divorce was granted on 26 September 1935, with Mama Jean citing mental cruelty which in this instance was more than appropriate.

The second event involved Harlow's hair. The *Time* cover heralded the closure of an era – the last time fans would see her as a platinum blonde. The change came about when Mayer and Thalberg watched the rushes for *China Seas* – the fact that they were convinced that if *they* could tell that Harlow was wearing a wig, so would everyone else. Persistent bleaching had damaged her hair irreparably, not just causing split ends but damage to the roots. Advice was sought from Sydney Guillaroff, who had made Harlow's wigs for *Reckless* and the new film. He suggested that the split ends be trimmed back an inch or so, and a specialist confirmed that if Harlow kept on applying peroxide to her scalp, not only would her hair fall out, she might suffer actual brain damage. For what little remained of her life, she would be publicised as a 'brownette'.

CHAPTER NINE

No Sad Songs For Me

'In a sense, perhaps, she was the victim of her own body because she looked what she simply was not – she was a child who happened to look like a vamp.'

Barry Norman, film critic

Later in the year, once her new image had been tested and approved by fans and critics, Harlow would tell *Picturegoer*, 'I've always hated my hair, not only because it limited me as an actress, but because it limited me as a person. I had to live up to that platinum personality.' What she did not say was that she enjoyed living up to her on-screen reputation because, like Gable and Crawford, there was little difference between the on-and off-screen persona. Each had been created and customised to fit her like a glove.

When she first went 'brownette', it was another story. Harlow fought against MGM wanting to change her hair colour, assured that her career would collapse as quickly as it had ascended. Truthfully, in a profession where typecasting was the norm, she may be considered lucky to have survived so radical a transition. To stop being the Platinum Blonde while at the very zenith of her success was the equivalent of the sultry Garbo turning up for her next movie with a 'Bronx honk' like Clara Bow. The *New York Times* observed, 'Not even a brunette rinse can dim the platinum potency of Harlow's allure,' – though she would have to wait until January 1936 to read this.

Harlow refused to discuss her concerns over her new image when interviewed by *Screen Book*'s Sonia Lee. The magazine had commissioned her 'life story', and had wanted Ben Maddox to write this. Maddox, keeping Clark Gable company on and off the set of *Mutiny On The Bounty*, would have nothing to do with the idea: he was too involved with his subject, and deplored any notion of divulging details of her private live to the public. Lee described Harlow, 'Like a little girl who has just discovered there in no Santa Claus,' but managed to get some sort of scoop, which she promised Harlow she would not print but then reneged on. She was thinking of marrying again, but would not name the lucky man other than to say that he was a good friend. Everyone knew who this friend was, of course – William Powell – and Lee had her own opinion concerning the difference between friendship and love. Indeed, with her fondness for often speaking in the third person, these could just as easily have been Harlow's actual words:

> It was this near genius for friendship which had brought her into a close relationship with Paul Bern. The same thing happened when she married Hal Rosson. Love is selfish. Friendship never is. Jean couldn't understand the trans-mutation of a friend into a jealous husband, but that change had come equally in Paul and Hal. Needless to say, a marriage based on friendship only has neither the glamour nor the excitement nor the ecstasy of a marriage for love. It is difficult to admit that friendship is insufficient for marriage, that it can only be a small part of marriage. Whether she will make that mistake again depends largely on the next year.

In the meantime, Harlow's next leading man was Spencer Tracy, with whom she had starred in *Goldie*, but not really had much to do with away from the set. Born in Milwaukee, Tracy (1900–67) had studied with the American Academy of Dramatic Art before joining a New York stock company. His stage break had occurred in 1923 when he had played the heavy in *Royal Fandango*, with Ethel Barrymore, but his most accomplished role had been that of death-row prisoner Killer Mears in the 1929 Broadway production of *The Last Mile* – Clark Gable had taken this on the tour circuit, on the eve of making it big in Hollywood. Tracy was a rare bird in Hollywood in that he detested the glamour and attention that came with being a star, though in the late autumn of 1935 he was already a rebel, a complete law unto himself and drinking heavily. He got off to a bad start with Harlow, turning up for work one morning half-drunk from the night before after quaffing the proverbial hair of the dog for breakfast. Harlow complained to the director, J. Walter Ruben, and Tracy was sent home to sober up. What few knew is that she too had been drinking fairly heavily since her divorce, her favourite tipple being gin because the odour did not linger on her breath. Rather than lose his rag with her, as was his wont, the incident drew Tracy towards her and they became friends who would insist on working together again.

Scripted by Frances Marion, H.W. Hanemann and Anita Loos from a story by Frances Marion, and co-starring Una Merkel, the tagline for *Riffraff* was, 'When A Red-Headed Woman Meets A Red-Headed Man!' – which did not make that much sense. In a role far too similar to the ones being portrayed by Joan Crawford (*Possessed* and *Mannequin*, also with Tracy and with a storyline not too dissimilar to this one), Harlow played Hattie Tuttle, a cannery worker who lives in near squalor on the waterfront with an extended family which includes a flighty sister, Lil (Merkel) and a brattish baby brother (Mickey Rooney in an early role). Hattie is madly in love with fisherman Dutch Miller – Tracy typecast in one of his gung-ho, over-swaggering roles, cynical, conceited and indifferent towards her. 'What has a tuna fisherman got to be conceited about?' *Variety* would pompously demand. The pair get close after Dutch ends up in a dance-hall brawl with Hattie's boss, Nick Appopolis (Joseph Calleia) who cannot keep his hands off her. 'I love dames with spirit – dames and fishes,' he growls. They marry, and in a juxtaposition of fiction and fact things go wrong at once. The fishermen elect Dutch as their union leader and go on strike for better working conditions and more pay – action which in those days was regarded as cowardly and unmanly. Dutch is fired and Hattie, who has urged him against militancy, takes the blame – he leaves her and the waterfront. Later, Hattie learns that he is ill, and when Nick refuses to loan her the money to visit him she steals it and ends up in jail. By now, Dutch has come to his senses and wants to spring her, but she has secretly given birth to his child, which she has handed over to Lil, and wants nothing more to do with him. Dutch promises to go straight and wait for her, and returning to the waterfront he gets a job as night-watchman. He catches a man sabotaging one of Nick's boats, and this puts him back in the boss's good books: he is reappointed as union leader. Thinking he was hurt during the sabotage, Hattie escapes from prison, but when she sees that he is okay, she tells him about the child and hands herself in to the authorities so that she can serve out her sentence, knowing that he will be waiting when she gets out.

It had been done before, said the critics – and better, by Joan Crawford, the undisputed queen of shopgirls and factory workers. This was the Depression, there were millions of Hattie Tuttles in America, fighting to survive. Was it therefore necessary to turn abject poverty into screwball? Of the broadsheets, only Bland Johaneson of the *New York Daily Mirror* found *Riffraff* worthy of applause: 'Lively, daring, meaty and rough, it is the best film Jean Harlow has made for a long time, and she gives a rich performance as the unhappy belle of a fish cannery.'

Harlow complained of yet more back pains while shooting the film, but the studio doctor merely suggested that she was suffering from muscle strain through playing too much golf. Arthur Landau is said to have been sufficiently concerned to have contacted Louis B. Mayer with a request that she see a specialist. The Messiah, however, had 'other fish to fry' – a pun, in view of the movie, picked up on by the press. Mayer was served with a writ by California's State & Industrial Welfare Committee on behalf of 40 female extras who had been drenched during the prison rainstorm sequence. These women claimed that they had not been forewarned of the scene, otherwise they would not have taken the job, and that they had subsequently lost work owing to illness. Mayer, who could worm his way out of a straitjacket, had his lawyers fight the case and each extra ended up with a paltry $15 in compensation. Harlow's much more serious condition, meanwhile, was completely ignored.

Stenographers had represented the archetypal allure for bosses with roaming hands since Wallace Beery had slobbered over Joan Crawford in *Grand Hotel*. With this in mind, and allowing her a mere three weeks respite despite Arthur Landau's protestations that his client was far from well, Mayer put her into *Wife vs. Secretary* with Clark Gable and Myrna Loy. This was the fourth Gable–Loy outing, and his fifth with Harlow. Angered by the suggestion in *Time* that Harlow was not particularly bright – when the opposite applied – Mayer insisted that this time she should display her articulacy to its fullest extent. She played Whitey Wilson, secretary to magazine editor Van Stanhope (Gable), an 'It' girl who wears gold lamé gowns and whose duties extend beyond the typewriter when she redecorates his office while he is away on vacation. He is happily married to Linda (Loy), who initially does not find Whitey much of a threat because she is convinced that her husband has eyes for her alone, though she only pretends not to be upset when he pretends to have forgotten their wedding anniversary – until she sees that he has hidden a diamond bracelet inside the fish he serves her for breakfast. 'She's sitting on his lap and he hasn't even touched his trout,' the maid remarks of their constant canoodling in front of the servants. Van's mother (May Robson) on the other hand suspects them of having an affair, and brings Linda around to her way of thinking: Whitey is far too intelligent to be a mere secretary, and Linda feels that she should be promoted and moved to another department to keep them apart. Whitey is in fact in love with the much less articulate Dave – James Stewart in an early role – who dumps her when she refuses to give up her job to marry him. Suspicion turns to anger when Van flies off to Cuba for a business transaction, then summons Whitey to help him clinch the deal. For one moment, 'it' almost happens, but they resist temptation. Then Whitey takes a call from Linda in his bedroom, she jumps to the obvious conclusion, and when he gets home he finds that she has packed her bags – not to go on the vacation he has promised her, but to his mother's. At first, Mrs Stanhope thinks she should forgive him: he is after all only a man, and most men are like children when faced with temptation. 'You wouldn't blame a little boy for stealing a piece of candy,' she says, 'if left alone in a room with a whole box full!' Linda argues that this was not temptation: Whitey was in her husband's room during the early hours of the morning, therefore the act can only have been pre-planned.

All ends well, of course, according to the rules laid down by the National League of Decency. Whitey catches up with Linda as she is about to board a ship for Europe, and convinces her that nothing has been going on between her and Van – though she assures her that this will be the case, if Linda leaves: 'If he ever turns to me, I'll never turn away. You're a fool, for which I'm grateful!' The film ends with the Stanhopes reconciled, while Whitey finally gives up her job to marry Dave, who has suddenly reappeared on the scene and been apparently sitting in his car, out in the street, these last three days waiting for her to make this decision!

Variety singled out Whitey Wilson as Harlow's best role ever: 'She clicks in every scene without going spectacular. She shows she really can act something beside the vamp roles with which she has been chiefly identified.' James Stewart claimed in interviews that, of all his leading ladies – which had included Dietrich, Ginger

Rogers and Margaret Sullavan – Harlow had been his favourite. Speaking to his biographer, Michael Munn, he said, 'I was just this skinny guy from Pennsylvania, and she had this [platinum] hair and this beautiful face like a little angel with attitude. And she kinda slouched because slouching was fashionable then, and she had this low-cut dress on and...well, she had nothing on underneath. And *I* had to kiss Jean Harlow!' According to Munn, Stewart and Harlow had a fling while making the film, but never dated on account of his fear of Marino Bello and his mobster connections. This does not add up, and was doubtless wishful thinking on Stewart's part. He managed to get her most vital feature (the colour of her hair) wrong, and shooting did not commence until November 1935, by which time Bello had been out of the picture. The film also has a crafty little 'in-joke', slipped into the script by one of the writers. Van is poring over a magazine article penned by Alice Duer Miller, when he drawls, 'Hey, Alice has written a very nice article here!' Miller was one of the *Wife vs. Secretary* scriptwriters!

MGM had forced an unprecedented change of direction for Harlow, by changing her hair, and now with the studio no longer using her to sell sex in the movies. Yet sadly with this change came the gradual decline in her health. During the morning of 11 December she collapsed on the set of *Wife vs. Secretary*, nothing to do with the back pains she was still suffering – which Mama Jean vowed would be cured by a few choice readings from Mary Baker Eddy – but on account of nervous exhaustion. Despite her mother's protests and Bible rantings, director Clarence Brown took Harlow to see the studio doctor, who prescribed less work and more fresh air. She took a few days off to play golf, and the week before Christmas returned to the set. Her recovery coincided with rumours that, at 24, she might be planning her retirement from the movies. Her romance with William Powell was still going strong, and she had already told friends like Ben Maddox that, if she married again – and at this stage this seemed likely – she would no

longer wish to juggle family life with a Hollywood career. She
hammered home this point by not attending the *Riffraff* premiere
on 3 January 1936 – telling reporters that it was much nicer,
'staying home and darning Poppy's socks.' The columnists began
hearing imaginary wedding bells while the outlook for Harlow's
contribution to the MGM coffers looked bleak.

Louis B. Mayer expressed more cause for concern when Harlow
announced that she was moving out of Beverly Glen into a smaller,
rented property at 512 North Palm Drive – describing this as the
perfect little love nest for William Powell and herself. Mama Jean
moved in with her, naturally, though initially she did not spend
much time here: there was a new man in her life, 40-something
Henry Brand, of which little is known other than he had a property
on Catalina Island. Free of Marino Bello, Mama Jean now had
another costly passion – collecting antiques, not for herself, she said,
but because she and Brand were thinking of opening a shop. Why
the new beau did not finance her latest foible was never asked.
Harlow paid her mother a weekly allowance and let her please
herself – anything it would appear to remove her from under her
and Powell's feet.

The real reason for the move was that, solely on account of the
Bellos' extravagances, Harlow was more than $50,000 in debt, most
of this to Arthur Landau for bailing her out more times than he
cared to remember. The Beverly Glen house was put on the market,
fully furnished, for $150,000. It was purchased by Nat Levine of
Republic Studios, who asked for $25,000 to be knocked off the price
in exchange for a quick sale. Harlow did not mind this. The place
may have been advertised in the real estate agent's window as
'Glamour Star's New Ancestral Mansion', but she had never been
really happy there with Marino Bello prowling around, incapable of
keeping his hands to himself, and even though he was gone his
ghost must still have been present to make her feel uncomfortable.

In mid-April, Harlow began shooting *Suzy* with Cary Grant
and Franchot Tone – directed by George Fitzmaurice, who was

unofficially assisted (via telephone) by Howard Hughes. MGM had decided that, rather than spend money shooting aerial combat scenes, they would use some of the leftover footage from *Hell's Angels*, and this shows rather badly. She had known British-born Grant (1904–86), arguably her most debonair co-star, for a while courtesy of Ben Maddox, who frequently stayed at Grant and Randolph Scott's beach house for weekends of discreet fun. Such was the naivety of the day, that Maddox even got away with doing a spread for *Modern Screen* where the 'blissful bachelors' were photographed in the gym, in the pool, and in the kitchen wearing aprons, seemingly without raising any suspicions at all. Only the columnists saw through the charade, and with some of these it is not too difficult to read between the lines to discern what was going on. A former roommate of William Haines, which probably said enough about his sexuality, Grant was used to working with man-eating sirens. He had worked with Dietrich in *Blonde Venus*, and with Mae West in *She Done Him Wrong* and *I'm No Angel*.

Suzy Trent (Harlow) is an American chorus girl working in London on the eve of World War I – there is no explanation of how she got there, but this being a Harlow movie, one does not have to guess too hard. 'Blondes never go broke,' she tells best friend Maisie (Inez Courtney) backstage after their final appearance in *Melodies of 1914*, having handed over her pay packet to a needy colleague, 'Besides, I got a rich uncle!' When Maisie says this is the first she has heard of this, Suzy responds, 'I haven't got any relatives anywhere, but I got a rich uncle!' Maisie is leaving to work in a Paris revue, but Suzy will stay put and look for a wealthy husband. There are echoes of the closing scene from *Dinner At Eight*, and the same look of surprise when she announces, 'I've been reading a book' – and of *The Girl From Missouri* when Maisie suggests that maybe she has set her hopes too high, and Suzy offers her theory, 'It's just as easy to fall for a big shot as a little one.' In the next scene she attends an audition and, asking for a part with lines this time, is told by the manager that this will be forthcoming providing she hops onto the casting couch. Naturally, she refuses – Harlow back to being a virgin once more – and in a fluster over this she is knocked down outside the theatre by Irish inventor Terry Moore – Franchot Tone, with an accent that wavers back and forth between County Down and New York. Terry runs her back to her lodgings in the Rolls-Royce he has 'borrowed' from his German boss, Mrs Schmidt (Greta Meyer).

Evicted from her lodgings, Suzy has to find a husband faster than she anticipated. Terry takes her to the factory where he works as an inventor. Mrs Schmidt arrives unexpectedly, and while Suzy hides, fires Terry for using her equipment after hours. He celebrates losing his job by marrying Suzy, but their marriage gets no further than a first kiss in his apartment. The couple have found out that Schmidt is using the factory as a cover for a spy ring and one of her cohorts, Diane Eyrelle, has followed them home. She shoots Terry, and Suzy, assuming that he is dead and that she will be blamed for his murder, flees to Paris. The newspaper headline she reads aboard the cross-Channel steamer declares, 'Archduke Ferdinand Assassinated In Sarajevo', heralding the start of World War I.

In Paris, Suzy meets up with Maisie, who finds her work at her cabaret. Here, the scriptwriter has Harlow juxtaposing with Suzy Solidor (1900–83), the legendary chanteuse who ran La Vie Parisienne, a nightclub on the rue Saint Anne. MGM had hired Eadie Adams to overdub her voice for this scene, but she was not used: Harlow emulates Solidor, nicknamed The Girl With The Flaxen Hair, beginning her chanson – 'Did I Remember?' – leaning against the shawl-draped piano, then wandering around the tables, serenading the women as well as the men. She halts at the table of airman, André Charville (Cary Grant) – a part based on the famous French aviator, Jean Mermoz (1901–36), whose plane would plunge into the Atlantic, en route to Brazil, later that year. Like Mermoz, Charville is an undisputed hero, but a rat where women are concerned. His wealthy father (Lewis Stone) knows this, and has been bailing him out of scrapes for years. When

Charville sweeps Suzy off her feet, weds her and takes her home, M. Charville is initially disapproving. When his son leaves for the Front, gets decorated for gallantry but prefers to spend his leave with floosies rather than with his wife, the old man warms to her and they become very close.

This being a Hollywood movie aimed at raising morale during the Depression – and with a real-life situation developing in Europe as war-clouds slowly gathered – MGM injected a little fantasy into the proceedings by making Suzy's world just that little bit smaller. Terry turns up in Paris, hale and hearty, sent here by the War Office to deliver a plane he has invented to Charville. He and Suzy meet at the hospital while visiting Charville, wounded in action, but Terry refuses to believe why she left London in a hurry – to his way of thinking, she is an opportunist, and now a bigamist. 'When this war's over, if a bullet doesn't set you free, I will,' he growls. Suzy intends confessing all to Charville, but finds him in the arms of his mistress – Diane Eyrelle, who is planning to kill him. Terry now realises that Suzy is genuine, and they set off to confront Eyrelle at her chateau, but before they can save him, Charville is shot by one of her henchmen. As Charville expires, Terry pursues the spy in the new plane, blowing up her car and also finding time to bring down a few enemy aircraft before crash-landing back at the chateau – actual scenes purloined from *Hell's Angels* this time. The film ends with Charville's body being placed next to the plane, allowing everyone's secrets to remain intact, while the emotion to Charville's 'loss in action' is so great that even the mighty Baron Von Richtofen (courtesy of Howard Hughes again) flies overhead and drops a wreath!

The reviews for *Suzy* were surprisingly average. Critics could cope with her change of hair colour, but they were still unused to Harlow not playing the siren. And was that really Lola Burns comforting Lewis Stone, and looking so sincere? Richard Watts of the *New York Herald Tribune*, who had loathed then loved her, now took a step backwards and opined, 'I will go on screaming in

my customary wilderness that it is a great shame to waste Miss
Harlow in such a role, when she should be exercising her vast gifts
as a half-sophisticated, half-innocent comic.' The *New York Post*'s
Irene Thirer agreed. Declaring that the laughs fell to Cary Grant
and Franchot Tone – Thirer must have been watching another
film, for despite the perennially witty Dorothy Parker's contribution
to the script there are few intentional laughs to be had anywhere in
this one – she added, 'Jean plays practically straight – and she
oughtn't to. She's a swell comedienne, and not too adept at drama
– especially tragedy.'

   Suzy wrapped on 20 May 1936. Seven days later, Harlow filed to
change her name by deed poll. On 1 July her application was
heard, and she appeared at the Los Angeles Superior Court. She
gave her name as Harlean Carpenter McGrew Bern Rosson, and
20 minutes later left the building as 'plain old Jean Harlow', telling
reporters that she would not be changing her name again in any
hurry. 'The goddess walked upon her earth and found it good,'
Arthur Landau observed. If this did not give William Powell a less
than subtle hint that she was no longer interested in marrying him
– though so far as is known, there had been no arguments between
them – her next move very definitely did. Already breaking her
pledge by signing the register as 'Mrs Jean Carpenter', she booked
herself into the Good Samaritan Hospital for what can only have
been her third abortion. This time, there was no meddling by the
Christian Scientist movement. Inasmuch as he had investigated
Marino Bello's nefarious activities, William Powell knew
everything that was happening in Harlow's life, and would not have
stood for such nonsense. Mama Jean, who accompanied her
daughter for the procedure, signed the visitor's book as 'Mrs Webb'.
As had happened with her supposed appendectomy, Harlow was
installed in Room 826, where she remained for just three days
before being discharged to North Palm Drive. Louis B. Mayer and
Irving Thalberg kept the incident out of the press, along with the
fact that Harlow was fast becoming addicted to gin.

While Mayer's hypocritical moral side may have wished to see Harlow joining the dole queue, his pocket dictated otherwise: she was earning way too much money for the studio for them to risk letting her go. Mayer therefore took the unusual step of rewarding her for her next movie: a $5,000 bonus and top-billing above whichever leading man she chose for herself – on the proviso that she 'cleaned up her act'. She was given time to do this – the whole of June, and the first half of July, on full pay. Throughout much of this time she steered clear of William Powell, dividing her time between Kay Mulver and her son – buying the boy a pony and teaching him to ride and improving her golfing handicap with the recently retired Leo Diegel. If she did see Powell, it was at chaperoned dinner parties hosted by Carey and Carmelita Wilson.

Because of the adverse reviews for *Suzy*, it was back to the old routine when Irving Thalberg assigned her to *Libeled Lady*, with Myrna Loy (replacing Rosalind Russell) and Spencer Tracy already cast. Harlow chose William Powell as her co-star. Their affair had started to cool by now, but the two were close – Powell never bore grudges, and remained on good terms with both of his ex-wives, and Carole Lombard was a frequent visitor to the set, never failing to turn the air blue with her caustic humour and colourful conversation. Thalberg saw no problem in letting Harlow and Powell work together: both were free agents, therefore the columnists hopefully would not unearth any scandals and the National League of Decency would be happy. Shooting began on 13 July, and with a few interruptions – sadly, Harlow's health was starting to fail – wrapped at the end of August.

In *Libeled Lady*, Harlow plays divorcée Gladys Benton, who for the past two years has played second fiddle to the newspaper which employs her fiancé, Warren Haggerty (Tracy). 'You'd make your crippled grandmother do a fandango for that paper,' she scathes. Today is her wedding day, and for the third time he stands her up, though this time he has a good excuse: the paper has printed a fabricated story accusing mega-rich socialite Connie Allenbury

(Loy) of stealing another woman's husband, and now she is threatening to sue for $5 million. To get her off his back, so to speak, Haggerty comes up with an idea which leads to one of silliest plots in any Hollywood movie. Connie has never been involved in a scandal, so he will frame her and force her to drop the suit – enter former disgruntled employee Bill Chandler (Powell), 'a double-crossing heel who can beat anyone from Gandhi to Garbo.' The plan is that Chandler will be the husband Haggerty catches Connie having an affair with – his only problem being that he is a confirmed bachelor, a problem he promptly solves by having him marry Gladys, be his wife in name only, then divorce her once Connie has been fixed!

The rest of the story is equally contrived but, though they have their moments, aside from a hilarious fly-fishing scenario the ensuing scenes between Powell and Loy are nowhere near as sparkling as in their *Third Man* films. A ship, Chandler decrees, will be the ideal environment to conduct an affair – therefore he sails to England just so that he can board the ship which will be bringing Connie and her tycoon father (Walter Connolly) back to England. She is unbelievably snooty and initially frosty towards him, but when he rescues her from being mauled by reporters – a situation he has arranged – she gradually warms to him. The pair meet up again on home territory, and Connie falls for Chandler after a midnight swim, by which time he is starting to feel guilty about the whole set-up and wants out. Suffice to say, after numerous complications – mixed-up divorces, punch-ups and slanging matches – we get the impression that everyone should be living happily ever after, though the ending is so rushed, contrived and silly, who cares? Harlow later said that she had achieved her ambition to marry Powell, if only on the screen – though it was quite clear by this time that marriage was the last thing either of them wanted.

The reviews for what is almost certainly Harlow's worst film were surprisingly excellent, and resulted in her occupying the throne recently vacated by Marie Dressler as MGM's top female star after Garbo. The *New York Telegraph* hailed her 'a luminous comedienne'. The *New York Herald*'s Howard Barnes wrote, 'Miss Harlow has a part cut to her talents. Her insulting cracks at the editor are gems of brash comedy and she vitalizes the material throughout.' Barnes was referring to the moment when an exasperated Gladys yelled at an ever-deliberating Haggerty, 'Marry the paper – and be the proud father of a lot of headlines!' An appreciative Frank S. Nugent concluded in the *New York Times*, having watched the scene where Harlow accepts a peck on the cheek from husband Powell before flinging herself into Tracy's arms, 'Moments like this compel us to condone a certain slackening of pace toward the picture's conclusion, and we are pathetically grateful to Metro for restoring Miss Harlow to her proper metier that we could have forgiven even more serious lapses.' The film was nominated for a Best Picture Award at the 1937 Oscars, but lost out to *The Great Ziegfeld*, also starring Powell and Myrna Loy. Harlow attended the ceremony with Powell, arriving in the same limousine as Clark Gable and Carole Lombard, by this time very much of an item.

Meanwhile, on 14 September 1936, two weeks after Harlow completed *Libeled Lady*, MGM's Boy Wonder, Irving Thalberg, suddenly but not unexpectedly died at the age of 37, sending the movie capital into a state of profound shock. Many of those who had worked with him genuinely grieved – though many more did not. A few weeks earlier, a simple cold had developed into lobar pneumonia. Clark Gable and Douglas Fairbanks Sr were ushers at his funeral at the B'na B'rith Temple on Wilshire Boulevard, and anyone who was anyone was there to pay their respects – or disrespects, depending on how they had got along with the precocious mogul. Only the crowd-hating Garbo, currently adding the finishing touches to Thalberg's *Camille*, was absent, sending her excuses along with a huge wreath. Harlow and Joan Crawford, briefly reunited by their hatred of this man, exchanged pleasantries outside in the autumn sunshine. Both had fought against being there – Joan because Thalberg had always overlooked her to offer the choicest roles to Norma Shearer, Harlow declaring him the most obnoxious, tight-wad creep she had ever known. Gable too was there under extreme duress. At the time of Thalberg's death the two had not been on speaking terms because Thalberg had wanted him to don tights for his latest big budget production, *Romeo and Juliet*. Rightly pointing out that at 35 he was way too old to be playing the teenage Romeo, Gable had spat out, 'Besides, I don't do that Shakespeare shit!'

Thalberg had died at the height of his powers, but may have been about to take a plunge in popularity among his peers. Rumour had it that he had been planning to leave MGM and set up his own production company, and that some MGM stars would follow him: Norma Shearer without any doubt, Garbo almost certainly, Gable and Crawford perhaps with a different attitude towards Thalberg once Mayer had been removed from the equation. Of his last works, *Romeo and Juliet*, had been panned by the critics because Leslie Howard (older than Gable) and Norma Shearer were far too old as the tragic lovers – a 'problem' Thalberg had solved by ageing up the rest of the cast. *The Good Earth*, released a few months after his death, was on the other hand a huge success and earned its star, Luise Rainer, an Oscar. Thalberg would later serve as a model for F. Scott Fitzgerald's *The Last Tycoon*, and from 1937 onwards the Motion Picture Academy would present an annual Best Producer Award in his memory. Thalberg's funeral was the second that Harlow and Powell had attended that year. On 9 January, John Gilbert had died of a heart attack, aged 40. The difference was that she had wanted to say goodbye to Gilbert because, like herself, he had been treated like dirt by MGM.

For Harlow, Thalberg's death marked the beginning of the end. It was as if she had been made acutely aware of her own mortality, or maybe the fatalist within her caused her to suspect deep down that her days may have been numbered. There was scarcely a day afterwards that she looked robust, even when made up. Maybe hoping that they might live together, now that marriage was no longer on the cards, Harlow accompanied William Powell to San Francisco, where he was to film *After The Third Man* with Myrna Loy. If reports are to be believed, she travelled with a raging temperature. On 28 August she had appeared on NBC Radio's *Elza Schallert Reviews*, and breathlessly told the host, 'I've got pneumonia' – though with her sometimes warped sense of humour, she could have been pulling his leg.

In San Francisco, she booked herself and Powell a suite at the St Francis Hotel, which on account of the edicts laid down by the National League of Decency they were not allowed to share – Powell took a room on the next floor, and Loy moved into the suite. Much of the time when Powell was filming, Harlow stayed here. The other guests later recalled her going down to breakfast with her face all puffy and grey – a combination of the gin she had quaffed the night before, and a 'mysterious illness' which, when questioned, she said was fatigue. Much was made of the $20,000, 85-carat sapphire ring that Powell had bought her the previous Christmas, with the press speculating that it must have been an engagement ring as she wore it on her left hand. Harlow was not letting on if Powell had popped the question or not: she amused reporters by telling them that from now on she would never be naked again because the ring stayed on her finger, even when she was in the shower.

Powell was similarly reticent to speak about their relationship. 'Ask Bill what truth there is in the persistent rumours of a near-future marriage, and he shrugs his shoulders non-committally,' James Reid observed in *Modern Screen*. Reid had been given the task of questioning Powell about his lack of sociability so far as Hollywood parties and receptions were concerned. In his piece, 'He Wants To Be Alone' (a pun on Garbo's famous utterance), Reid tried to work out why this curmudgeonly 'hermit' preferred his own company to that of his colleagues, and asked what had

happened to the luxury home in Southern California which Powell
had reputedly commissioned for Harlow and himself.

> Into it went every known comfort, device and glamorous
> decoration. In fact, he had the help of Jean Harlow in the
> decoration, a circumstance that provoked surmises that he
> and Jean were about to marry, and that Bill was about to
> forsake forever his non-party existence. But, to the best of
> everyone's knowledge both are single. And the house is no
> longer his.

Reid had also tried to interview Harlow, to no avail:

> Neither will Jean talk about Bill. But intimate friends of both,
> not so reticent, say,'They're very fond of each other. Very.
> There probably isn't a more companionable couple in
> Hollywood today. They're both lonely people who have
> discovered that, together, they aren't lonely. They have a
> million laughs together. But it's companionship, not love.
> That breathless, eager note just isn't there – yet.'

There it was again – that word 'companionship', with its echoes of
Paul Bern and Hal Rosson, enabling Harlow's fans and the
columnists to draw their own conclusions on how such a wedding
would turn out, should it take place.

When the boredom became too much for her, Harlow hired a
seaplane to take her to Catalina Island, where she spent a few days
relaxing with Mama Jean and Henry Brand, themselves rumoured
to be close to tying the knot. While here she spent too much time
in the sun, and suffered second-degree sunburn. One hour after
arriving back in Hollywood she collapsed with a fever of 103
degrees. Mama Jean was contacted by Howard Strickling, and
immediately called William Powell, who had rushed to North Palm
Drive to comfort her. Mama Jean insisted her daughter should not

receive medical treatment for a condition that had been accidentally caused by God, and which would therefore disappear with the intervention of prayer. Powell ignored her, and summoned Dr Burnhap, the medic who had taken care of her abortions. Burnhap prescribed a (then) primeval remedy which caused almost as much suffering to the patient as the actual malady: the blisters on Harlow's back and limbs were lanced, drained and sprayed with a solution of boracic acid which must have caused her tremendous pain. She was also told to avoid strong sunlight from now on, and when Dr Burnhap suggested that in the future, MGM should acquire special 'cold' lighting for her indoor scenes and that she should always wear dark glasses for outdoor locations, the press drew two conclusions. One, the peroxide which for years she had been massaging into her scalp had now affected her entire body. Two, she was actually an albino who had *not* been lying at the time of *Hell's Angels* when she had denied bleaching her hair.

On 14 December, smiling radiantly but looking bloated and far from well, a bespectacled Harlow appeared on Cecil B. DeMille's *Lux Radio Theater* in a one-off performance of Victorien Sardou's comedy set during the French Revolution, *Madame Sans-Gene* (Madame Free-and-Easy). She played the title role: supporting were Claude Rains, C. Henry Gordon and, fresh from his success in *Camille*, Robert Taylor. She proved herself an able radio actress with the arty script – 12 years earlier, Gloria Swanson had camped up the movie version. Though she had done numerous radio broadcasts, usually being interviewed at premieres or appearing as herself in variety programmes, aside from re-enacting a few scenes from *China Seas* with Clark Gable and Rosalind Russell in August 1935, this would be her only appearance in a legitimate drama – more's the pity.

Robert Taylor (Spangler Arlington Brough, 1911–69) was Harlow's co-star in the remake of *The Man In Possession*, based on the play by H.M. Harwood: the 1931 original had starred Robert Montgomery and Charlotte Greenwood. Shooting began on

29 December with W.S. 'One-Take Woody' Van Dyke at the helm. Harlow had visited Taylor on the set of *Camille*, hoping to be introduced to Garbo, but the elusive Swede had refused to see her, just as she had refused to meet Joan Crawford – aside from a rapid one-minute cast photo-shoot – on the set of *Grand Hotel*. Taylor, along with Gable, Cesar Romero, William Haines and his long term lover Jimmy Shields, and Francis Lederer was already regarded as 'one of the gals' in the discreet circles in which he moved. They, along with Joan Crawford or Carole Lombard, would frequently hit the gay bars and cruising area around Los Angeles' Pershing Square, using their female companions as 'beards'. Again, Thirties' naivety prevailed: two men would never be perceived as gay if a woman was with them. Taylor was also one of the many conquests of Ben Maddox.

In January 1937, most of these people were guests at a high-camp dinner party thrown at the Brentwood home of Joan Crawford and Franchot Tone in honour of the legendary French revue star, Mistinguett, about to open in her own Hollywood show. La Miss, whose 'date' for the evening was 32-year-old Robert Montgomery – 30 years her junior – loved nothing more than to shock. She had especially asked Joan to invite Harlow, bringing the acid response, 'While there's breath in my body, I won't have that trollop in my house!' William Powell was invited, and turned up with Myrna Loy, his co-star in *The Great Ziegfeld* – red rag to a bull, so far as La Miss was concerned. In MGM's costliest extravaganza since Ramon Novarro's *Ben Hur*, director Robert Z. Leonard had copied, feather-for-feather, Mistinguett's most recent *Folies Bergère* revue. Now, she took Loy to one side and asked if she could appear in her next Paris show. Loy was delighted, until the older star crowed for all to hear, 'Good, then I'll push you head first down *my* staircase and break your pretty neck!'

Harlow went to see Mistinguett's show, and found out why she had wanted her at the Crawford party: the playbill listed 'Jean Harlow'. This was actually Guilda, her Harlow lookalike dresser, a transvestite and so convincing, she observed in her memoirs, that Robert Montgomery had not learned the truth until they had been between the sheets – not that this had made any difference. On opening night, Guilda was halfway through his 'Platinum Bombshell' routine when a man in the audience stood up and yelled, 'I've heard that dame's a guy!' After the show, La Miss was in her dressing room when a reporter wanted to know why France's biggest export after Maurice Chevalier should wish to work with such 'freaks'. She stunned him by snarling that, where she came from, sexual orientation had always been secondary to artistic merit – adding, 'Only you Americans keep your dirty secrets under cover. If Guilda was good enough for Robert Montgomery – and if one of my boys was good enough for Robert Taylor, then my freaks as you call them are more than good enough for me!' Had this remark reached the press at the time, the careers of Montgomery and Taylor would have been finished. Following persistent rumours concerning their sexuality, in 1939 MGM would force Taylor into a lavender marriage with 'baritone babe' Barbara Stanwyck.

Shooting on Harlow's *The Man in Possession* had been underway less than a week when the title was changed to *Personal Property*. The story, set in England, is somewhat trite but it is an attractive production, if only for the combined beauty of its two stars, particularly in their many close-ups. Robert Dabney (Taylor) is released from prison after serving time for stealing a car. His stuffy family do not want to know him, so he finds work guarding the house of widow Crystal Wetherby (Harlow), whence the neo-Feydeau farce begins. Crystal is facing bankruptcy, though Dabney does not suspect this, even when told to ensure she does not remove anything from the property to sell it. She is hoping to get out of her fix by marrying Dabney's brother, Claude (Reginald Owen), who she thinks is loaded. In fact, the Dabneys too are on the verge of bankruptcy, and Claude is hoping that Crystal's money (which she does hot have) will bail them out. Naturally, she and the younger, better-looking Dabney fall in love, though not without having their share of rows. There is a hilarious exchange when Crystal demands, 'And while we're asking so many questions, why were *you* sent to jail?' When he tells her, 'Murder,' she hits back, 'I wish it had been suicide!' For a time, money provides the stronger pulling power, and the wedding to Claude is arranged – only to be called off when the bailiffs arrive to remove Crystal's furniture. Together at last, the lovebirds kiss as they leave in the back of the furniture wagon.

'Miss Harlow is hoydenish and coy in her own inimitable style,' *Variety* enthused. 'She wears some striking costumes which cleverly convey the ideas the designer had in mind. There is more of Miss Harlow on display when she's all dressed up than some girls reveal in their step-ins.' *Personal Property* was one of the few Harlow films to be reviewed by the *New York Times'* Bosley Crowther. Other critics and even some movie moguls hung on to every waspish syllable which spewed forth from his vituperative mouth: a 'Johnny Opposite' law unto himself he believed that he was *always* right, Crowther (1905–71) would subsequently applaud commercial flops as *Cleopatra*, while panning successful productions such as *Laurence Of Arabia*. He loved this film only because he was a cloying Robert Taylor fan. Having squired Janet Gaynor, Irene Dunne, Joan Crawford and most recently Garbo, Crowther added of his idol,

> If they will only be patient, all the girls on the MGM lot are going to have a twirl at him, it seems. This week it is Jean Harlow who loves Robert Taylor at the Capitol, and the gilded welkin of that deluxe establishment is ringing with feminine coos and delighted soprano laughter. For Mr Taylor being a card is just as irresistible as Mr Taylor being deadly serious, with those large Nebraska eyes, whereas Miss Harlow – sweeping or flouncing through expensive sets in that eternal negligee of hers – is positively the indignant lady of a Peter Arno drawing.

'I'll give him indignant, if ever I get my hands on him,' Harlow is alleged to have said after reading of Crowther's comparing her with a caricature cartoon. Sadly, she would not live long enough to afford herself this privilege – though had she got around to exacting her revenge on this obnoxious individual, she would have found herself waiting in a very long queue.

CHAPTER TEN

Saratoga

'*After Bill's rejection, Jean seemed to lose interest in everything and when stricken she refused to put up a fight. It was as if she took advantage of a minor ailment to escape from life.*'

Anita Loos, Kiss Hollywood Goodbye

On 9 January 1937, exactly one year after John Gilbert's death, Harlow sent flowers to the funeral of her friend, 29-year-old Ross Alexander, who like Clark Gable she met by way of Franchot Tone. She had openly cursed the movie moguls for bringing about yet another fine star's demise with their double standards, hypocrisy and greed – Harlow had experienced such behaviour first-hand, of course.

Alexander's body had been found at his ranch: in a fit of despair, he had shot himself. As happened with Paul Bern, Jack Warner and the studio police had been first at the scene to search for a suicide note. This time there had been none, so Warner had made up the story that Alexander, deeply in debt, had never recovered from the shotgun suicide of his first wife, Aleta Freel two years earlier. The reason for this tall tale was that Warner had unearthed Alexander's diary, full of his indiscretions and containing a blackmail letter from a young drifter he had picked up for sex over the Christmas holidays. Additionally, upon learning that he had been pencilled in for her next film, Bette Davis had branded him a 'dirty queer'. Warner had given orders for Alexander's ranch to be ransacked, to make it appear that he had 'gone nuts' before killing himself.

His death came as a huge shock to Hollywood's closeted gay community and their 'fag-hag' supporters, chief of which were Harlow, Joan Crawford and Carole Lombard who personally attended the funeral with Clark Gable. In the wake of their own past discretions which, he declared might one day 'creep up and bite them on the ass', Mayer summoned Gable to his office, and called Harlow at North Palm Drive. Both were given the same warning: 'There but for the grace of God go you!'

Mayer's tyranny and complete lack of compassion knew no bounds. Inasmuch as he had kept Marie Dressler working right up to the grave, squeezing that last ounce of strength out of her when she had been literally at death's door, so he was wholly unsparing of Harlow. Mayer did not give a damn for her welfare, but he had invested a lot of capital in Robert Taylor, and in a last-bid attempt to quell the rumours of his homosexuality, later in the summer would be taking him to London personally to supervise him in MGM's first British production, A *Yank At Oxford*. As *Personal Property* would not be premiered until 19 March, this would give the studio ample time to get a few glowing reports over how well it treated it stars, and how much they were respected in high places – in this instance, inviting Harlow to attend another Presidential Ball at the end of January, this one to honour Roosevelt's 55th birthday.

Arthur Landau complained that his client was too ill to travel all the way to Washington by train, even on the luxurious Santa Fé Chief which covered the first leg of the journey between Los Angeles and Chicago – and to appear at 22 official events in just three days. The Ball itself was spread across seven hotels, and Harlow was expected to dance with all of the invited dignitaries at every one of them. Then there were the official luncheons and dinners, including one with Eleanor Roosevelt at the White House. She gave in gracefully, and appeared to be having fun most of the time. She even attended a machine-gun demonstration, in the company of J. Edgar Hoover, and surprised everyone with her knowledge of the subject. It was widely rumoured that, during her 'gangster's moll' period with Al Capone, Bugsy Siegel and Abner Zwillman, she had actually fired one.

Harlow had wanted William Powell to accompany her on the trip, but he had other commitments. Therefore, reluctantly this time, she took Mama Jean. For once, perhaps, she had made the right decisions, for only her mother could control her drinking. When she boarded the Washington–New York express for the start of the homeward journey, she had developed a cold which she said she had caught from kissing Robert Taylor for the publicity photographs.

By the time she transferred to the train for Chicago, to rejoin the Santa Fé Chief, she had a raging fever. Much of America at this time was ravaged by a flu epidemic, and the train's purser was taking no chances – he exercised his authority to quarantine Harlow and Mama Jean to their sleeping compartment so that whatever had laid her low would not spread to the other passengers.

Harlow recuperated for a few days at North Palm Drive before travelling to Palm Springs, where she spent a month alone at the Desert Inn. Because of her apparent allergy to sunshine, she ventured out of her bungalow only in the evening once the sun was down, accompanied by a Cahuilla Indian guide who escorted her on trips to San Jacinto Mountain and the Tahquitz Canyon.

Upon her return to Hollywood, she had barely recovered when she fell ill again: on 23 March she was admitted to her 'second home' – Room 826 at the Good Samaritan Hospital. While in Washington she had developed what she had thought to be a gumboil, but the problem was actually impacted wisdom teeth. On account of her recent suspected bout of flu, and in the wake of the boracic acid treatment she had received for her sunburn, the dental surgeon who examined her, Dr Leroy Buckmiller, diagnosed her too weak to undergo a lengthy operation, and suggested that she have her teeth removed one at a time, at weekly intervals. With William Powell out of town, Mama Jean was ruling the roost once more and declared that Mary Baker Eddy, faced with such a dilemma, would have had *all* of the teeth out in one go. The procedure was carried out the next morning, and as Dr Buckmiller had predicted, there were complications: Harlow suffered cardiac arrest, and very nearly died on the operating table.

Because this was supposed to have been 'no more than a visit to the dentist', the incident barely made the press. The *New York American* reported, 'The four wisdom teeth which put Jean Harlow in the hospital have brought about a much more serious condition than anyone suspected' – but this piece did not appear until the end of the month. Even so, Louis B. Mayer ordered an enquiry. So far as he had been aware, Harlow had been resting at home until 24 March, the date she was scheduled to begin working on her next film, *The World's Our Oyster*, with William Powell. Now he learned that she was still at the Good Samaritan Hospital, where she would most likely remain for another week. Pyorrhoea had developed in her gums: the poison from this had entered her bloodstream. Harlow received much sympathy and daily visits from Clark Gable, who had suffered the same malady during the summer of 1933 – the infection had reached his gall bladder, and almost cost him his life.

When Mayer found out that Harlow was seeing more of Gable than William Powell, he cancelled *The World's Our Oyster* and decided to cast them as sparring partners in *Saratoga*, a racing drama for which Lionel Barrymore had already been signed. This would be directed by Jack Conway, who would be travelling with Louis B. Mayer and Robert Taylor to London, to direct *A Yank At Oxford*. The change of plan brought about a few expletives from Joan Crawford, who had already been told that she was going to be in the film.

Harlow was discharged from the hospital on 10 April, and driven under cover of darkness to North Palm Drive. Once again, Mama Jean had turned her daughter's bedroom into a mini-clinic, and taken her nurse's uniform out of mothballs. Henry Brand had returned to Catalina Island.

In the winter of 1936–37, Harlow was often seen in the company of Donald Friede (1899–1965), the much-travelled former publisher of T.S. Eliot and Ernest Hemingway, currently freelancing in Hollywood as a seller of film rights. Friede had successfully negotiated works by Somerset Maugham and H.G. Wells, among others, and was hoping to get Harlow on side with a view to representing her novel, *Today Is Tonight*. Many years later, Friede's widow (he went through six wives, the most famous being the writer M.F.K. Fisher) would claim that he had asked Harlow to marry him, but this was just wishful thinking. Harlow had already decided, for the time being at least, that if she could not marry William Powell, then she would never accept second best. And as soon as Friede learned that MGM owned the rights to her book, as an extension of her persona, he moved on to his next target in the hope of making a fast buck.

Another companion at this time was Jesse Lasky Jr (1910–88), son of the Hollywood pioneer who had helped found Paramount Studios. Lasky writes of Harlow with great tenderness in his autobiography. Theirs was a brief relationship which came at exactly the right time, when she needed a friendly shoulder to lean upon: also, unusual for a confidant, he was her own age. She was suffering from depression, reflecting far too much on her failed marriages, and no doubt wondering if she had done the right thing in deciding not to marry William Powell. Lasky was obviously sexually interested in her – as indeed was every red-blooded man in America – yet their liaison remained platonic because she wanted it this way, and he respected her far too much to push things further. By day the pair went golfing at the Riviera Country Club, and spent their evenings shooting craps – Harlow was also an expert

with the dice. They took trips to Santa Monica Pier and the Venice
Amusement Park. 'Jean enjoyed the sensations she created
everywhere, the riots of demonstrative fans,' Lasky recalled. 'No
Garbo, hiding her light from the world, when the local police had
to extract us from the too-physical adulation of autograph hunters,
she was unruffled and vastly entertained. Fun to her was the
unexpected, the unplanned, the unconventional.'

Meanwhile, Harlow began working on what would be her last
film, *Saratoga*. To punish her for going into hospital without
informing him, Mayer had demoted her to second billing after
Clark Gable. This she did not mind. The movie and fan
magazines, however, who had adored Gable's pairings with Harlow
and Crawford, protested because they believed that he should have
been given another chance to work with Carole Lombard. He and
Lombard had made just one film together, *No Man Of Her Own*,
back in 1932 when they had been just colleagues – and now, as
Hollywood's number one couple, everyone agreed that they would
have proved box-office dynamite. Mayer had been all for the idea
until the National League of Decency had deemed it unsuitable
because Gable was still married.

While shooting *Saratoga*, Gable and Carole saw little of each
other. Lombard the actress was completely removed from Lombard
the party animal. When working it was an almost Spartan regime of
early to bed, early to rise and absolutely no nights out. She was
making her first Technicolor film, *Nothing Sacred*, with producer
David O. Selznick, and trying to keep in his good books in the hope
of acquiring her most important role ever – Scarlett O' Hara,
opposite Gable's Rhett Butler in *Gone With The Wind*. Here she was
not alone – virtually every young actress in America was vying for the
part which would eventually go to Vivien Leigh, though in the spring
of 1937 the clear favourites in 'The Scarlett Stakes' were Lombard,
Bette Davis and authentic southern belle Tallulah Bankhead. Gable
therefore spent much of his free time with Harlow, and there were
absolutely no rumours of a romance because the press were still

describing her and William Powell as 'joined at the hip'.

Gable observed a distinct change in his co-star since last seeing her at Irving Thalberg's funeral. She had piled on the pounds, her features were bloated, and she had started having blackouts. She was also suffering from the shakes, and her hair had started to fall out – the years of bleaching really had begun taking their toll. Gable initially suspected that her health problems could only have been attributed to drinking – on some of their soirees he had watched her polish off an entire bottle of gin in one sitting. Yet she handles herself well in the film, and only occasionally does one see her fading before one's eyes.

The film opens at the Brookvale Farm stud, once the finest in Saratoga, where grumpy Grandpa Clayton (Lionel Barrymore) is about to yield his last stallion to his creditors. He runs the place with his son Frank (Jonathan Hale), who has gambled away practically everything they ever had. Enter disreputable bookmaker Duke Bradley (Gable), who saves the day by buying the horse for the old man because he loves him. Indeed, Duke loves everyone, including the chubby black maid Rosetta (another inspired performance from Hattie McDaniel) who says, 'Ah's fix up for him any time. If only he was the right colour, ah'd marry him!'

When Clayton's granddaughter Carol (Harlow) arrives from England with her stuffy millionaire fiancé Hartley (Walter Pidgeon), Duke devises a scheme to get the stud farm back in business. She is stuck-up, with a phoney King's English accent, while Hartley is 'the perfect chump with a bankroll the size of the US Treasury'. Initially, Frank is in with the plan, giving Duke the deeds to the farm to cover the money he owes him: this way it will be in safe keeping for Carol to inherit some day. When Frank drops dead at the racetrack, however, Carol says that she will get Hartley to cover the debt so that she will never be beholden to Duke, who she suspects only wants the stud for himself. To ensure that Hartley coughs up, she agrees to marry him sooner than they anticipated, bringing the strangled response from Duke, 'A gal that put the bite on a bridegroom for 60,000 smackers before she even gets him to the altar is awfully full of larceny!'

From this point in the film, Carol pretends to dislike Duke, though she is secretly in love with him. She finally comes clean on the Race Special express train – this scene was borrowed from Gable's earlier *It Happened One Night*, where all the passengers engage in a lively sing-song. She makes an effort to impress him, putting on her best *kimonah* (the Harlow–Gable in-joke from *Red Dust*), before admitting him to her sleeping berth *and* allowing him to rub embrocation on her chest and back. Then she is back to hating him again when, upon learning that her 'chump' fiancé is about to be sent packing, Duke offers her a percentage if she can keep stringing him along. She vows revenge: when she has finished with him, Duke will have been reduced to begging on a street corner with a tin cup!

The film's ending is disappointing. Hartley bets a fortune on his own horse, which Carol convinces him will win the race and thus bankrupt Duke. In a photo finish, the horse loses, Clayton gets to keep his stud farm, and fate throws Carol and Duke together during another singalong on the express train – actually a scene saved over from the *first* singalong.

On 3 May, Harlow appeared on the cover of *Life* magazine, though the photo-shoot with Hungarian artist Martin Munkácsi was a disaster. Her make-up kept flaking and her face was puffy and grey-tinged. Munckácsi took all the required shots – then tactfully informed her that none of the photographs had developed properly, therefore *Life* had dipped into their archives to use a portrait he had made of her during the summer of 1935. Entitled 'Harlow In Hollywood', it is a nice shot: soberly dressed in a waisted jacket and medium-length skirt, she glances over her shoulder at the photographer as she strolls away from him along the pavement.

Shortly afterwards, she and William Powell celebrated their 'third anniversary' – actually the third anniversary of their first unofficial date. Powell had a cake delivered to the *Saratoga* set, which Harlow shared out among the crew. Attached was a card covered in kisses, and the message which more or less summed up the basis of most of her relationships: 'To My Three-Year-Old From Her Daddy'. As Louella Parsons was present, for the first and last time Harlow transferred Powell's sapphire ring to her right hand – almost a waste of time, because Louella claimed that she had whispered, 'Of course, I know we'll never be married!'

During the afternoon of Saturday 29 May, Harlow and Gable filmed the scene which comes towards the end of *Saratoga*, where Duke is supposed to carry Carol across a room and, to raise a few laughs, unceremoniously drop her onto a chaise longue. Gable abandoned the scene and called cut when she went limp in his arms, and a few minutes later Harlow passed out. The studio doctor, smelling urine on her breath, repeated the diagnosis pronounced by the Good Samaritan Hospital: a gall bladder infection caused by the poison leaking into her system from her unhealed gums. This had already been brought to director Jack Conway's attention by Walter Pidgeon, whose character Hartley declares that he cannot bear to kiss his fiancée. Pidgeon very ungallantly protested that even asked to kiss Harlow, he would refuse, because her breath 'stank of piss'. The doctor also diagnosed water retention, unusual in a woman so young. Additionally she was suffering from stomach cramps associated with her menstrual cycle.

Conway suggested that the set should be closed at once, and Harlow taken to the hospital – no one informed Mama Jean, knowing that she would virulently oppose this. In the meantime, Harlow came to and asked one of the technicians to drive her to the set where William Powell was shooting *Double Wedding* with Myrna Loy. Powell was in the middle of a scene, and advised her to go home – he would follow on as soon as he could.

Mama Jean was at North Palm Drive when she arrived: someone had contacted Louis B. Mayer, who had been honour bound to call her mother. She now called Powell and informed him that her daughter was simply tired and in need of rest, therefore there was no need for him to come to the house. Naturally, medical treatment was out of the question. Against the express wishes of her family, Powell and the fools at MGM had coerced 'Baby' into entering a hospital, and this had only aggravated her condition: if anything happened to her now, these people would be held accountable. Prayer would cure her, but it would now have to be more intense than ever and conducted in absolute privacy. Mama Jean therefore dismissed the household staff for the rest of the weekend, so that she and Harlow could be alone while Mary Baker Eddy effected a miracle cure. She vowed that by Monday, Harlow would be back on the set of *Saratoga*, as hale and hearty as she had ever been.

Throughout the weekend, Mayer persistently tried to contact Harlow, but her mother had taken the phone off the hook. Eddie Mannix and Howard Strickling went to the house: the doors were locked, and Mama Jean shouted for them to go away. A few hours later, she called the studio and said that Harlow was feeling much better – well enough to work the next day. When she failed to show on the Tuesday morning, Jack Conway shot just one scene with Clark Gable which did not involve her, before Gable stormed off the set, declaring that he would sort out 'that fucking woman' – Mama Jean – once and for all. He at least managed to get her to talk from the other side of the door, but she would not let him see her daughter. Gable returned to the set and called Arthur Landau. Between them they formulated a plan wherein they, assisted by Frank Morgan (one of the actors from *Saratoga*), producer Bernard Hyman and Jack Conway would 'storm' North Palm Drive and *force* Mama Jean into letting them see Harlow. The idea was that Landau would ring the front door bell and gain admittance to the house – he was convinced this would happen, for he was one of the few people Mama Jean trusted – and then the other men would emerge from their hiding place behind the bushes, barge into the place, and take over.

The plan worked, but only so far. Gable and his friends gained access to Harlow's bedroom, where they found her lying semi-conscious on the bed, extremely bloated, and clearly in great pain. The stench, Gable later said, was overpowering. Later he told John Lee Mahin (as quoted by critic Barry Norman in *The Hollywood Greats*), 'Clark told me that when he leant over to kiss her he could smell the urine on her breath. He said it was so shocking it was like kissing a dead person, a rotting person. He said that it was a terrible thing to walk into and that he hardly recognised her.' Frank Morgan, who had some medical knowledge, took her temperature. This was sky-high, and he made for the telephone to call a doctor. Arthur Landau recalled, via Irving Shulman, 'Laughing, Mrs Bello told them that they were two Jews and three ignorant amateurs. Then she ordered them to go and take their evil thoughts with them.' Mama Jean, apparently prone to fits of hysteria at a moment's notice, only calmed down when threatened with exposure in the press: unless she allowed her daughter to see a medical professional, the whole world would be made aware that her silly beliefs had put Jean Harlow's life in grave danger.

Landau brought in a Dr Ernest Fishbaugh, who agreed with all the diagnoses so far: Harlow had cholecystitis, or inflammation of the gall bladder, and needed immediate surgery. By this time, she was semi-comatose and barely able to speak, let alone protest against her mother's decision to still deny her professional help. The best Dr Fishbaugh achieved was getting Mama Jean's permission, under duress, to administer a morphine injection to lessen the pain, and to allow two nurses into the house to assist with keeping the sickroom and the patient clean – when conscious, Harlow was projectile vomiting much of the time. These nurses arrived within the hour, and Mama Jean had another screaming fit, threatening to smash over their heads any 'medical contraption' they brought with them that Mary Baker Eddy would have disapproved of. Clearly, this religious founder had much to answer for, for this included the intravenous drip required to keep the patient alive. This time Harlow's mother was threatened with Whitey Hendry's studio police: the drip was attached, and blood and urine samples taken and dispatched to the laboratory at the Good Samaritan Hospital.

It was either Gable or one of his friends who alerted the press, to bring this selfish woman's irresponsible actions out into the open. The next morning anxious reporters turned up at North Palm Drive – not interested in scandal, but wanting reassurance that one of their favourite stars was all right. All that Mama Jean would say was that Harlow had had a peaceful night, and that she was resting. Dr Fishbaugh, fearful that Mama Jean would exercise her legal authority and have him ejected from the house, lied to reporters that Harlow had a mere cold. Ben Maddox was allowed to see her, quite simply because everyone trusted him and knew that he would keep what he saw to himself.

Also, the press had bigger fish to fry. That same day, in England, the former Edward VIII (who had abdicated his throne the previous December) had married Wallis Simpson, and this story monopolised the front pages, though the *Los Angeles Times* did run the headline, 'Jean Harlow Seriously Ill'. Had it not been for the conclusion of the Edward and Mrs Simpson scandal, Harlow might have been afforded the same coverage that had been given to Valentino, 11 years earlier.

On the morning of 4 June, one of the nurses tending Harlow observed that her gums and lips were swollen, and that she could not swallow properly – that also she was drooling what smelled like very acrid urine. She called Dr Fishbaugh, who diagnosed an erythema of the mucous membranes brought on by the gall bladder infection. If this was not serious enough, he further diagnosed uremic poisoning and kidney failure – in pre-transplant pre-dialysis days almost always fatal. There was no doubt whatsoever in his mind that the condition had been building up for some time. Mama Jean claimed that she must have developed this after suffering polio as a child – a malady she had unquestionably invented – or after her teenage bout of scarlet fever, a slight possibility. Others speculated that the condition had been brought about by an over-surfeit of gin, but she had not been drinking long enough for this to be the case. Arthur Landau, referring to the beating Harlow had received on her wedding night, firmly laid the blame at Paul Bern's door, telling Irving Shulman, 'If Jean died, a dead man might have succeeded in murdering her years after his own suicide.'

The real villain, of course, was Harlow's by now clearly deranged mother. Dr Fishbaugh brought in a colleague, Dr Richard Chapman, and requested a second opinion which of course supported his own prognosis: if Harlow had an emergency operation to remove her gall bladder, she just might pull through by the skin of her teeth. And *still* Mama Jean refused to allow her to be taken to hospital. She even ranted that her daughter was only pretending to be ill to make a fool out of her religious beliefs, and to force Louis B. Mayer into giving her a badly needed increase in salary so that he would not feel responsible for her 'fatigue'. Eddie Mannix was summoned again, and asked to locate Marino Bello and Montclair Carpenter: in her delirium, she had called out their names, and Mannix was hoping that Mama Jean's ex-husbands might be able to drill some sense into her. Montclair was in Detroit, and Bello somewhere in Mexico.

Saturday dawned, with little happening. Harlow's father had not been found, but Bello was on his way to Hollywood and threatening his former wife with a fate worse than death if anything happened to his 'Baby'. Mama Jean had devised a new plan to save her daughter: she wanted everybody out of the house, and every last piece of medical equipment removed from the sickroom. She had arranged for a quartet of Christian Science readers to sit at Harlow's bedside. As Christ had risen from the dead on the third day, she declared, so these cranks would have her daughter on her feet and well again by Monday. Amazingly, no one had thought of informing William Powell until now (or any of her close friends) of Harlow's illness – the last time Powell had seen her, on the evening of 29 May, he had swallowed the exhaustion and period pains story. When on the Sunday morning he learned from producer Bernard Hyman what was really wrong with her, he hit the roof – and to his credit promptly took over. While he headed for North Palm Drive, he dispatched Hyman to Louis B. Mayer's house with the instruction that he should not leave until the mogul had been made fully aware of the facts surrounding Harlow's imprisonment by her mother, and of Mama Jean's only too obvious willingness to just sit back and watch her daughter die for the sake of her selfish principles.

Mayer made a single telephone call, and within 10 minutes an ambulance drew up outside North Palm Drive. The matter was now out of Mama Jean's hands. At 7pm on the Sunday, Harlow was installed in her old suite, Room 826, at the Good Samaritan Hospital. With no time to lose, she was given two blood transfusions and placed in an oxygen tent, while surgeons declared her far too weak to survive any operation. Mama Jean and William Powell, glaring at each other across the sickbed, sat with her throughout the night while Dr Fishbaugh kept watch from a darkened corner of the room – in a room across the corridor Marino Bello, Aunt Jetty, Henry Brand and Jack Conway held a vigil. At 6am, Dr Fishbaugh reported that Harlow's head was so swollen that it might be necessary to drill holes in her skull to relieve the pressure. In preparation for this, an intern shaved her. Two hours later, she slipped into a coma from which she would never emerge. Her lungs became filled with fluid, and as a last resort Dr Fishbaugh summoned the Los Angeles Fire Department to pump more oxygen into them, to no avail. At 11.38am on Monday 7 June 1937, Jean Harlow's suffering finally ended as she slipped peacefully away.

EPILOGUE
Baby

All Hollywood went into a state of shock, as did much of the country. Nothing like this had happened since the death of Valentino, back in 1926, and would not happen again until the death of James Dean. The MGM switchboard was jammed. The news was that much harder to bear because within hours of Howard Strickling announcing that Harlow was seriously ill, he was saying that she was dead. The Good Samaritan Hospital was besieged by hundreds of reporters, cameramen and grieving, confused fans. The staff were ordered, upon pain of dismissal, not to discuss Harlow's final illness. To cover her own back in the event of a public backlash, Mama Jean leaked the story that Harlow had died because *she* herself had refused medical aid.

All the major studios closed for the day. Cinemas and theatres all over America dimmed their lights and held two-minutes silences. Even the National League of Decency and religious groups who had condemned her reacted with intense sadness: everyone had loved Jean Harlow because, deep down inside she had been a good, caring person. Eddie Mannix called her, 'A sweet child – a great artist, wonderfully sincere, and an honest human being.' Marlene Dietrich said, 'I admired her so much for her courage at what must have been a very painful time in her life.' Louis B. Mayer, that arch hypocrite, issued a 'personally composed' statement which Clark

Gable said had only made him want to throw up.

> This is the end of a rich, personal friendship. This girl whom
> so many millions adored was one of the sweetest persons I
> have known in 30 years of the theatrical business. I have lost
> a friend. The world has lost a ray of sunshine. She was one of
> the most charming, thoughtful and reasonable players with
> whom I have been associated. She made all who had
> anything to do with her in an executive capacity ever anxious
> to please her, to contribute to her happiness.

Gable, who threatened to bawl out Mayer for being such an 'out
and out shit', changed his mind when he learned that the statement
had actually been written by Howard Strickling. Somehow, coming
from Strickling, the sentiments sounded genuine.

For practical reasons, there could be no decent period of
mourning: with the warm weather, and with Harlow's body still
leaking urine after death, the funeral had to take place as soon as
possible. There was no inquest. Today, almost certainly, Mama
Jean's behaviour during her daughter's final days would have been
investigated. She would have been castigated by the tabloids, and
accused of neglect, if not actual manslaughter. Though unable to
prevent her daughter from falling ill, she alone had been
responsible for her death. True, she had gone against her beliefs
and allowed some medical intervention, but this had been limited
and controlled, under extreme duress every step of the way. The
fact remains that had Harlow been operated on at once, the
surgeons would have stood a good chance of saving her. Like all
religious maniacs – and there is no other way of describing her –
Mama Jean was incurably headstrong and did not know how to
compromise. She would go to her grave protesting that she had
been right in permitting her daughter to die. Insane does not even
begin to describe this foolish, manipulative woman.

While her friends and fans lamented her passing, and her loved ones were making hasty preparations to say goodbye, MGM were left with a (for them) bigger dilemma: what to do about the unfinished *Saratoga*. Initially, Mayer declared that the film would be scrapped. The press saw through his ruse. The film had cost MGM $850,000 which they would be able to claim back from their insurers. Caught out, Mayer considered a re-shoot, and asked Carole Lombard to take over Harlow's role – bringing the response, 'Fuck off, you obnoxious old shit. Now we know what the B stands for in your name – *bastard!*' Jean Arthur and Virginia Bruce were similarly but more politely dismissive. Then the *Los Angeles Examiner* published an 'open letter' to Mayer from Harlow's fans – actually penned by one of William Randolph Hearst's reporters at his bequest:

> Thousands of devoted admirers of Jean Harlow are demanding that they be given the consolation of seeing their beloved film actress in her unfinished motion picture. They protest [against] Louis B. Mayer's announced plan of remaking *Saratoga* with a new personality, and refuse to accept a substitute for their beloved Jean. Great pieces of art, unfinished novels and paintings interrupted by death have been in the past handed over to other artists to complete. Jean Harlow was an artist and did her work up to the time she was called. That work should not be disregarded. May it be suggested, Mr Mayer, that Jean's friends in Hollywood, those who loved her best, the stars in the motion picture colony, and the thousands of men and women who discovered her and created her a star be consulted? *Let the public be the judge.* May it also be suggested, Mr Mayer, that in Hollywood there is some young actress who would be glad, in tribute to Jean Harlow, to play those remaining scenes? It would indeed be a gracious gesture for some actress to step forward and finish the picture in memory of a great little trouper who has been called upon to play another and greater role.

This prompted Mayer into changing his mind. He would complete the film, and release it as a tribute to Harlow – an announcement that attracted only the worst criticism. As had happened in the wake of Valentino's sudden demise, the studio was accused of exploiting a tragedy. Mayer was now effectively trapped between the devil and the deep blue sea. Shooting was resumed at once. Lookalikes Geraldine Dvorak and Mary Dees were hired for the scenes which Harlow had not completed – though Dvorak (1904–85), whose claim to fame had been portraying one of the evil count's wives in Tod Browning's *Dracula* – was only used in the long shots. Dees (1911–2005) had stood in for Harlow in *Dinner At Eight*. Because her voice was unlike Harlow's, her lines were overdubbed by radio actress Paula Winslowe (1910–96), best remembered for voicing the little deer's mother in *Bambi*. The film would wrap on 29 June, undergo a rapid edit, and be released to near mass hysteria on 23 July. It became the highest grossing film of the year, and in a strange twist of irony Clark Gable's new film, *Parnell*, would be removed from most cinema bills to accommodate it.

Cinema audiences and critics alike would try to work out which was the real Harlow in some scenes, and which was Mary Dees, and frequently get it wrong. In fact, between the two train singalong scenes, there are no others with Harlow. This explains why, during the first train scenario where Carol feigns illness to gain Duke's attention, her violent coughing fit was regarded as distasteful by those believing that *Saratoga* was shot in sequence, and that Mayer had left in Harlow's final scene to acquire maximum publicity. This was not the case. Her *final* scenes were shot at the racetrack, where Carol is first introduced to Duke – Harlow's features here are very bloated. During the last four racing scenes, her features are partially obscured by binoculars, or she (aka Geraldine Dvorak) is shot from behind. Similarly, in the sequence where the party guests dance the Saratoga, when Harlow dances through the French windows and on to the patio: the less buxom Mary Dees emerges from the other side. Worse still is the film's closing scene with

Hattie McDaniel, where Carol takes a consignment of tin cups sent by Duke as a prank – her entire head and shoulders are hidden by a ridiculously large picture hat which all but fills the screen.

Harlow's funeral took place at Forest Lawn's Wee Kirk O'The Heather Chapel on 9 June. Mama Jean had wanted a small family ceremony, followed by cremation, even though this was against her Christian Science beliefs – many thought as a means of destroying the 'evidence', should someone later decide to conduct an enquiry into how her daughter had died, and request an exhumation. She was overruled by Mayer, who rightly pointed out that the press would then definitely think she had something to hide. Neither would the mogul consent to burial in the Carpenter plot, in Kansas City. Jean Harlow had been a great star, he declared, and would be treated accordingly with the massive turnout she merited. William Powell agreed, and announced – many thought because he felt guilty for deliberating over whether to marry her or not – he would be paying for her final resting place: a $25,000 multi-coloured marble, three-space, 9 x 10 foot shrine in the Sanctuary of Benediction Mausoleum. The inscription says it all: OUR BABY. Irving Thalberg reposed next door: friends Ross Alexander and Marie Dressler were close by.

Like Thalberg's funeral, this one was tantamount to a royal occasion, albeit one lasting just 28 minutes. Unlike Thalberg's, it was an event where all of the 250 invitees wanted to be there because they had genuinely adored her. The exceptions were Nelson Eddy, who sang 'Oh, Sweet Mystery Of Life', and Jeanette MacDonald, who warbled 'Indian Love Call'. Both charged for their services.

The ceremony had originally been scheduled to take place at 11am, but when by 6am a 10,000-strong crowd had already gathered at Forest Lawn, the Los Angeles Police – fearing a riot, as had happened with Valentino – called Mayer, and it was brought forward by two hours. Genevieve Smith, one of Mama Jean's Christian Science readers who had filled her head with nonsense, and who therefore shared some of the responsibility for her daughter's death, read several short passages from the Bible, along with an extract from Mary Baker Eddy's *Science & Health With A Key To The Scriptures*. On Mama Jean's request she delivered an eulogy which lasted all of 30 seconds: in keeping with her beliefs that there was no such thing as death, Harlow's mother did not shed a single tear.

Clark Gable was one of the pallbearers – ignoring Mayer's orders to bring his wife along, he came accompanied by Carole Lombard. The other mourners included friends Wallace Beery, Ben Maddox, Myrna Loy, Norma Shearer (representing the 'much lamented' Irving Thalberg), both Barrymores, Spencer Tracy, Mickey Rooney and Ronald Colman. Hattie McDaniel and George Reed, aka the preacher who had married Harlow and Gable in *Hold Your Man*, wanted to attend but were prevented from doing so by Mayer, who felt that it would be 'undignified to have blacks at a white woman's funeral'. A few years later, Gable would refuse to attend one of the premieres of *Gone With The Wind* because Hattie and the other black actors were barred from entering the whites-only theatre. Then there were those who Harlow would not have wanted there. Mayer, weeping crocodile tears for his 'dear daughter', and a whole host of studio executives who had praised her to her face, but never had a good word to say about her otherwise.

The family group also included Montclair Carpenter and his wife, Aunt Jetty, Marino Bello, Hal Rosson, Carey and Carmelita Wilson, and Henry Brand. Montclair and Bello acknowledged each other, but virtually ignored the wife they had shared. William Powell arrived with his mother, Nettie, and wept throughout the ceremony.

For one hour, Harlow had lain on view in her $5,000 bronze and silver casket, while a police guard had hovered in the background – at least two reporters had tried to break into Forest Lawn's Tennyson Room to take photographs of the body. The morticians had concealed her shaved head with one of her wigs from *Red-*

Headed Woman, and dressed her in the pink negligee she had worn in *Saratoga*. Her face, which had turned almost black on account of the uremic poisoning, had been covered with a square of white silk. In her hand was a white gardenia, to which had been attached an unsigned note (almost certainly from Powell, though columnist Walter Winchell claimed that it had been placed there by Donald Friede) which read, 'Goodnight, my dearest darling.' Sophie Tucker, who Harlow had emulated in *Hold Your Man* but never met, sent a massive display of delphiniums, while Howard Hughes sent rare cottage roses. When those closest to her had paid their last respects, the casket was closed and surmounted by a blanket of 2,000 lily-of-the-valley and gardenia, Mayer's 'personal' contribution to what the press estimated to be more than $15,000 worth of flowers.

****

Because Harlow had not been permitted to lie in state for the fans to file past her casket, because of the sheer hastiness with which her funeral had been arranged and the last-minute change of time, rumours were rife as to how she had died. As with 31-year-old Valentino, many thought it inconceivable that someone so young and beautiful could die so young, and of a complaint most of them had never heard of. The Latin Lover had died of complications following what should have been a simple appendectomy, but this had not stopped the suggestions of murder by a jealous husband or suitor, or even by the studio itself because of his homosexuality and belligerent attitude towards his peers who had used him just as their successors would use Harlow.

With her, it had to be something equally sensational: a botched abortion, suicide, venereal disease, alcoholic or opiates poisoning. Other 'reliable' sources claimed that the peroxide used on her hair had seeped into her skin and caused brain damage. Clairvoyants came forward claiming that they had spoken to Harlow 'from beyond the grave', and been told by her what had really happened. Naturally, they had promised to keep this information to themselves. And virtually every story was raked up: the Paul Bern–Dorothy Millette scandal and other Harlow 'indiscretions', real or invented, and always wildly exaggerated. The Los Angeles Police were inundated with requests to launch a full investigation, but never did. In 1937 there seemed little point, though today things would have been very different. Many years later, Irving Shulman said aloud what many dared only think back then:

> It was all over. Best just to bury the girl and all her secrets. She was only 26, but she had lived full dream lives with millions of men, had been the ideal of millions of women. Her immortality would continue – even though Bern and Mama Jean had murdered her.

For a time, there was talk of a permanent memorial, a life-sized statue which Mama Jean planned having erected in the Rockefeller Center. She raised enough money herself to hire several sculptors to draw up designs, but what she really needed was a lump sum to pay for the work itself. When she petitioned Louis B. Mayer, he told her that it would be a waste of good money. Harlow was gone, others had taken her place, and it was time to move on – utter rot, of course. The project was abandoned.

The retainers, good and bad, are all gone. Harlow had never got around to making a will – hardly surprising, considering her age – but after probate, everything went to her mother. Mama Jean was expecting to inherit a fortune: estimates put Harlow to have been worth over $1 million, but at the time of her death she owed $100,000 in unpaid taxes, unpaid rent on the North Palm Drive House, and money loaned to her by Arthur Landau. She had however recently invested money in a number of retirement annuities, which suggests that she really had been thinking of giving up her movie career. From these Mama Jean would eventually receive $300 a month, for life. MGM also assigned her to a seven-year, $137 a week contract as a 'scriptwriter and talent scout', though it is doubtless she did much of either. Mayer was merely keeping her on side so that she would not go blabbing to the press about her daughter's personal life, and scupper the posthumous popularity of her films. Most of these were re-released soon after Harlow's death, and did great business at the box office. Only *The Public Enemy* was refused a certificate.

In 1944, Mama Jean married Henry Brand. The marriage lasted less than two years, and after her divorce she 'realised her dream' by opening an antiques shop on Palm Desert. For the rest of her life she dined out on 'Baby' stories, though very few of those she came into contact with respected or even liked her. She had also kept most of her daughter's clothes, storing them in a warehouse and visiting them weekly until prevented from doing so by obesity and a heart condition.

She died, aged 69, on 11 June 1958, and lies in Forest Lawn – next to Harlow, as she had wanted – but in a tomb that remains unmarked. Montclair Carpenter died in 1974, aged 96. Marino Bello married twice after his stepdaughter's death, and continued with his nefarious activities, most especially with mobster Bugsy Siegel. He died in 1953. Chuck McGrew married twice after Harlow – to socialite Marion Webb, then to rocket scientist Margaret Wood. He died in 1971, aged 65. Hal Rosson married three more times and died in 1988, aged 93. In January 1940, having just recovered from colonic cancer, William Powell married a 21-year-old starlet named Diana 'Mousey' Lewis. They had known each other less than a month, but the marriage lasted until Powell's death, aged 91.

It was inevitable that Hollywood would attempt to re-tell the Jean Harlow story. Irving Shulman sold the film rights to his *Harlow: An Intimate Biography* for $100,000 to Paramount. The book had been lambasted by critics and so-called 'friends' such as the horrendous Adela Rogers St Johns for not painting the star in a favourable light

– Adela had obviously forgotten some of the things *she* had written about Harlow – and for accusing Mama Jean of murdering her daughter. This and a rival film by Magna both bombed spectacularly and deservedly at the box office, and though there has been talk in recent years of making another biopic, this is yet to happen. Clearly, there will only ever be one Jean Harlow.

The Films Of Jean Harlow

Between 1928 and 1929, Jean Harlow appeared in innumerable films with various studios, as an extra or bit-part player. In most of these she was unbilled at the time, though when she became known new credits were commissioned for her name to be added, sometimes above those of the major stars. Some of these are now lost, and there may well be other productions in which she appeared, without this being noted at the time. The following therefore represent as much as is known about her very early work, and are not in any particular order:

Fox: *Honor Bound*; *Fugitives*; *Masquerade*

Pathé: *This Thing Called Love*

Al Christie Comedies: *Weak But Willing*

First National: *Why Be Good?*

Paramount: *Moran Of The Marines*; *Close Harmony*

Hal Roach Studios: *Thundering Toupees*; *Chasing Husbands*; *Double Whoopee*; *Bacon Grabbers*; *Liberty* (billed as Harlean

Carpenter); *The Unkissed Man*; *Why Is A Plumber?*

THE LOVE PARADE   Paramount, 1929
Director: Ernst Lubitsch. Script: Guy Bolton, Ernest Vajda.
   Photography: Victor Schertzinger. With Maurice Chevalier, Jeanette MacDonald, Lillian Roth, Lupino Lane. Harlow, unbilled, played an audience member. 107 mins.

THE SATURDAY NIGHT KID   Paramount, 1929
Director: Edward Sutherland. Script: Ethel Doherty.
   Photography: Harry Fischbeck. With Clara Bow, Jean Arthur, James Hall, Frank Ross, Edna May Oliver. Harlow was 11th billing. 62 mins.

NEW YORK NIGHTS   United Artists, 1929
Director: Lewis Milestone. Script: Jules Furthman.
   Photographer: Ray June. With Norma Talmadge, Gilbert Roland, Lilyan Tashman, Roskoe Karns. Harlow (along with Al Jolson, unbilled) played a party girl. 81 mins.

HELL'S ANGELS   United Artists, 1930
Director: Howard Hughes. Script: Howard Estabrook, Harry Behn, based on a story by Marshall Neilan and Joseph Moncure March. Additional dialogue/direction: James Whale.
   Photography: Gastano Gaudio, Harry Perry, E. Burton Steene, Elmer Dyer, Zech and Dewey Wrigley. Music: Hugo Riesenfeld. Began shooting as a silent, 1927. With Ben Lyon, James Hall, John Darrow, Frank Clarke, Roy Wilson, Jane Winton, Lucien Prival. Harlow was third billing. 123 mins.

CITY LIGHTS   United Artists, 1931 *
Director/Script: Charlie Chaplin.
   Photography: Gordon Pollock, Roland Totheroh. With Charlie Chaplin, Virginia Cherrill, Florence Lee, Harry Myers, Allan

Garcia. Harlow, unbilled (her scene was filmed in 1929), played a
restaurant customer. Her mother is thought to be the Jean
Carpenter on the list of extras. 86 mins.

  * Filmed 1927–31

THE SECRET SIX   MGM, 1931
Director: George Hill. Script: Frances Marion.

  Photography: Harold Wenstrom. With Wallace Beery, Johnny
Mack Brown, Lewis Stone, Clark Gable, Marjorie Rambeau,
Ralph Bellamy, Paul Hurst, John Miljan. Harlow was fourth
billing. 82 mins.

THE IRON MAN   Universal, 1931
Director: Tod Browning. Script: Francis Edward Faragoh, based
on the novel by W.R. Burnett.

  Photography: Percy Hilburn. With Lew Ayres, Robert
Armstrong, John Miljan, Eddie Dillon, Mary Doran. Harlow was
third billing. 74 mins.

THE PUBLIC ENEMY   Warner Bros, 1931
GB: *Enemies Of The Public*
Director: William Wellman. Script: Harvey Thew, based on a story
by John Bright and Kubec Glasmon.

  Photography: Dev Jennings. With James Cagney, Edward
Woods, Joan Blondell, Mae Clarke, Donald Cook, Leslie Fenton,
Beryl Mercer, Mia Marvin. Harlow was third billing. 82 mins.

GOLDIE   FOX, 1931
Director: Benjamin Stoloff. Script: Gene Towne, Paul Perez.

  Photography: Ernest Palmer. With Spencer Tracy, Warren
Hymer, Lina Basquette, Maria Alba, George Raft, Eddie Kane.
Harlow was third billing. 68 mins.

PLATINUM BLONDE   Columbia, 1931

Director: Frank Capra. Script: Jo Swerling, based on a story by Harry E. Chandler and Douglas Churchill. Dialogue: Robert Riskin.

Photography: Joseph Walker. With Robert Williams, Loretta Young, Louise Closser Hale, Reginald Owen, Halliwell Hobbs, Donald Dillaway. Harlow was third billing. 86 mins.

SCARFACE   United Artists, 1932*

Director: Howard Hawks. Script: Ben Hecht, based on the novel by Armitage Trail.

Photography: Lee Garmes, L.W. O'Connell. With Paul Muni, Ann Dvorak, George Raft, Osgood Perkins, Boris Karloff. Harlow was unbilled cameo. 91 mins.

* Filmed 1931

THREE WISE GIRLS   Columbia, 1932

Director: William Beaudine. Script: Agnes Johnson, Robert Riskin, based on a story by Wilson Collison.

Photography: Ted Tetzlaff. With Mae Clarke, Marie Prevost, Andy Devine, Walter Byron, Natalie Moorhead. Harlow was top billing. 67 mins.

THE BEAST OF THE CITY   MGM, 1932

Director: Charles Brabin. Script: John Lee Mahin, based on a story by W.R. Burnett.

Photography: Barney McGill. With Walter Huston, Wallace Ford, Jean Hersholt, Dorothy Peterson, Mickey Rooney, John Miljan. Harlow was second billing. 87 mins.

RED-HEADED WOMAN   MGM, 1932

Director: Jack Conway. Script: Anita Loos, based on the novel by Katharine Brush.

Photography: Hal Rosson. With Chester Morris, Lewis Stone, Leila Hyams, Henry Stephenson, Una Merkel, May Robson, Charles Boyer, Harvey Clark. Harlow was top billing. 73 mins.

RED DUST   MGM, 1932
Director: Victor Fleming. Script: John Lee Mahin, based on the
stageplay by Wilson Collison.
    Photography: Hal Rosson. With Clark Gable, Gene Raymond,
Mary Astor, Donald Crisp, Tully Marshall, Forrester Harvey.
Harlow was second billing, 82 mins.

HOLD YOUR MAN   MGM, 1933
Director: Sam Wood. Script: Anita Loos (from her story), Howard
Emmett Rogers.
    Photography: Hal Rosson. With Clark Gable, Stuart Erwin,
Dorothy Burgess, Garry Owen, Muriel Kirkland, Paul Hurst,
Theresa Harris, George Reed. Harlow was top billing. 86 mins.

BOMBSHELL   MGM, 1933
GB: *Blonde Bombshell*
Director: Victor Fleming. Script: John Lee Mahin, Jules
Furthman, based on the play by Caroline Franke and Mack Crane.
    Photography: Hal Rosson, Chester Lyons. With Lee Tracy,
Frank Morgan, Franchot Tone, Pat O'Brien, Una Merkel, Ted
Healy, Isabel Jewell, Ivan Lebedeff, Louise Beavers, C. Aubrey
Smith, Mary Forbes. Harlow was top billing. 90 mins.

DINNER AT EIGHT   MGM, 1934
Director: George Cukor. Script: Frances Marion, Herman
Mankiewicz, Donald Ogden Stewart, based on the play by Edna
Ferber and George S. Kaufman.
    Photography: William Daniels. With Marie Dressler, John and
Lionel Barrymore, Wallace Beery, Lee Tracy, Billie Burke, Edmund
Lowe, Madge Evans; Jean Hersholt, Karen Morley, May Robson,
Louise Closser Hale, Phillips Holmes, Grant Mitchell, Edward
Woods, Hilda Vaughn. Harlow was fourth billing. 112 mins.

THE GIRL FROM MISSOURI   MGM, 1934
GB: *100 Per Cent Pure*
Director: Jack Conway. Script: Anita Loos, John Emerson.

Photography: Ray June, Hal Rosson (uncredited). With Lionel Barrymore, Franchot Tone, Lewis Stone, Patsy Kelly, Alan Mowbray, Clara Bandick. Harlow was top billing. 75 mins.

RECKLESS   MGM, 1935
Director: Victor Fleming. Script: P.J. Wolfson, based on a story by Oliver Jeffries (aka David O. Selznick).

Photography: George Folsey. Principal Songs: Jerome Kern, Oscar Hammerstein. With William Powell, Franchot Tone, May Robson, Rosalind Russell, Ted Healy, Mickey Rooney, Allan Jones, Nat Pendleton, Henry Stephenson. Harlow was top billing. 94 mins.

CHINA SEAS   MGM, 1935
Director: Tay Garnett. Script: Jules Furthman, James Keven McGuinness, John Lee Mahin (uncredited).

Photography: Ray June. With Clark Gable, Wallace Beery, Lewis Stone, Rosalind Russell, C. Aubrey Smith, Dudley Digges, Robert Benchley, William Henry, Hattie McDaniel. Harlow was second billing. 88 mins.

RIFFRAFF   MGM, 1936
Director: J. Walter Ruben. Script: Frances Marion, H.W. Hanemann, Anita Loos, from a story by Marion.

Photography: Ray June. With Spencer Tracy, Una Merkel, Joseph Calleia, Mickey Rooney, Victor Kilian, Paul Hurst. Harlow was top billing. 88 mins.

WIFE VS. SECRETARY   MGM, 1936
Director: Clarence Brown. Script: Norman Krasna, Alice Duer Miller, John Lee Mahin, based on a story by Faith Baldwin.

Photography: Ray June. With Clark Gable, Myrna Loy, May Robson, James Stewart, Gloria Holden. Harlow was second billing. 87 mins.

SUZY   MGM, 1936
Director: George Fitzmaurice. Script: Dorothy Parker, Alan Campbell, Horace Jackson, Leonore Coffee, based on the novel by Herbert Gorman.

Photography: Ray June. With Franchot Tone, Cary Grant, Lewis Stone, Benita Hune, Greta Meyer, Inez Courtney, Una O'Connor. Harlow was top billing. 95 mins.

LIBELED LADY   MGM, 1936
Director: Jack Conway. Script: Maurice Watkins, Howard Emmett Rogers, George Oppenheimer, based on a story by Wallace Sullivan.

Photography: Norbert Brodine. With William Powell, Myrna Loy, Spencer Tracy, Walter Connolly, E.E. Clive, Cora Witherspoon, Hattie McDaniel. Harlow was top billing. 96 mins.

PERSONAL PROPERTY   MGM, 1937
GB: *The Man In Possession*
Director: W.S. Van Dyke. Script: Hugh Mills, Ernest Vajda, from the play *The Man In Possession* by H.M. Harwood.

Photography: William Daniels. With Robert Taylor, Reginald Owen, Una O'Connor, Henrietta Crosman, E.E. Clive, Cora Witherspoon, Marla Shelton. Harlow was top billing. 84 mins.

SARATOGA   MGM, 1937
Director: Jack Conway. Script: Anita Loos, Robert Hopkins.

Photography: Ray June. With Clark Gable, Lionel Barrymore, Frank Morgan, Walter Pidgeon, Una Merkel, Cliff Edwards, George Zucco, Hattie McDaniel, Margaret Hamilton. Harlow was second billing, 92 mins.

(Harlow died while making this film: her unfinished scenes were completed by body doubles Mary Dees and Geraldine Dvorak, while Paula Winslowe doubled for her voice.)

APPENDIX II
Biopics

HARLOW   MAGNA, 1965

Director: Alex Segal. Script: Karl Tunberg. 109 mins.
Jean Harlow: Carol Lynley, *Mama Jean*: Ginger Rogers, *Marino Bello*: Barry Sullivan, *Paul Bern*: Hurd Hatfield.

Filmed in monochrome 'electronovision', the Magna biopic was shot in just three days – and it shows – to compete with the big budget movie being filmed at the same time by Paramount. Carol Lynley *looks* like Harlow, and (at 23) is the right age, but is completely void of charisma. William Powell threatened to sue, should his name be mentioned: he becomes the flimsily disguised William Mansfield, woodenly portrayed by Efrem Zimbalist Jr. A slight plus was the signing of Ginger Rogers, in what would be her last film, as Mama Jean. She was fourth choice for the role after Judy Garland, Rita Hayworth and Eleanor Parker had turned it down. All had worshipped Harlow, and loathed her mother for just letting her die. Ginger Rogers had no such principles. An interesting cameo came from eccentric British actress Hermione Baddeley, as Marie Dressler. The film was rush released on 14 May 1965, a clear month ahead of its rival. Distributors considered it so mediocre that it was invariably screened as a second feature.

HARLOW Paramount, 1965

Director: Gordon M. Douglas. Script: Arthur Landau. 125 mins.
Jean Harlow: Carroll Baker, *Mama Jean*: Angela Lansbury, *Marino Bello*: Raf Vallone, *Paul Bern*: Peter Lawford, *Arthur Landau*: Red Buttons.

'Harlow Stood For Only One Thing, As No Woman Has, Before Or Since!' So reads the tagline for this monstrosity. Allocated a whopping $2.5 million budget, the story was based on the book by Irving Shulman, so it was bound to be controversial. Paramount cast *Baby Doll* actress Carroll Baker as The Platinum Blonde, at 35 way too old, but glamorous enough – especially in the *Bombshell* scene. Angela Lansbury, just six years Baker's senior, was unconvincing as Mama Jean, though Raf Vallone was suitably creepy as incestuous stepfather Marino Bello. Howard Hughes would not allow his name to be used in the film, so here we have Richard Manley (Leslie Nielson). As Paul Bern, brat pack hell-raiser Peter Lawford is hopeless: one is almost relieved when he kills himself because of his impotence. The most ridiculous aspect of the film, however, is that 'message' that failed relationships and alcohol contributed to Harlow's 'downfall' – the producer had obviously not done his homework, otherwise he would have learned that Harlow had died at the very zenith of her career – of uremic poisoning, and not from pneumonia, as seen here. Few who had known her were in the least surprised when this dreadful mishmash bombed at the box office.

Bibliography: Primary and Secondary Sources

BOOKS

Alpert, Hollis: *The Barrymores* (Dial Press, 1964)

Anger, Kenneth: *Hollywood Babylon I & II* (Arrow, 1986)

Bankhead, Tallulah: *Tallulah* (Harper & Bros, 1952)

Bret, David: *The Mistinguett Legend* (Robson, 1991)
   Tallulah Bankhead (Robson, 1996)
   Rock Hudson (Robson, 2004)
   Joan Crawford (Robson, 2006)
   Clark Gable (J.R. Books, 2007)
   Interviews With Marlene Dietrich

Eames, John Douglas: *The MGM Story* (Octopus, 1979)

Eyman, Scott: *Lion of Hollywood: Louis B. Mayer* (Robson, 2005)

Greif, Martin: *The Gay Book Of Days* (W.H. Allen, 1985)

Harlow, Jean: *Today Is Tonight* (Dell, 1965)

Hay, Peter: *MGM: When The Lion Roars* (Turner, 1991)

Lasky, Jesse Jr: *Whatever Happened To Hollywood?* (W.H. Allen, 1975)

Loos, Anita: *Kiss Hollywood Goodbye* (Viking, 1974)

Mann, William: *William Haines: Wisecracker* (Penguin, 1988)

Munn, Michael: *Jimmy Stewart* (Robson, 2005)

Norman, Barry: *The Hollywood Greats* (BBC, 1979)

Parish, James Robert: *The Hollywood Book of Death* (McGraw Hill, 2001)

Parsons, Louella: *Tell It To Louella* (Putnam, 1961)

Porter, Darwin: *The Secret Life of Humphry Bogart* (Blood moon, 2003)

Quinlan, David: *Quinlan's Film Stars/ Character Actors* (Batsford, 1981, 1986)

St Johns, Adela Rogers: *Love, Laughter & Tears* (Doubleday, 1978); 'The Private Life of Jean Harlow', *Liberty*, 1933

Shulman, Irving: *Harlow: An Intimate Biography* (with Arthur Landau) (Mayflower, 1964)

Stenn, David: *Bombshell: The Life & Death of Jean Harlow* (Doubleday, 1993)

Stuart, Mark: *Longy Zwillman* (Lyle Stuart, 1985)

Thomas, Bob: *Thalberg: Life & Legend* (Doubleday, 1969)

Tornabene, Lyn: *Clark Gable: Long Live The King* (Putnam, 1976)

Wallace, Irving: *The Secret Sex Lives of Famous People* (Chancellor Press, 1993)

PERIODICALS

Albert, Katherine: 'What's Wrong With Hollywood Love?', *Modern Screen*, undated

Camp, Dan: 'Career Comes First With Loretta', *Motion Picture*, undated

Gable, Clark: 'What I Think About Jean Harlow', *Hollywood Magazine*, 1935

Grant, Jack: 'The Story Jean Harlow Has Never Told', *Screen Book*, 1933

'Jean Harlow: Chicago Society Girl With Caddo', *Los Angeles Examiner*, 1929

'Jean Harlow: Tired of Being A Vamp', *Kansas City Star*, 1933

'Jean Harlow Answers Your Questions', *Motion Picture*, 1933

'Jean Harlow: I Shall Marry Again', *Motion Picture*, 1933

'Jean Harlow: The Authentic Story of My Life', *New Movie Magazine*, 1934

'Jean Harlow: The Facts About My Romance & Marriage', *New Movie Magazine*, 1933

'Jean Harlow: My Advice To Myself!', *Motion Picture*, 1937

Lee, Sonia: 'Jean Harlow: From Extra To Star', *Screen Book*, 1935

Maddox, Ben:
  'What About Clark Gable Now?' *Screen Book*, undated, part-spiked
  'Jean Harlow: The One Star Who Has No Enemies', *Screen Book*, undated, part-spiked
  'Jean Harlow Carries On', *Screen Book*, 1932
  'Why Girls Say "Yes!"', *Screen Book*, undated, part-spiked

Mank, Gregory: 'Jean Harlow', *Films In Review*, 1978

Manners, Dorothy: 'Is Jean Harlow Hollywood's Most Underpaid Star?', *Motion Picture*, 1933

Ramsey, Walter; 'Franchot Tone: Gentleman Rebel', *Photoplay*, undated

James Reid: 'Bill Powell: He Wants To Be Alone', *Modern Screen*, 1936

Tully, Jim: 'The Truth About William Powell', *Screen Book*, 1935

Vantol, Jan: 'How Stars Spend Their Fortunes', *Screen Book*, 1933

'The Truth About Jean Harlow's Marriage', *Screen Book*, 1933

Index